Mallam Ali Obaje, C.B.E., the Ata of Igala

THE
IGALA KINGDOM

by

J. S. BOSTON

PUBLISHED FOR
THE NIGERIAN INSTITUTE OF
SOCIAL AND ECONOMIC
RESEARCH

IBADAN
OXFORD UNIVERSITY PRESS
1968

Oxford University Press, Ely House, London W.1

GLASGOW NEW YORK TORONTO MELBOURNE WELLINGTON
CAPE TOWN SALISBURY IBADAN NAIROBI LUSAKA ADDIS ABABA
BOMBAY CALCUTTA MADRAS KARACHI LAHORE DACCA
KUALA LUMPUR HONG KONG TOKYO

Oxford House, Iddo Gate, P.M.B. 5095, Ibadan, Nigeria

Printed in Great Britain by
Butler & Tanner Ltd, Frome and London

To
Charles and Phyllis Black

PREFACE

THE work on which this study is based began in March 1960, when I was appointed to a Research Fellowship in the Nigerian Institute of Social and Economic Research, and ended in December 1964, when the study was presented as a thesis for the D.Phil. degree in the University of Oxford. During this period twenty-two months were spent in the field, divided equally between two centres in the metropolitan area of Igala Division in Kabba Province, Northern Nigeria. In the first eleven months I lived at Idah, the Igala capital, and studied the traditional system of central government. For the second phase, in which the emphasis shifted to traditional local government, I moved to the village of Igebije in Gwolawo District, about 25 miles north of Idah.

I should like to thank the present and past Directors of the Nigerian Institute of Social and Economic Research for their encouragement and for the freedom which they allowed me in carrying out the research. I am also grateful to the Ata Igala, Mallam Ali Obaje, C.B.E., for his kind personal interest as well as for his official support of my work. The Igala Native Authority, of which the Ata is President, gave me access to official files and court records, and in addition gave financial help by paying part of the salary of my chief assistant. The local office of the Northern Nigerian Administration was also generous with its facilities. And the progress of my work owed much to the hospitality and kindness of many Government and Native Authority officials and of the members of the local Catholic and Qua Iboe missions. I remember with gratitude the friendship of T. Healy, B. J. Stafford, C. J. Sykes, P. S. Achimugu, M. J. Lander, E. Wennen, W. M. Holley, P. Belgrave, Fr. P. Roberge, J. Naylor, S. Johnson, and J. Lomax. And in acknowledging the kindness and hospitality of the Igala people in general I should like to thank in particular Amana Edime, the Ochai Ata of Igala, who worked with me throughout my stay, and my two interpreters, Alhaji Aduku and James Udekwe, who worked with me for shorter periods.

vii

Among many friends at Igebije I am particularly grateful to Ada Onyẹbẹ, Itanyi Ọmonu, Edime Ọmonu, and Odaudu Itodo.

For academic guidance in the course of this research I wish to thank Professor E. E. Evans-Pritchard. And for earlier training in Social Anthropology I am indebted to Professor Fortes and his colleagues at Cambridge and to Professor Evans-Pritchard and his colleagues at Oxford.

University of Ibadan,　　　　　　　　J. S. BOSTON
Ibadan

CONTENTS

LIST OF PLATES

LIST OF FIGURES

LIST OF TABLES

NOTE ON ORTHOGRAPHY

WITH one addition I have used the orthography which has become familiar to Igala through the publications of the Stewards Company at Ikka. This system uses o̩ and e̩ to represent the open vowels o and e. Diacritical marks are also used to indicate nasalized vowels, as in *ou̯n* and *e̩nw*. The addition that I make to the conventional orthography consists of a subdotted i for the vowel that occurs in *okĩkilĩ* and *kĩ*. It has the same sound as the vowel of the English word, bit. The original orthography uses e for this sound as well as for the e sound that occurs in *ene* or *ere*. But there are two different sounds to be represented here, and the ambiguity of the old orthography can best be avoided by creating a separate letter for the short i.

Tones have not been marked but it should be borne in mind that the language has a complex tonal system.

CHAPTER ONE

ENVIRONMENTAL FACTORS

THE Igala kingdom is skirted on two sides by the great waterways that divide Nigeria into its major natural and cultural regions, the river Benue and the river Niger. In shape it is roughly triangular, with the confluence of the two rivers forming the apex and the base extending irregularly into Idoma and Ibo country. Its strategic situation is of key significance in the historical development of the kingdom. Their geographical position has brought the Igala into contact with a wide range of peoples and a great variety of cultures, including contact with the Ibo, the Yoruba, the Edo-speaking peoples, and the Jukun, to name only the principal groups. Idah, the Igala capital, is situated on the river Niger, and it is clear both from written records of nineteenth-century exploration and from the traditions of the many peoples who trace their rulers' descent to Idah that the Igala kingdom has dominated the affairs of this riverain zone for many centuries.

But although the Igala are deeply involved in the system of contacts and common economic, political, and cultural interests engendered by this riverain network, they are not a riverain people in the strict sense of the term. The main axes of settlement run inland from the capital in the south-west corner of the kingdom; moreover, the Igala have withdrawn from the rivers in the region of the confluence itself and from the south bank of the Benue to make way for various immigrant groups. And further south, along the left bank of the Niger, the border of the river is occupied mainly by clans who regard themselves as Igala by assimilation rather than by origin.[1] The Igala utilized the river for trade in slaves, foodstuffs, and imported goods. But their traditional economy was based on arable farming, and they value hunting more highly than watermanship or any form of riverain activity.

[1] These immigrant groups are of Bassa and Gwari stock in the immediate vicinity of the confluence. Further south, the left bank of the Niger is peopled by Igala-speaking groups of Igbirra stock.

1

District boundary
Provincial boundary
× — × — Regional boundary
● District headquarters
Main roads
========= Secondary roads

0   4   8   12 Miles

FIGURE 1. IGALA DIVISION

2

Igala describe specialist watermen and other people born to the water somewhat disparagingly as *amọmọnya,* children of Ọnya, which is a far-off[1] town representing the extreme limit of Igala contact with the peoples inhabiting the Niger delta.

Ecologically, the Igala live in an area of transition between the high forest conditions of the coastal belt and the drier and more open conditions of the savannah belt. The rainfall, averaging about 50 inches a year, is high enough to support the principal crops of the forest zone, such as yams, cocoyam, maize, pumpkins, and cassava. But conditions also favour the crops on which drier areas rely exclusively, namely millet, guineacorn, benniseed, and various types of beans. The transition is also reflected in the tree crops that play an important part in the Igala diet and in womens' trading. These include the fruits of the oil palm and of *Irvingia,* which are both typical forest trees, together with the fruits of *Prosopis* and *Parkia,* which reach their southern limit of distribution in Igala. Igala farming, which is carried out principally by the men, is based wherever possible on a combination of yams and maize supplemented by the other crops mentioned above. The farmers practise shifting cultivation, planting yams in the best land available and following this up with a rotation of maize and other crops when the initial fertility is lost and it becomes necessary to shift the yam sequence to a new area, cleared from either secondary bush or from fallow land.[2]

The present boundaries of the Igala kingdom are defined by the configuration of the Igala Division, an administrative division of Kabba Province in Northern Nigeria. These boundaries do not coincide exactly with the traditional limits of the kingdom, which were slightly more extensive, but the difference is not great, and the modern nucleus includes all but an insignificant minority of the Igala-speaking peoples known to reside in this area. In this study I identify the traditional kingdom with its modern configuration, which is justifiable if it is borne in mind that the Ata formerly exercised a loose form of suzerainty over Igbirra and Kakanda groups near the

[1] In the delta region of the Niger.

[2] The success of yam cultivation in Igala depends on making skilful use of the dry season watercourses with their plentiful reserves of high forest and well-shaded land.

confluence, and that he also made appointments to titles, and in some cases exercised direct control, over many Ibo- and Idoma-speaking settlements that lie beyond the present boundary.[1]

The total area of the kingdom today is roughly 4,900 square miles, with a total population, in the 1952 census, of 361,119 persons. This gives an average density of seventy-four persons per square mile, which is slightly lower than comparable figures for the Idoma to the east, and much lower than the averages that occur among the neighbouring Ibo in the south and south-east. The low overall density of population, in a fertile and productive area, is a factor of great sociological significance. It can be associated with the system of residence in small, scattered, and impermanent hamlets which traditionally obtained over much of Igala. In the southernmost areas, along the left bank of the Niger, annual flooding of low-lying territory restricts settlement to a few higher ridges, and the traditional pattern here is one of compact, large, and permanent villages. But elsewhere in Igala, and particularly in the central districts to the north and north-east of the capital, the typical pattern is one of small dispersed settlements, loosely grouped together in villages.

The mobility of the traditional pattern of settlement in Igala cannot be over-emphasized, although this situation is changing rapidly today with the establishment of a permanent network of improved communications. In the past hamlets were often short-lived, with an average life span of from two to three generations, and in this period of their existence it was common for their composition to alter considerably owing to the abandonment of homesteads and the establishment of new living sites in other hamlets or villages.[2] The question as to whether a householder should move or not is one that frequently occurs in oracle consultations, and moves are made as a reaction to political oppression, to sickness and to misfortune of various kinds. The impermanence of settlements is

[1] cf. Boston, J. S., 'Notes on Contact between the Igala and the Ibo', *Journal of the Historical Society of Nigeria,* Vol. 2, no. 1, 1960.

[2] The verb *echodo,* 'to set up a new dwelling', is an extremely significant term in the Igala political vocabulary. The corresponding noun for an abandoned dwelling is *aláche.*

4

reflected in Igala material culture, which has developed few of the arts that seem to go with long continuity of settlement and prolonged occupation of the same set of dwellings. For instance, the principal altars and shrines used by the Igala are all capable of being uprooted and moved to a new environment. They comprise staffs and masquerades, representing the dead, calabashes and pots to contain medicines and fetiches, and simple mud pillars and mounds which can be made anew and rededicated by a series of appropriate offerings if the householder decides to move.

The influence of this pattern of dispersal and population movement on social life and on the social and political institutions of the Igala is less obvious. But it is probable that the characteristic emphases of the social and political system can be explained as part of the system of ecological adaptation. The balance of ties of descent against ties of kinship is related to this factor; similarly the existence of a dual system of administration, combining hereditary and non-hereditary modes of grouping in equal proportions is ultimately an expression of the underlying pattern of residence and settlement.

5

CHAPTER TWO

THE PERSPECTIVE OF IGALA ORAL TRADITION

THE Igala tend to validate knowledge in general by saying that it comes from the past, and their way of saying that a fact belongs to the widest order of human experience is to say that it was known to the ancestors of long ago, *abogujo igbili*. Within the category of knowledge so validated they distinguish between narratives that record facts with certainty and, as it were, objectively, and those that embellish the truth by allowing fancy to play upon the sequence of events and accepted connexions between facts. Narratives in the first class are described by the term *ita*, whilst the second category is termed *ohiala* or *ohiaka*. The former group includes proverbs, myths, legends, and other forms of inherited objective comment. The latter includes folk tales, fables, and a wide range of popular and imaginative stories. *Ita* are told for a serious purpose, however comic their actual content may be. *Ohiala,* on the other hand, exist to stimulate the imagination, and facts whose true nature and relationship is recorded in *ita* can be arranged freely in any order in *ohiala*.

Ita are not strictly historical in character and represent the infinite in human experience rather than the dimension in which knowledge accumulates through processes of cause and effect. An essential feature of all *ita* is that they try to define the essential character of their subject, subordinating historical development to a statement of the subject's basic relations with the other major features of the world in which it exists.

One typical *ita* explains the difference between the bushfowl and domestic fowl by saying that the former grew tired of being used for sacrifice, and decided to run away and live in the bush. In this way the two related species came to lead separate lives. But the bushfowl shows its relationship to the domestic fowl by returning daily, before daybreak to inquire whether fowls are still being used for sacrifice. And the domestic cock replies to this by complaining that *ma che ololoo,* 'they are doing so, much too much'.

Within the general corpus of *ita,* the Igala distinguish clan histories as a separate category, *ita olopu.* They are distinguished in this way partly because they refer to the basic divisions of the social world in which the Igala live, but also because they co-ordinate oral tradition in a chronological as well as a structural sense. In so far as the Igala measure the exact sequence of past time they do so dynastically: each clan chronicles the past by the succession of generations of its own members. And these diverse traditions are co-ordinated and synchronized to some extent by reference to the dynastic history of the royal clan. The Igala identify the history of their nation with the history of the royal clan, and represent both its structure and the traditions of its origins and development by reference to the relationship of the royal clan with other leading descent groups that are representative of the widest divisions of Igala society.

Previous accounts of Igala oral tradition have used the Igala king lists as though they are basically equivalent to the linear time scale employed in European historiography, and they have attempted to translate the legends that record the origins and foundation of the ruling house by the concepts of sequence and historical development that are associated with this type of time scale. The difficulties that arise in this connexion, however, constitute major objections to the mode of analysis itself, and in order to show the necessity for a different approach I will summarize briefly some of the ways in which the oral traditions resist any attempt to translate them literally as an objective record of the actual succession of events in the past.

The principal objection to regarding the Igala king lists as an exact dynastic record is that their total time span does not coincide with the much longer span of time which seems reasonable for the history of the kingship on other historical grounds. There is much evidence, as I will show later, which points to a connexion between the Benin and Igala kingdoms in the first decades of the sixteenth century, and evidence of a still older cultural connexion with the Yoruba-speaking

7

peoples suggests that kingship at Idah may be contemporaneous with the period of the late Yoruba and early Benin kingdoms, which fall roughly between the thirteenth and sixteenth centuries. But the fullest known list of Igala kings cannot be made to cover a period of more than a few centuries. Clifford wrote of the immigration which is supposed to have established the dynasty:

> So began the regime of the Atas at Idah. It is not possible to fix any reliable date for this event, but we shall not be very far wrong in assigning the colonization of the Agatu–Ocheku–Amara area to the early part of the Seventeenth Century, and Ayagba's arrival at Idah towards its close.[1]

From internal evidence of borrowing in other directions, it seems fairly certain that Clifford based this date on arguments advanced in an unpublished note by a previous administrator at Idah, who calculated the average time span of recent generations and extrapolated this backwards to arrive at a total of 250 years for the whole dynasty. This author wrote:

> On the analogy of the past 68 years the rule of the Igara in Idah cannot have extended over a period of more than 250 years. Basing our calculations on the average period from generation to generation at 30 years (a generous allowance), we get a total of 220 years back to Indoko. Numerous other pedigrees collected in various reports in Ankpa and Dekina show a maximum of six generations taking us back to the earliest Attahs. It would appear therefore that the dynasty was founded about the end of the Seventeenth Century.[2]

At the present time, when approximately 30 years have elapsed since this calculation was made we are in a position to assess the average length of the last ten reigns, which span a period of roughly 120 years, from c. 1834 to 1956. Applying the average of 12 years per reign to the full king list, which contains twenty-five names, a time span of approximately 300 years emerges for the entire dynasty. Allowing for the difference in date between the two calculations, this second assessment is roughly in agreement with Monsell's estimate.

[1] Clifford, Miles, 'A Nigerian Chiefdom . . .', *J.R.A.I.*, Vol. LXVI, 1936, p. 397.

[2] Monsell, C. N., *Historical Notes on the Attahate of Idah*, ms.

The comparatively short period of an average reign can probably be explained by the rotating system of succession, in which three other lineages hold the royal office in turn before the cycle is completed and a son succeeds his own father. Igala kings tend to be old, or comparatively mature, when they come to the throne, and the whole system favours relatively short periods in office.

Clifford, and other writers who have dealt with this problem of chronology, assume that the king list and associated traditions refer only to the last two or three centuries, and that any earlier developments, antedating this period, fall largely outside the scope of Igala oral tradition. This view, that the Igala retained no formal knowledge of their history before the seventeenth century, is essential to Clifford's argument that kingship was established at Idah by a migration from Wukari, in which a branch of the Jukun royal house was involved. He maintains that there was no earlier dynasty at Idah, but only a system of clan government in which the heads of the indigenous families, or Igala Mela, participated.[1] In Clifford's thesis Igala history literally begins with the kingship, and with the arrival of the immigrant rulers from Wukari. The early ancestors of the royal house are regarded as shadowy, but nevertheless essentially historical, figures who migrated by a well-defined route through the north of Igala, stopping for two generations in the vicinity of Amagedde near the Benue river, before they finally moved across country to settle at Idah.

This analysis, however, gives an entirely false impression of unanimity and agreement in Igala oral tradition, and misrepresents the perspective of Igala legends in order to evade the analytical difficulties created by the inadequate chronology of the king list and by the diversity that actually exists in the traditions. In a published study of these traditions I have tried to show that there are at least three different attributions of royal origin, existing side by side in the corpus of legends.[2]

---

[1] '. . . There was in those early days no form of central organization, the tribe consisting of a number of moieties each under its own patriarch or petty chieftain; these latter, nine in number, were the primitive fathers of Igala . . .', Clifford, op. cit., p. 395.

[2] Boston, J. S., 'Notes on the Origin of Igala Kingship', *Journal of the Historical Society of Nigeria*, Vol. 2, no. 3, 1962, pp. 373–83.

Clifford's emphasis on the Jukun connexion overlooks earlier published evidence of Yoruba and Benin influence, and my own research has confirmed the existence of traditions of Benin origin within the ruling house itself. Clifford's bias towards the Jukun attribution is clearly related to the interest aroused by Meek's study of the Jukun kingdom, and to Meek's support of the hypothesis that kingship diffused into Nigeria from Hamitic sources along the valley of the Benue river.

It cannot be too strongly emphasized that the Igala hold divergent views about the origin of their kingship, and that this divergence occurs *within* the dynastic framework that Clifford related solely to the period of Jukun contact. In other words the king list and associated traditions represent a total view of Igala history, covering contacts with other peoples and historical developments in the remote past as well as in more recent times. The fact that traditions of Jukun, Yoruba, and Benin origin can exist in the same corpus of legends shows that the king list is not bound by the conventions of sequence that occur in a linear time scale. Igala oral tradition clearly takes a synoptic view of the past, selecting important events from different periods and bringing them within a narrower compass of past time. And the fact that these different traditions coexist with one another, as alternatives, is also highly significant. It suggests that the perspective imposed by attempts to translate the material into a strictly historical sequence is largely artificial, and that the oral traditions have a perspective of their own which has not been fully explored. I suggest that the early part of the dynastic record, down to and including the period of political foundation represented by the period of Ayagba ọm Idoko, is largely mythological in significance and that the early ancestors are not to be regarded as historical figures in a literal sense, but rather as mythical archetypes of structural arrangements that must have taken a longer period of time to evolve than is suggested by the idiom of associating events with single reigns. The effect of regarding the king lists as a substitute for written history is to overlook the mythological content of Igala tradition and ultimately to misrepresent the perspective in which the Igala see the past. If the traditions are seen in their true perspective it at once appears that the mythological phase of the past is of para-

mount importance, and that historical function is correspondingly subordinate to the political function of the myths contained in these traditions.

The mythical character of the early period of the Igala
kingship is reflected in uncertainty about the genealogical
status of the first royal ancestors. Genealogically, the apical
ancestor of the royal clan is the fifth in line of descent, and
there are four Atas, including one woman, before Ayagba ọm
Idoko, to whom most branches of the royal clan trace their
descent. Ayagba's forbears are:

> Abutu Ẹjẹ   Agẹnapoje   Ẹbẹlẹjonu   Idoko

Idoko immediately precedes Ayagba, and is fixed in this
position by the fact that Ayagba's name is invariably given as
Ayagba ọm Idoko, son of Idoko. But the relationship of the
other three ancestors is uncertain, in the sense that there are
different versions of their connexion, amounting virtually to a
complete series of variations on the genealogical positions of
these three names. These early ancestors are both structurally
and historically protodynastic, they do not belong to the main
pedigree of the ruling class and they also represent a different
order of time. Ayagba and his father are transitional figures,
mythological with regard to their achievements and the compression of historical events, and historical in the sense that
they mediate between the period of creation and the later
period of development in which events occur within the
dimension of historical time.

The protodynastic ancestors tend to be represented in
kingship ritual by a single figure or by a single symbolic cult
object. In Ọjaina, the royal burial ground at Idah, there are
only twenty-two royal graves, and the grave of Ẹbẹlẹjonu is
symbolically equivalent to the graves of Agẹnapoje, Abutu
Ẹjẹ, and Idoko, who are not represented by individual graves.
There is, similarly, a single ritual staff, Otutubatu, which represents all the protodynastic ancestors collectively in the
royal ancestor cult; when sacrifices are made their names are
not called individually as are those of the dynastic kings, but
their presence is manifest in the ritual staff, which is placed
to one side of the other ancestral staffs and first receives

11

offerings.[1] We can relate to this collective ritual role the tendency in oral tradition to regard these early reigns as belonging to the same dimension in time. The protodynastic ancestors are not sharply differentiated from each other, and it is frequently not clear in which of the early reigns the events described are supposed to have occurred. They represent collectively the age before Ayagba, and the emphasis on their common function may account for the blurred outlines and indistinct sequence of the mythical epoch.

The transfer of sovereignty

The myths that describe the protodynastic epoch place events in a sequence that is governed by rules of logical development rather than by objective historical conventions. There are three principal stages which in a sense lead on from one another but nevertheless fit together awkwardly in a historical sequence, because of the omission of intervening stages and also because the historical details given in the legends are specific to each phase and do not always relate exactly to the details of the other phases. The argument proceeds logically rather than historically, and on the whole its development bears out Professor Levi-Strauss' suggestion that the division and symbolism of myths are frequently based on a procedure of modifying ideas that are initially predicated as opposites.[2] It will become clear to what extent this idea is useful in the context of Igala tradition if we analyse the principal myths separately and consider the inter-relationship of their symbolism.

The first phase of Igala protodynastic myth is contained in different legends describing the transfer of sovereignty from the autochthonous population to an immigrant group of royal or noble descent. These legends vary with regard to the tribe or centre to which they attribute the origin of the immigrants. But they coincide in stating that the immigrant founder of the

[1] The staff, Otutubatu and the grave of Ębęlęjonu are correspondingly more important than the other staffs and graves reserved to single rulers. Otutubatu is cared for by the senior priest, Atębǫ, and has its own shrine near the palace. See p. 107.

[2] Levi-Strauss, C., 'The Structural Study of Myth', *Journal of American Folklore*, Vol. 68, 1955.

Igala royal house was himself of royal origin, the scion of an older and senior royal line in another kingdom. The migration to and arrival in Igala may be described in detail, with supporting circumstantial evidence of a geographical character. Clifford's account of the migration from Wukari is a good instance of this, and there is a counterpart, making a different attribution, in the legend of Benin origin that forms part of the inner tradition of the royal house. But this migration can also be represented symbolically, and there is an important myth of totemic identity between the royal clan and the leopard which avoids the difficulties of historical attribution by attributing the foundation of the royal clan to a union between an anthropomorphic leopard and a woman of the autochthonous group. Mockler-Ferryman gives a version of this myth in which the royal baby was exposed by its mother and then found and fostered by the leopard until it became old enough to re-enter human society. The numerous other references that occur in unpublished and published literature to a 'man who came out of the bush' probably also refer to this myth, although they often graft the purely mythical allusion on to the stem of legends belonging to later phases. Monsell writes, for example:

> Ebelejawno who became the first Atta of Idah was grinding corn one day when a handsome youth came out of the bush. She asked him to come and help her, and afterwards took him to her house, bathed and fed him, and ultimately married him . . . he became the first Ashadu.[1]

The full text of the royal version of the leopard myth, as told me by one of the elders of the ruling subclan at Idah, is as follows:

> The first rulers had a daughter who went daily from the capital to collect firewood in the grove that is now called Ojaina. As she was visiting this grove she met a leopard there who took the form of a young man. He made advances to her and was accepted, so the young girl was going daily to meet her husband in the bush. He killed game for her and made presents of bushcow and other animals to her parents who began to be curious about the mysterious husband and asked repeatedly to see him. When the

[1] Monsell, C. N., op. cit.

girl told him of this the leopard promised to appear and fixed a time at which he would show himself to his inlaws. But when the leopard came out of the bush the girl's parents ran away in terror. So the leopard ran and hid himself again in the thick bush at Ojaina and went into the ground there. His wife later delivered a child, Abutu Ẹjẹ, who was the founder of the royal clan. The Ojaina grove is the spiritual centre of the royal clan and forms the last resting place of all dead Atas.

The theme of these different legends of royal origin is that the foundations of the Igala state were laid by the transfer of sovereignty from a group of clans representing the local population to an immigrant lineage of royal descent. This explanation is only partially, or incompletely, historical in character. As we have seen, the historical aspect is subordinate to the mythical function to the extent that different historical attributions exist as alternatives to one another, and the central idea, of a royal migration, can be expressed in a purely mythological form by using the idiom of ritual unity implicit in the totemic attribution. The function of these legends as a form of myth is to contrast the political implications of royal descent with the principle of non-royal descent. The transfer of sovereignty expresses the royal group's inborn right to rule and fulfils the destiny of the migrant prince created for him by the fact of birth to an older royal line. Other more explicit reasons are added for this transfer of power. In Mockler-Ferryman's version of the leopard myth, when the leopard's foster-child emerged from the bush his first public act was to settle a dispute between two men who were fighting. The legend says

> He at once took upon himself the duties of arbiter, rebuking the one and commending the other. So astonished were the people who had during the incident crowded around him that they immediately proclaimed him their King, and refused to permit him to leave the town. This was the first Atta . . .[1]

Another, unpublished, version of the king's arrival says:

> The Okpoto were much struck by the skill of the newcomers in hunting and also by their knowledge of the art of poisoning arrows, in which up to then they were not very expert. Ayagba

[1] Mockler-Ferryman, A. F., *Up the Niger*, 1892, pp. 308–9.

moreover seemed to be possessed of a very powerful medicine, probably taught him by his father, who was a noted medicine man.[1]

A third explanation says:

> The story about this is that a man called Aiyagba or Ajagba, came from a far country called Apa. He settled in Idah and married an Okpoto woman. He was successful in war and became chief of the whole tribes and country.[2]

These stories embellish the main theme that the immigrant stranger was of royal blood, and if we survey the whole corpus of tradition on this subject it is clear that the principal reason given for the transfer of sovereignty is the personal nobility of the immigrant, reflecting the high status of his own forbears. In other words the first origin myth is concerned wholly with hereditary status, and with the different implications, in terms of political function, between royals and non-royals. This image of a polar relationship between the two classes, in which one is permanently super-ordinate and the other permanently inferior, reflects a basic division of political functions between clans in the Igala political system. I analyse this difference fully in the later sections of this study, and need only say here that in this political system rights of political sovereignty, in the widest geographical sense, are vested in large-scale clans of high rank, whilst rights of local sovereignty are vested in small-scale, localized clans who are often regarded as being the 'landowners' of the areas in which they are settled. The myth represents this basic division of functions and attributes its origin to the introduction of notions of aristocratic rule from other kingdoms with whom the Igala have been in historical contact.

The peaceful nature of the transfer of sovereignty is significant, since it implies a high degree of continuity from the older system and also stresses the complementary nature of the

---

[1] From a legend collected by C. N. Monsell from the chief of Mozum in 1929, Monsell, C. N., op. cit.

[2] Byng-Hall, F. W., 'Notes on the Okpoto and Igala Tribes', *Journal of the African Society*, Vol. VII, no. XXV, 1907, p. 166.

relationship between the two classes of descent group involved. At this stage of the myths the political functions of the indigenous clans after the transfer of power are not defined precisely. But it is implied that the king co-ordinates their relations without modifying the earlier structure. Furthermore, the myth leaves open the question of relations between the two groups in future generations; it is clear from the structure of the situation that the king's sons inherit a right to rule, but it is also clear that the descendants of the landowning clans inherit something of their forefathers' position as kingmakers.

The Achadu and the kingmakers

Whereas the first phase of these origin myths is not associated with any particular reign in the protodynastic period, the second phase is usually placed in the reign of the female Ata, Ẹbẹlẹjonu. This female figure plays a key role in the legends that describe this phase of development, mediating a marriage alliance with the non-royal elements of the Igala population and reversing the direction of the alliance recorded in the first myth, so that the royal clan, from being a wife-receiving group, reaches the position of giving its own women to the non-royal descent groups that make up the bulk of the population.

A version of this legend told in the royal subclan at Idah says:[1]

> When Ẹbẹlẹjonu became Ata she was a young girl and had no husband. She was fond of festivals where there was singing and dancing and one day went to a celebration arranged by the Igala Mela clans at Igalọgwa,[2] in their own section of the capital. At this festival she saw a slave belonging to the Igala Mela, who was of strikingly handsome appearance. He was a man of Ibo origin who had come to the Igala area for hunting, had lost his way in the bush, and had been found and taken as a domestic slave by the Igala Mela, in whose territory he was hunting.
>
> Ẹbẹlẹjonu was so much attracted by this person that she had him transferred to her own service, and eventually made him her

[1] For other, closely similar, versions of this legend see Seton, R. S., 'Installation of an Attah of Idah', *J.R.A.I.*, Vol. LVIII, 1928, pp. 269–70, and Clifford, Miles, 'A Nigerian Chiefdom . . .', *J.R.A.I.*, Vol. LXVI, 1936, p. 395.

[2] The name Igalọgwa means 'the first (or premier) Igala'.

consort. The Igala Mela and her own followers were jealous of the husband's position and began to abuse him in her hearing. But she retorted that apart from the slave, *ochai adu*, there should be no one with power like her own.[1] This description was incorporated in the title of Achadu which the Ata then bestowed on her consort. It was also determined that this title would be hereditary in future, and that the Achadu would control all the land lying beyond the river Anambra to the east of Idah as his own hereditary fief.

Ẹbẹlẹjonu died childless, and the kingship passed to her brother, Agẹnapoje. But the Ata is still described as *ọy'Achadu*, the Achadu's wife, in memory of this early marriage, and this is also why Igala kings have their ears pierced like a woman's.[2]

In all probability the historical events alluded to in this myth are compressed in time, so that developments which may have spanned several generations are assigned to a single reign. The rise of the Achadu's clan to a position of dominance within the federation of kingmakers is described aetiologically rather than historically. Similarly, the brief references to contact with the Ibo and to the Achadu's connection with the trans-Anambra region condense a wide range of historical associations covering a long period of Igala expansion into Ibo territory in this eastern sector of the Igala-Ibo border.[3] We can conclude from this synoptic treatment of historical material that is well-known to the Igala in other contexts, that the function of this tradition is to summarize the historical trends for a mythological purpose.

In this phase of the mythical epoch both the elements of the previous stage are present, the immigrant royal clan being represented by a female ruler, and the indigenous clans being identified explicitly with the Igala Mela. There is also a third element, however, in relation to which these other two elements, previously opposed to one another, symbolically merge and form a unity. In the first myths the principle of opposition is the distinction between royal and non-royal descent. But in this new phase of development descent itself is contrasted

---

[1] This etymology is not accepted by the members of the Achadu's clan.

[2] Text from the Ochai Ata, Amana Edime, who claims that it belonged to the series of legends formerly taught by the palace eunuchs in the royal history school.

[3] cf. Boston, J. S., 'Notes on Contact between the Igala and the Ibo', *Journal of the Historical Society of Nigeria*, Vol. 2, no. 1, 1960.

with change in a descent system, the status and qualities transmitted by the descent principle are contrasted with the principle of achieved status and with the realignments that this can create in a system based on inherited status. In relation to this new principle of opposition the two elements of the former antithesis merge with one another since they are both examples of the transmission of status by descent and as such are logically opposed to the symbolic figure of the slave, cut off from his antecedents and owing his position entirely to his own personal qualities and to political opportunism.

In one sense the first Achadu, Omẹppa, appears in the traditions potentially as an historical figure, as the actual mediator of a marriage alliance between two groups of clans and of a wider political alliance between the border areas whose fortunes are closely involved with the Ibo and the home districts of the kingdom. But in another sense this itinerant hunter who from being the slave of the landowners rose to be their overlord is a purely conventional figure, whose standard attributes and qualities are directly opposed to the conventional attributes of the other royal and non-royal clan heads as representatives of an on-going descent system. In a paper on the significance of the hunter figure in Igala oral tradition I have shown that the origin legends of local communities in Igala tend to fall into two classes, one centring upon founders of noble birth or aristocratic descent and the other upon founders who are said to have been hunters by profession.[1] This second type of legend is difficult to analyse by historiographic methods, since it is usually lacking in the kind of detail that is useful to historians, and is frequently embellished with dramatic incident that appears to be either fanciful or imaginative in character. But if we interpret this class of legend sociologically, and regard the hunter figure as an archetype rather than an actual historical figure, the details and even the shortcomings of these legends become meaningful.

The approach that I have adopted to the hunter legends, and which I suggest corresponds to the true perspective of this figure in Igala tradition, is to regard its symbolism as a co-ordinate of the symbolic notions expressed in the myth of

[1] cf. Boston, J. S., 'The Hunter in Igala Legends of Origin', *Africa*, Vol. XXXIV, no. 2, 1964.

the landowners and the royal dynasty. There is often a direct complementary relationship between the two sets of notions. The hunter legends, for instance, use the idiom of an un-inhabited area and of a wandering hunter to stress the absence of descent and kinship ties which are of such vital importance in the opposite class of legend. Again, the hunter acts in a field of human relationships where leadership is not institu-tionalized, and where the competitive and egalitarian aspects of human activity are strongly emphasized. The distinctive feature of the hunter's position is his lack of previous com-mitments. Hunting is, in terms of hereditary status relation-ships, a neutral zone, and achievement in this field is not contingent upon an existing structure of relations as achieve-ment in war, trade, or in the accumulation of wealth would be in the context of the Igala social system. This complementarity of achieved and hereditary status can be extended, if we widen the analysis to include the widest associations of these legends, to ritual, where it appears as an opposition of cosmological principles. The king, and the heads of the landowning clans, are strongly associated with the ancestral dimension of Igala religion. The hunter on the other hand, is usually credited with surpassing skill in the use of magic and medicines; in a sense he personifies the world of magic, since he moves in the world of plants and trees from which almost all medicines and magical substances are compounded.

If this analysis of the hunter figure in oral tradition is correct, we can suggest that the emergence of the Achadu's clan symbolizes the possibility of realignment in a political system based on descent. Political offices are hereditary in patriclans in the Igala, and the distribution of power is governed by the division of functions between clans grouped in classes. But the descent model does not cover all the contingencies that arise from the inter-action of clans within the system. The frame-work is an open one in the sense that the clans are not tied together by the descent principle as lineages are within a seg-mentary system of lineage relations. Through marriage, and through the purely political inter-action of the constituent units, new groupings can arise, which may consolidate older alliances, as in the case of the Igala Mela, or create an entirely new pattern, as is predicated in the case of the hunter legends which do not admit the existence of an earlier population. In either case structural change comes about through the realignment of lineage genealogies so that they either meet in the person of the hunter, or become coeval with the foundation of the hunter's own lineage. In the case of the Achadu both processes occur. There are many lineages in the trans-Anambra area that claim direct descent from Omẹppa and are thus full members of the Achadu's clan. The Igala Mela, on the other hand, have traditions of separate foundation, and claim to be older in point of time. But their genealogies are in fact no greater in depth than that of the Achadu's clan. And in fact also the succession of generations within the Igala Mela genealogies tends to be synchronized with the pattern set by the Achadu's lineages, so we can regard the former as being to some extent structurally dependent upon the latter.

The relationship indicated by this myth between the principles of inherited and achieved status is ultimately one of superordination and subordination. In the legend the Achadu owes his elevation to royal patronage, and similarly in many hunter legends the founder consolidates his achievement by marrying one of the king's daughters and obtaining the grant of a title. But this ideal ascendancy of the royal group is modified by the role assigned to their representative in this myth as *oy'Achadu*. The king, as 'wife' to the head of this clan, is in some respects in a subordinate position. The Achadu's authority over the king is a function of his duties as head of the kingmakers, and is expressed again in the ritual of accession when the Achadu beats and abuses his 'wife', and sends the candidate for the throne to his own senior wife for the ceremony of piercing the ears. The myth uses the idiom of domestic kinship relations to describe this authority, and in the same way that some of the other kingmakers are described, in the context of accession as the 'father' and 'mother' of the king.[1] I will show later that the division of powers in government between the royal clan and the federation of kingmakers tends to be concentrated on the opposed offices of Ata and Achadu. This concentration and opposition is symbolically expressed

[1] cf. Monckton, J. C., 'Burial Ceremonies of the Attah of Idah', *Journal of the African Society,* Vol. XXVII, 1927–8, p. 17, and Seton, R. S., op. cit., pp. 260–4.

in the myth by the idiom of a wife–husband relationship. And the associations of these positions counterbalance those that are implicit in the description of the Achadu as a slave and hunter who was ennobled by the favour of the Ata.

Ayagba ọm Idoko

The third, and concluding phase, of Igala mythology describes the achievements of the apical ancestor of the royal clan, and identifies his contribution to the kingship with the emergence of an autonomous and fully organized state. Ayagba's reign forms a reference point for most of the office-holding clans in Igala, from which they measure their position in the state. These clans sum up and conceptualize their functions in the state system by the mythical relationship that existed between Ayagba and their own founders. Each of these clan traditions makes a separate contribution to the Ayagba myth, and a correspondingly wide survey would be necessary to do justice to its importance in Igala tradition. But some of these secondary sources will be considered later, and it is sufficient here to consider the main outline of Ayagba's reign, about which most of the traditions agree. This divides naturally into three major series of events, corresponding to the stages by which the kingdom achieved its independence from alien rule. I give below versions of these legends told by a member of the royal house at Idah:[1] they agree closely with similar legends told in other parts of Igala.[2] The first legend tells the story of Ayagba's accession and of the way in which he provoked a conflict with the Jukun.

The Ata had been paying tribute to the Jukun from a remote period. The Jukun came here and made war so that we would give them something. When the Igala grew tired they decided to pay tribute to avoid further war, and went on paying until Ayagba's time. Idoko was ruling at that time and Ayagba, his son, was being trained by a palace eunuch with the title of Ẹnẹfọla; Ẹnẹfọla looked after Ayagba until he grew up, and taught him to prepare medicines. Ayagba became powerful and made medicines that

[1] Amana Edime.
[2] A remarkably similar version of this legend was given me by an elder from Akpodo, about 20 miles north of Idah.

were successful. God showed him the way in this. Then Ayagba said that at the end of the year he would go to the Jukun himself. His father approved, being sick at the time, and authorized Ayagba to take the tribute on his behalf.

Ayagba took dried excrement and put it into nine calabashes of the kind that they use today in festivals, he put it inside them and covered it over. Then he bought tobacco wrapped up in the ancient manner and got that ready. He travelled with these loads, accompanied by palace servants, and on arriving in the Jukun court said that he would rest and present the tribute in the morning. So he was shown somewhere to stay.

After Ayagba had gone in, the son of the Jukun chief came to look for Ayagba, but found only a young girl there. He greeted her and asked if she was Ayagba's wife, but the girl replied that she was Ayagba's younger sister. The prince said that he found her attractive and would ask Ayagba for her when he came back. The girl agreed.

This prince then made gifts of food to the girl who said that she needed a special ritual vessel, *aṇẹ*, before she could eat. The prince replied that he would bring his own father's vessel if she would agree to spend the night with him. She consented, so the chief's son stole the *aṇẹ* after his father had finished eating and brought it to the girl, not knowing that she was Ayagba in another form. That night, when the time came for the girl to go to the prince, he fell asleep, and Ayagba woke his followers telling them to make haste because he had found what he came for. They ran, and were on the road next day when the Jukun rose and began to call Ayagba.

When they failed to find him, the Jukun decided to uncover the tribute without waiting any longer. They uncovered the calabashes and pulled out a piece of tobacco which they gave to the king, sitting on his box stool. The king smoked it and swooned; his people ran to support him, but he did not revive. So the Jukun looked up and down for Ayagba but did not find him. They sent a messenger to Idah, who returned to say that Ayagba had not returned, but that the old king, Idoko, was dead. The Jukun asked about the succession and were enraged when they heard that Ayagba was the heir. They said that war would reach there first, and that they would destroy the city of Idah.

The main themes of this legend, the king's tactical skill in adversity and his need of the *aṇẹ* symbol as an emblem of sovereignty are discussed elsewhere in this study, and need not be dealt with fully here. It is a significant comment on the Igala conception of royal power that Ayagba inherits a fundamentally weak position from his ancestors. The notion that the king has to work within the framework of given circumstances is a constant theme of kingship tradition in this society, and this legend is one of many parables which show that political solutions are achieved by intrigue and cunning rather than by the application of force. It is typical of this attitude that the symbolic transfer of sovereignty in which the *ane* vessel stands for the king's rights over the land, is accomplished by a stratagem involving the use of medicines. In this context the Jukun overlords represent a whole complex of external forces with which the Igala king has to deal, and possibly also symbolize the opposition of physical force to the qualities of rank inherent in the Igala royal clan.

The second phase of this myth follows on chronologically from the first legend and describes the defeat of the Jukun in their punitive campaign against Ayagba. This legend has become well-known in the literature of Igala and is recorded by both Seton and Clifford. I give below Seton's version, which condenses the essential features and differs only in a few details from Clifford's account and from other versions that are told in Igala today.

> Inikpi was the daughter of Ayagba Qm'Idoko. She is reputed to have been very beautiful and of a noble disposition and her father loved her more than anything else in the world, and she him.
>
> In Ayagba's reign the Jukuns under Appah attacked Idah, and he was unable to make any headway against them. He asked a certain learned Nupe, Mallam, what he could do to change the fortune of the war. He replied: 'If you do not wish to lose both your title and your land you must sacrifice the daughter you love so much to the spirits of this place.'
>
> When Ayagba heard this he was overcome with grief, and appeared prepared to lose all that he had rather than carry out the sacrifice. She, however, heard what the Mallam had said, and went to her father and begged him to save himself by sacrificing her. She is said to have gone nine times before he consented.
>
> A large hole was dug in the market place, and she went down into it with nine slaves and with all her jewels and charms. She called to the people above to throw in the earth. This was quickly done. She was unmarried at the time of her death. . . .

23

After her death the Mallam supplied the Attah with some charms, which were thrown into the river Nasallu (near Idah). The Jukuns, who were camped on the far bank, ate the fish taken from the river, and many of them died. The remainder were scattered by Ayagba and his followers.[1]

This version does not make it clear, as do texts in the original language that both the sacrifice and employment of the Nupe magician were advised by the Ifa oracle. Nor does it reveal the important fact that the oracle specified that the sacrifice should be made to the land. Igala versions of the immolation say that Ayagba offered his daughter to the land, i momanw du nyanẹ.

This central incident again reflects the myths' constant pre-occupation with the ritual relationship existing between the king and the land. This connexion is shown to be the one dimension in which the king's powers are incomplete, and in which the royal clan cannot fulfil its destiny to rule without external assistance. The sacrifice of Ayagba's daughter shows this incompleteness in an extreme form; the king is in imminent danger of defeat, and his failures are ascribed to the 'spoiling of the land', anẹ ekpabiẹ. Other versions of this Inikpi legend emphasize the threatened extinction of the dynasty by saying that Ayagba had no male children, and that the sacrifice of his daughter was made to ensure the birth of male heirs to continue the line. Both interpretations attribute this situation to the failure of the king's duties towards the land, and they make the survival of the dynasty conditional upon the restoration of this relationship.

This myth, in other words, restates the theme of the initial phase of the protodynastic period, which is also expressed indirectly in the legend of Ayagba's quest for the anẹ symbol of the Jukun king. The Ata's powers embrace every aspect of government with the exception of ritual control of the land. The royal clan's control of this aspect of the state is variously represented as being due to a voluntary transfer of sovereignty, the theft of an emblem of sovereignty from the Jukun, and, finally, to a sacrifice in which the Ata gave up his most valued

---

[1] Seton, R. S., op. cit., pp. 270-1.

24

possession. The theme common to these different formula-
tions is that sovereignty over the land exists, as it were, apart
from the royal clan, and is not part of the hereditary qualities
which are transmitted by descent and form the birthright of
each member of the royal group. This conceptual distinction
corresponds, as I suggested earlier, to the division in political
functions between clans of high and low rank in the Igala,
and is the basis of the opposition between royals and non-
royals. The full associations of ritual responsibility for the land
will become clearer as I describe the detailed working of the
political system, and it will then also be clear how these mythical
references to the land cult symbolize a basic aspect of Igala
political organization.

The myth of the last phase of Ayagba's reign is the common
property of the many clans that trace their foundation to this
period and begin their history with an account of their founder's
connexion with Ayagba. Perhaps the most important theme
that emerges from their different accounts of this epoch is the
role of Ayagba as the creator of the system of hereditary titles
on which the Igala political organization depends. These titles
are usually described as rewards given by Ayagba to the clan
founders for their assistance in the Jukun war, for specialized
services that have become hereditary within the clan, or, finally,
to mark some special kinship connexion with the founder of
a particular clan.

In many cases the award of a title by Ayagba forms the charter
by which immigrant clans justify their arrival and presence in
Igala, and by which, at the same time, they demonstrate their
assimilation into the state system and into the pattern of Igala
culture. A majority of the clans living along the left bank of
the Niger fall into this category, and hold titled offices whose
duties are concerned with riverain affairs and with contact
between the capital and the other nations using this riverain
highway. In this instance, the compression of the historical
dimension into a single transaction between the king and the
clan founder emphasizes the equality of the groups concerned
with other clans, and the completeness of their assimilation
into the Igala system. The historical difference between these
immigrant groups and the indigenous inhabitants of Igala is
focused upon differences of hereditary political function, and

does not imply the notion of cultural difference or of qualified membership of the political community.

In other cases the award of a title redefines an older relationship between the royal clan and an indigenous group, crystallizing functions that are implicit in the earlier traditions and giving them a constitutional form. This is especially true of the kingmakers, who in the earlier mythical phase are identified with the kingmaking role of the autochthonous population, and have authority over the Ata, but do not have precise political functions of the kind associated with the award of a title. Ayagba, after his victory over the Jukun, included the Igala Mela in his distribution of titles: this is recorded in the traditions of the Igala Mela themselves, and is also made explicit by the name of one of the titles, Agbẹnyọ, which is popularly said to mean that the holder forgot, egbẹnyọ, to allocate land to his own clan when he was appointed by Ayagba to fix the boundaries of the Igala Mela territories.

In both these sets of tradition the contractual element of the relationship between the king and his office holders is pronounced. The effect of placing these political connexions in the mythical period of time is to give them permanence and make them unalterable in principle. They become the subject of rituals that are performed annually to renew the ideal connexion between the ruling house and subordinate clans. And the rite sets the seal on a perpetual alliance between two descent groups, in which each has its part to play in maintaining a wider structure to which they both belong. One of the functions of historical compression here is to emphasize the contractual nature of the relationship, by balancing the king's inherent superiority directly against his dependence upon the specialist services of others and upon the nexus of kinship ties that form an inevitable corollary of the descent principle.

This series of formal contracts that make up the title system also resolve the problem of the king's relationship with the land which was posed by the earlier myths. In awarding titles to his followers Ayagba is said to have defined the boundaries of clan land in all parts of the kingdom, and so to have fixed the relative position of the major clan centres for all time. The significant feature of this distribution of fiefs is that they were awarded principally to non-royal clans, who exercise the rights

26

of local sovereignty that are implicit in the roles of the non-royal population in the earlier myths. Ayagba's sovereign rights are limited by this distribution to rights of overlord-ship, entailing a share of the non-royal clans' perquisites, but curtailing the king's participation in local government by the intermediacy of the non-royal clan heads. Within the context of a hereditary system of government this in turn limits the rights of the royal clan as a whole, and defines their position in relation to the local landowning clans to whom they are superior in rank. These are the basic principles of structure whose working out dominated traditional politics in Igala. I have tried to show that oral tradition presents these principles, and so provides a model of the political system, by using the names and achievements of different groups of clan founders as archetypes. To some extent these archetypes are presented in the manner that Professor Levi Strauss has suggested is typical of the procedure of mythical thought. They form a series of polar types or complementary extremes, which are progressively mediated by the introduction of new terms and new contrasting pairs.

The logic behind this system of oppositions is probably an historical one and does not obey mechanical laws of philosophy or rules of logical necessity. It probably reflects a type of political evolution in which kingship emerged in a system where discrete clan units were associated with definite tracts of territory over which they held sovereign rights. It would be interesting, in this respect, to compare the Igala system with that of the neighbouring Idoma, where there is no traditional system of kingship but where the clans are organized on the basis of their local landowning rights. The Igala concept of the land chief, which I describe later, and which underlies the whole concept of royal power, is closely paralleled by the Idoma concept of the land[1] and there are also obvious affinities with the political concepts of many other West African peoples who have no system of kingship but nevertheless define clan functions in terms of land ownership.

[1] cf. p. 95. Armstrong, R. G., 'The Idoma-speaking Peoples', in *Peoples of the Niger-Benue Confluence*, Ethnographic Survey of Africa series, 1955.

CHAPTER THREE

THE HEREDITARY BASIS OF CENTRAL GOVERNMENT

I N the administrative system by which the Igala are governed at the present time, territorial considerations are paramount, and the division of the kingdom into districts and village areas would form a natural starting point for any analysis of the modern system of government.[1] But it is clear from the form taken by Igala oral tradition that in the past the hereditary aspect of political authority was the major focus of interest, and that the clan system was seen as providing the basic framework of government and administration. This difference is one of emphasis and does not involve a conflict of principle. Igala clans are usually localized, and the rights that they possess in land make up a major portion of their corporate functions. But although the territorial sphere formed a major dimension of clan consciousness and clan inter-relations, the clan system existed in its own right as a framework within which political authority was delegated permanently among clans of different orders. And the primacy of this mode of organization over the territorial distribution of power was such that spatial relationships were more fluid in the traditional than in the modern system and the geographical balance of power was correspondingly more dynamic than is possible in an administration tied to a rigid system of territorial divisions. I have tried to follow this bias and bring the main emphases of the traditional system to life by considering the hereditary and the territorial aspects of government in separate sections, and by giving priority to the workings of the clan system, divorced as far as possible from its territorial foundation.

Agnatic links are followed in Igala to determine succession

---

[1] The village areas of the modern network correspond to the districts, *anẹ*, of the traditional system, whilst the modern Districts are closely linked to the traditional spheres of influence of various royal subclans.

to hereditary political office and to the many different statuses involved in the inheritance of rights over persons and property. Hereditary rights of this order are vested in patrilineal groups, *olopu*, whose members exercise jurisdiction over succession and inheritance. These are the groups around which public and political life revolved in the traditional system, and to which much of Igala life is still orientated at the present time. In this society a man's status and expectations are still governed to a considerable extent by the basic fact of clan membership, inherited from the father's side, and in the traditional system clanship was even more important as a determinant of status.

Olopu[1] are unilineal descent groups in the sense that their members are related to each other agnatically and share certain rights in common that can only be transmitted through the male line. But they are unilineal groups of clan rather than of lineage type. Exact genealogical relationships are important over only a limited span in time, usually not more than three or four generations, and beyond this connexions with or through earlier generations tend to be abridged by naming the founder of the group.

When genealogies are collected from clan members it is common to find a basic uncertainty about the actual relationship above the third or fourth ascending generation. For instance, in a sample of six clans among the kingmakers, the Igala Mela, all the clan heads knew several names of previous office holders, but only three placed the series in exact genealogical relationships. The others explained that the first three or four men named in each case were patrilineally related, *ọmẹnẹkẹlẹ*, to each other, but that the details were unknown. Further inquiries into one of these imperfect genealogies had the same negative results, producing a shallow genealogy with a very wide span and a mainly putative connexion between the founder and the first generation. One informant, living 20 miles from the capital, was in frequent communication with

---

[1] This term has no other meaning in Igala. Its two roots, *ol'* and *ọpu*, may be cognate with the Idoma terms *ọlẹ*, family, and *ọpu*, council ground or doorway. Personal communication from Professor R. G. Armstrong. cf. also Armstrong, R. G., 'The Idoma-speaking Peoples', in *Peoples of the Niger-Benue Confluence*, Ethnographic Survey of Africa series, 1955.

the clan head at Idah, and went to him for advice and assistance on a number of family problems. But their mutual relationship could not be established in detail; it went back to two ancestors in the third ascending generation who were known to be patrilineally related and beyond this it was stated that 'we do not know who their progenitors were', *a mẹnẹ ki bi ma gen*.

In tracing agnatic relationship there are a number of conventional formulae which make it unnecessary to establish exact genealogical connexions. The procedure is simplified in the first place by concentrating on sibling relationships, in which the persons named usually belong to the same generation or are brought into line with other persons who do. The discussion then proceeds by steps from one generation to the next, each pair of names being *oji ẹgọ* or equal in generation. When no more names are known, or when it is wished to shorten the discussion the formula for sibling relationship is used and the last persons named are described as *ọmata*, 'children of one father'. This term is essentially a category of relationship and is not descriptive as the literal translation implies. It assimilates the relationship between siblings to the connexion between children. Intervening generations can be disregarded, provided the links are agnatic, and two members of any subsequent generations can be regarded as representing *ekoji*, the children, *ekojiọma*, of the original founder. The phrase *ata ka tịtị bi ma*, 'one father begot them', has the same significance, meaning that the connexion is an agnatic one and that the number of generations involved is irrelevant. If we represent this term diagrammatically it will show more clearly how the step from the founder of a clan to the first generation is often made.

The putative nature of the first level of clan genealogies also appears in the use of title names for clan founders instead of their own personal names. In the majority of clans, the office of clan head is combined with a political title, *ọfẹ*, having its own name and salutation. On appointment to the title the holder virtually gives up the use of his personal name and is known by the name of his office. As ancestors in the clan genealogy, former titleholders are known by their personal names again, together with any cognomens that may have

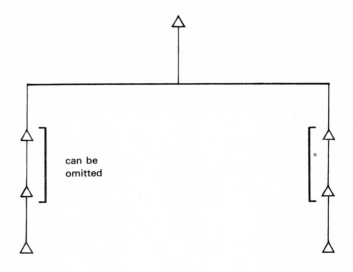

can be
omitted

FIGURE 2. AGNATIC DESCENT

become associated with them. But the clan founder can also be described, in the genealogies, by his clan title, and in many cases no personal name is given, but only that of the title. For instance, in the imperfect genealogy referred to above the founder's name was given as Aleji. But this is the name of a title that the clan heads hold in succession from the Ata, and also of the clan itself. In this instance the founder is purely a figurehead, personifying generations of early ancestors whose names have been forgotten. Forgotten is perhaps the wrong term for this process of genealogical adjustment; the shallow depth of the genealogies is related to a rotating system of succession which I describe later on, and it is mainly because they are irrelevant to this structure that the names of early ancestors can be discarded or subsumed under a class name.

Clans have individual names, which are often synonymous with the names of political titles. There are also individual clan salutations, used in polite address by non-members, and varying according to the sex of the person addressed. In titled clans, salutations for men usually take the form of a diminutive of the title salutation or of the clan name. This is formed by prefixing the term *ọma*, child, to either of these names, as in *ọmata,* 'royal clansman', which uses the name of the royal title, or as in *ọmanu,* 'Achadu's clansman', which makes use of the Achadu's title greeting.

In practice clan salutations are more commonly used towards women than men. In addressing men salutations can be borrowed loosely from a set of terms that properly denotes seniority within the clan. Thus the term *odaudu* strictly applies to the first-born son of the speaker's father, or, more generally, the eldest surviving member of one's own patrilineal clan segment. *Okolo* is the correct form of address for the second son or for the next in line to the head of the clan segment. *Wodi* and *adọgbaa* are the corresponding terms for the third and fourth sons respectively, or for the men in those positions in the order of clan seniority. The first two terms in this set are frequently used by non-members of the clan to acknowledge greater seniority or higher status in the person addressed, and in many contexts it may be more respectful to address a man as *daudu* than to use his correct clan greeting. In addressing women, there are two terms which denote seniority in relation to the speaker. *Iye* is used for a woman a generation above one's own, and *ouja* for a senior member of one's own age-group. But these terms have kinship associations through being used as familiar terms of address among women in the same local community. And it is often more respectful to address a woman by her clan salutation than by the term based on seniority, the reverse of the pattern that obtains in the salutations used for men.

Relative seniority is a major constituent of clan relationships, and in all Igala clans one of the chief functions of clanship is the creation of a pattern of authority based on descent. Seniority is also important in other social contexts, but outside the context of clanship or of clan inter-relations it does not have the same jural significance. And in many kinship contexts, as we shall see, the norms of behaviour between blood kin are patterned by contrasting their relationship with the formal relations expressing seniority that characterize the narrower field of agnatic relationships within the clan.

The most general distinction of seniority within the clan opposes the elders, *abogujo*, to the age-groups of younger men, *abokolobia*, and places these in turn above the lowest class of juniors or young children, *abimoto*. Within this broad classification there is a further distinction of generations. The Igala are extremely conscious of this distinction and classify men on the basis of their being *oji ego*, equal in age, with one another. The classification is co-ordinated roughly throughout Igala by reference to the sequence of generations in the royal house. In 1960, for instance, the Igala regarded the Ata Amaga's generation as being almost extinct,[1] and accorded great respect to anyone who was generally accepted as belonging to this group. Conversely, they used Atabo's reign[2] as a dividing line between groups that might have reached the age of discretion and those who, by definition, were too young to have any understanding of adult mores and the conduct of public life.

This distinction of seniority between generations vests the authority of the clan in a hierarchy of sibling groups, within which each group is free to manage its own affairs but is nominally subordinate to the senior groups above it. Within the sibling groups, again, relative seniority is distinguished, and an internal hierarchy of authority emerges in any context that brings clansmen of the same generation together. This internal distinction is nominally based on age, and is upheld by the use of kinship terms that denote relative seniority within the same age-group, *achogwa* for senior sibling and *okikili* for a junior person. But this criterion is affected by a number of other factors, including wealth, size and status of family, maternal and other cognatic kin ties, lineal closeness to office holders within the clan, personal ability, and so on. The hierarchy that emerges in a given situation is delicately poised in spite of its apparently solid foundations. And it may be the fictional and dynamic nature of this principle that accounts for the tensions and constraint that characterize sibling relationships within the clan. Here a pattern of authority that is outwardly stable and fixed in its order, is in fact competitive and open to change.

The logical outcome of this hierarchical arrangement is that the most senior member of the uppermost age-group has authority over the whole clan. The Igala recognize this by

[1] Amaga died in the year 1900.
[2] Atabo died in 1926.

33

making the position into an important clan office, of *ogujo olopu*. And they define the pattern of succession to this role by saying that when the *ogujo olopu* dies the person who is next in order of seniority should return home to the clan centre, from wherever he may be living, in order to look after the affairs of the clan, *Egba kogujo olopu lekwu ene ki charononw a liwunyi todu ki a de olopunw.*[1]

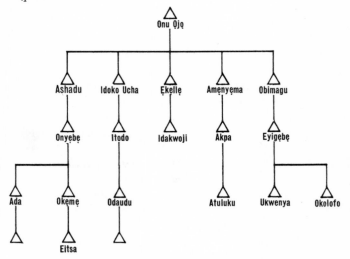

FIGURE 3. THE OJO CLAN

In the Ojo clan, centred on Igebije, some 25 miles from the capital, one branch of the clan had provided two or three *ogujo olopu* in succession. But after Okeme's death, his relatives sent for an elder, Idakwoji, living in the Ibaji district about 40 miles away. Idakwoji later quarrelled with Okeme's branch of the clan and gave up the post, so another elder, Odaudu, was invited to return to Igebije from a neighbouring district to become the *ogujo olopu* in his place.[2] When Odaudu died the office passed to Atuluku, who had moved to Igebije during Odaudu's lifetime.

The authority exercised by the *ogujo olopu* within the clan is

[1] 'When the senior member of the family dies the next in age should return home to look after the family.'

[2] This dispute is described more fully later. See pp. 161–2.

34

moral and ritual in character and the office is important not so much administratively as forming a symbol of clan unity. Its holder mediates between the living and the dead members of the clan by standing next in order of seniority to the ancestors themselves, and his home is an important centre for the ancestral cult carried on within the clan. Arbitration in disputes is often referred to this ritual function, by the *ogujo olopu* saying for instance that he intervenes 'so that the ancestors will not be angry'. The Ifa oracle, which is consulted in all serious misfortunes, often gives its verdicts in the same terms. A case was recorded for instance in which a son who had quarrelled with his father made sacrifices through the *ogujo olopu* to the clan ancestors who were said by Ifa to be incensed and to be punishing the offender by bringing sickness and other misfortune into his household.[1]

The administrative functions of the *ogujo olopu* are limited by the fact that Igala clans tend to be widely dispersed beyond their original centres. But, more especially, they are limited by the existence of other offices in which the external leadership of the clan is vested. In clans that are titled, as the majority are, the roles of external and internal leader are merged in a single office, to which succession is governed by formal rules of rotating succession. In bestowing titles the king, or other patron, uses the formula:

Inyini ẹ mudogujo olopu
'Today you become the *ogujo olopu*.'

In other words seniority by age is in this case entirely subordinate to the function of political leadership, which has its own rules of procedure. The duties of the ritual *ogujo olopu,* or most senior elder, are limited in these cases to deputizing for the titleholder during the succession. When the titleholder dies the ancestral cult symbols *okwutẹ* are transferred from his house to that of the senior elder, and the next incumbent formally takes on the duties of *ogujo olopu* when the *okwutẹ* are handed over to him after his appointment.

---

[1] In another case a married woman who became chronically ill, with tuberculosis, was sent home to her father when the oracle attributed her sickness to ancestral anger and discovered various ways in which the patient had offended her father's ancestral guardians.

The Igala also isolate and limit the administrative functions of the clan elder by distinguishing between the office of *ogujo olọpu* and that of *onu anẹ*, or 'chief of the land'. The second term describes the political head of the clan in his capacity of heir to the sovereign rights exercised by the clan over the land with which it is associated. In titled clans this function is merged with the political and ritual aspects of clan office to form a single entity. But during title disputes and the long periods of interregnum that are so characteristic of the Igala title system, the two offices tend to become separated and the demarcation of their respective spheres of jurisdiction and authority is frequently a matter for dispute. I postpone discussion of this complex relationship to the section in which territorial rights are described more fully.

One of the basic differences between the position of *ogujo olọpu* and other clan offices is its association with the horizontal plane of clan organization, in which the unity of sibling groups cuts across the vertical division of the clan into lineages or into subclans. The ritual duties of the office, for instance, present relations with the clan ancestors in the light of this unity rather than portraying them as an association of separate lineal groupings. Titled offices on the other hand, incorporating the functions of the land chief, *onu anẹ*, tend to emphasize lineal divisions, and vest the hereditary rights of the clan in one lineage or subclan at a time. This distinction will become clearer as we investigate the differences between clans in more detail, and at this stage we will illustrate only the principle of age-group unity without supplying the contrasting term of solidarity within the lineage.

In all matters concerning inheritance and succession, in which, by definition, all clan members have a common interest, the principle of sibling unity is upheld by the rule that seniors take precedence over juniors.[1] This rule is expressed in a traditional formula of inheritance which says that

> *achọgwa onẹ chẹnẹ ki a rọnonw*
> 'the senior sibling is the person to succeed.'

---

[1] A more detailed study of Igala inheritance custom is being published elsewhere. cf. Boston, J. S., 'Igala Inheritance and Succession', in Derrett, J. D. M. (ed.), *Studies in the Laws of Succession in Nigeria*.

36

When a person dies in Igala the transfer of statuses that the deceased held is discussed and put into effect by the agnates of the deceased when they assemble for the funeral ceremonies. The main stages of the funeral, which may be spread over years, correspond to different stages in the distribution and allocation of the deceased's property. At the first stage, centring on the interment, an interim arrangement is made. A further allocation of rights, over the dead man's wives and children, is made when the family reassembles for the rites that end the widows' mourning. And the final settlement is reached at a further stage of ritual, the Aku ceremony in which the ghost becomes an ancestor definitively.

These funeral assemblies reproduce the sibling organization of the clan in miniature and form one of the most important occasions for corporate action within the clan. The terse succession formula quoted above refers to the pattern of organization that emerges on these occasions and does not directly describe the actual heir or the mode of transferring property. It is related to the norm that clansmen have a common interest in property matters and a common voice in the determination of inheritance. When the clan, or its local section, meets to discuss inheritance, the sibling grouping takes precedence over division into lineages, and authority over the settlement rests chiefly with the senior siblings, *achogwa*, of the deceased. The number of those who actually attend varies with the social status of the deceased and the genealogical involvement varies accordingly. At the funeral of a wealthy noble most of the branches of his subclan or clan may be represented, and the inheritance issues are discussed informally over a wide range of clan relationships. At the other extreme a poor commoner living apart from his clansmen may have only his own and his brothers' children to represent the *olopu*. But the principle of agnatic right and sibling unity is unaffected by these variations in practice.

The clan group that meets to discuss inheritance and perform the funeral rites for a dead member of the clan is nominally under the authority of the *ogujo olopu* within the clan. If the deceased is a titleholder this may be symbolized when the funeral presentations are begun, by making the first presentation in the name of the *ogujo olopu*. But this symbolic authority is rarely put into effect unless a dispute breaks out

37

over the inheritance which is of such dimensions that the funeral procedure has to be suspended. Under normal circumstances, the effective head of the proceedings is the most senior male member of the dead person's sibling group. It is this relative who formally takes responsibility for the whole funeral and adopts the role of *ajïegwu*, 'He who buries the body.' He presides over the discussion of inheritance questions, and gives the final decision if there is disagreement within the sibling group. In between the formal assemblies the heirs of the deceased consult the *ajïegwu* before they alienate or convert any of the property. Similarly, clansmen who wish to take any of the widows, under the custom by which rights over widows are inherited agnatically, make their request to the *ajïegwu* who then brings it before the whole sibling group when they assemble at the end of the ritual period of mourning.

Traditionally, the *ajïegwu* should be chosen, where possible, from a collateral lineage of the clan and not from the deceased's own lineage. The lineage is the widest group within which self-acquired property and domestic rights over houses, land, and crops are normally inherited. But by the rule of funeral procedure this grouping is made subordinate to the clan as a whole in property matters, and the common interest of clansmen in this sphere is expressed and maintained by giving them authority over the inheritance settlement. Moreover, clansmen from collateral lineages are not excluded entirely from inheriting themselves. They can, for instance, inherit rights over widows and children and if the deceased had specially close ties with agnatic relatives outside his own lineage this might be recognized by allowing them to take small items of property, or by allowing them the use of any land or houses that had been granted them in the deceased's lifetime.

The pattern of co-operation and obedience that emerges in connexion with inheritance is so fundamental to the institution of clanship that the Igala frequently use the principle of responsibility for burial to characterize agnatic relations in general. In acknowledging other groups as clansmen they often say:

awa cholǫpu katiti a ji egwu ǫla wa
'We are one clan, we bury each other.'

38

Similarly in title contests, where candidates may try to disqualify their rivals by alleging that they are not full clan members, the person so challenged may reply by bringing evidence to show that members of his own lineage have buried or been buried by other lineages whose clan status is beyond question. If the evidence is accepted it counts as a proof that the persons named were agnatically related and that their descendants in the male line are members of one and the same clan.

As the context of this corporate activity shows, the notion of clan solidarity is essentially a ritual one, involving the totality of clan members both living and dead in an indivisible, but essentially spiritual, unity. Perhaps the clearest expression of the ritual identity between clansmen occurs in the agnatic inheritance of ritual prohibitions, *elifo*, on the use of various animals and plants as food, or on certain kinds of activity that are ritually proscribed. These clan avoidances, *elifo olopu*, are observed throughout the individual's life, and it is believed that sickness will result if the rules are knowingly disregarded.[1] After death, on the other hand, the prohibition has to be ritually broken as part of the obligatory funeral rites, *icholo*, that separate the dead from the living. In the Achadu's clan, for instance, a morsel of the prohibited *ouwe* fish is added to cooked food of which a portion is then placed on the grave of the dead person. Or, if a certain kind of behaviour is proscribed, such as using three forked sticks to support household vessels, this is done deliberately at one stage of the funeral to release the dead person from his bonds with the living members of the clan.

These hereditary avoidances form the basis of clan oaths which can be employed by a suspected person who wishes to swear his innocence. The Igala say that if a man swears by the thing which is forbidden to his clan his word is not to be doubted. The oath takes the form of saying 'If I am guilty of this thing may the prohibited thing (naming the food or action) be done to me this year.' In other words, the suspect swears by his own clan identity that he will die within the year if his words are untrue, and implies that his fellow clansmen

---

[1] Sickness caused by disregard of *elifo olopu* usually takes the form of boils and other chronic skin conditions.

will assemble to carry out the *icholo* connected with this prohibition.

These clan avoidances are like totemic prohibitions in that they often concern animals or plants. But there are also many differences between the Igala custom and the use made of animal and vegetable species in the classic system of totemism. The *elifo olopu* are in many cases not widely known outside the clan, and do not form public symbols of clan identity. By their nature, the prohibitions ought to be observed at all times, and potentially make a symbolic distinction between the members of a clan and those who observe different restrictions. But in practice it is mainly their role as funeral *icholo* that brings the *elifo olopu* into prominence in ordinary social life, and in this context they form esoteric symbols of the mystical bond on which clanship is founded.

In general the Igala do not rationalize the different ritual prohibitions observed by clans beyond saying that they belong to funeral ritual, *enw icholo,* or that they are an ancient custom, *enw ogwu.* This absence of aetiological myths and legends in connexion with the *elifo olopu* is especially typical of the avoidances connected with inanimate objects or with miscellaneous activities such as whistling at night or cracking palm kernels outside the house.[1] Where the prohibitions refer to animals, explanatory traditions are more common. Typically, this class of prohibition is explained by stories that attribute the hereditary relationship between a clan and its totem to the animal's intervention at a moment of danger in the life of the clan's founder. For example, the Ofojo clan at Achigili relates that in the distant past its members, who were then living together in one village, were asleep at night when an *ediikwu* monkey disturbed the rest of one of the elders by chattering in a tree above his house. Each time the man tried to get back to sleep the monkey became more insistent, and behaved in such an unusual way that the elder at last understood that it was giving warning of impending attack by a raiding party from another village. So the elder roused the village and led his

---

[1] In some cases the prohibited activities are carried out by masquerades, and to perform them in any other context would be to betray a secret of masquerading. For example, whistling at night is an activity associated with the *Ameli* masks which are performed by certain clans.

clansmen to safety, whilst a group of the *ediikwu* monkeys dispersed the footprints they left on the sandy paths, so that the enemy would not know which direction they had taken.[1]

This type of legend rationalizes the fact of clan dispersal in Igala by postulating the break up of an earlier, more concentrated type of patrilocal settlement through a war or series of wars. In upholding the myth that each clan originally had a common founder and a common birth place the legend transfers some of the loyalty owed to these geographical symbols to the special relationship with a particular animal species, which at once recalls the mythical unity of the clan in remote time, and the factors that led to the clan's dispersal. One other element stressed by this type of legend is the clan's solidarity in its external relationships with other descent groups. The prohibitions on inanimate objects and miscellaneous activities tend to be symbols of the internal unity of the clan and of the ritual bonds between members exclusive of their connexions with members of other clans. But the prohibitions on creatures tend to refer to the clan's participation in a wider scheme of political relations. For instance in respect of certain of their individual *ẹlifọ olọpu* the royal clan is opposed as a class to the non-royal clans and to the Achadu's clan. The royal clan taboos the flesh of dogs and has a positive affinity with the leopard. The Igala Mela clans, on the other hand, taboo *ewọlọ* or civet cat, and in this respect are typical of those indigenous clans throughout the kingdom who perform the Egwu Afia play, which uses a costume incorporating the pelt of *ewọlọ*. The Achadu's clan, finally observes an absolute prohibition on the *ouwẹ* fish. These three classes of totemism are widely known in Igala and to some extent serve to symbolize the identity and individuality of the clan groups concerned within a system of political co-operation.

Although Igala clans are basically similar in construction and in function, there are many differences between individual clans, and diversity is a characteristic of the clan system as a whole. The differences are partly differences of detail, in matters of burial custom, masquerading, and other features of ritual symbolism. But they also extend to clan structure in

[1] This story occurs also in Idoma country, and among some Ibo groups in the Nsukka area.

that there are marked differences of scale within the clan system, and variations in the order of internal segmentation. This structural variation is associated with rank and political ascendancy, the largest and most complex clans being those of aristocratic descent whilst the smallest and simplest descent groups tend to be low in the social scale and insignificant politically.

Some idea of the range of variation in the structure of Igala clans can be gained by considering two clans placed at opposite poles of the system. At one extreme the royal clan divides genealogically into at least five major subclans, which in turn subdivide individually into several maximal lineages. The subclans are centred in different parts of the kingdom, and the clan as a whole is so numerous and so widely dispersed that it has representatives in practically every village throughout the kingdom. It is difficult to calculate the total membership of this group, but a rough estimate can be made of the Idah subclan as totalling at least 35,000 members. In 1963 the Ocholi Descendants Union, comprising members of one of the four lineages that make up the ruling subclan, had a paid-up membership of 8,907 persons, mostly adults. The membership included some uterine kin in addition to agnates,[1] but this accession must be balanced against the fact that not all full members of the lineage belong to the Union. The four lineages of the ruling subclan based on Idah are roughly equal in size, and it would therefore be reasonable to estimate the total membership of this subclan at four times the total of any of its lineages.

The relationship between the numerical size of the Idah subclan and the other royal subclans located in other parts of the kingdom is even more difficult to estimate accurately. But we know that some of these groups are not far below the ruling house in rank and political importance, and that their role and pattern of dispersal closely parallels the position of the ruling

[1] Strictly speaking, the Igala term *olopu* describes the patrilineal nucleus of a clan and the term *aju* the descendants in either line of a common ancestor. In practice the second term is often used by Igala to mean a patrilineal clan with its membership increased by including uterine kin, *omonobulę*. The position of uterine kin in relation to the nuclear descent group is discussed in a later chapter, see pp. 135 et seq.

house within the metropolitan area. On a conservative estimate the combined membership of the provincial subclans at least equals that of the ruling house at Idah. So we can conclude that the total membership of the royal clan as a whole is in the order of 70,000 persons, which is equal to about 24 per cent. of the Igala-speaking population.

At the other extreme of clan structure are clans of low rank whose political functions are limited to controlling the district within which they are centred. A typical example of this type of clan is the Ọjọ clan centred on the village of Igebije in Gwolawo District. As the genealogy in figure 3 on page 34 shows, the clan divides into five major lineages and has no intermediate stage of subclan organization. Its total adult membership in 1963 was not more than twenty persons, or a maximum of forty if we include closely associated uterine kin.

The genealogical depth of clans in Igala seems to vary with their numerical strength and political importance. The subclans of the royal descent group, for instance, vary in depth between seven and nine generations. In the Ọjọ clan, and a group of similar clans in the surrounding area, the variation is between four and seven generations.

This discrepancy in size and scale between clans of high and low rank in Igala is a fact of great cultural and political significance. Apart from their overt political functions, the aristocratic clans perform a unifying and centralizing role through their great size and wide dispersal. In other words political control is a function of clan size and spread as well as of judicial administrative and military arrangements. Culturally also, these clans are regarded as the natural guardians and arbiters of tradition, and this may be connected with the fact that their corporate activities form a complete demonstration of the rules that are basic to Igala social structure. Offices held within the royal clan, for instance, represent the widest possible extension of the principle of seniority, and also demonstrate in full the relationship between this principle and that of lineal segmentation. Cases of inheritance and succession in the royal clan form an important class of legal precedent for this reason and are remembered and discussed long after similar cases concerning commoners have been forgotten. But above all, by their ubiquity and political ascendancy, the aristocratic clans provide the clan system itself with a framework within which clans are oriented to the centre by hereditary alliances and by ties of kinship and marriage.

The overall dominance of the royal clan within the clan system is balanced politically by grouping other, lesser clans together in opposed classes. I demonstrate this by discussing the grouping of clans within the capital and the division of functions between them. I then go on to show the repetition of this pattern in the provincial centres of government, leaving the purely local aspect of clan relations to be described in the following chapter.

The royal clan.

From some points of view the various groups claiming royal descent in Igala make up a federation of clans rather than a single unilineal entity. The royal subclans are localized in different parts of the kingdom and in the past were virtually autonomous within their own spheres of political influence. Relations between them were often hostile, and even today the branches are so jealous of their own prerogatives that they tend to regard each other as rivals in a struggle for political power. But in spite of the degree of separation between subclans, and of a recurrent absence of co-operation, members of the clan have a strong sense of royal identity, based on common descent and this sense of belonging to a class set apart from other, non-royal clans, compensates for the centrifugal tendencies inherent in the political functions of the clan.

The family tree of the Igala royal clan, like Igala clan genealogies in general is essentially an aggregate of individual lines rather than a balanced and symmetrical structure of the type that emerges in a lineage system. For convenience, since it provides a useful way of summarizing genealogical information about the different subclans, I have shown the pedigree of the royal clan in figure 4 on page 46 as a comprehensive genealogy. But it should be emphasized that this synthesis is to a large extent an artificial one and has no exact parallel in Igala concepts of clan structure. There is no occasion or context on which the pedigree is set out, recited, or otherwise preserved as a whole, and the total structure is beyond the knowledge and outside the interest of most of the members of the clan.

To some extent the genealogy of the royal clan is systematized through the fact that all royal titles, though hereditary within particular subclans, have to be submitted to the Ata at Idah for appointment when an office falls vacant. In investigating the claim of rival contestants the king, together with his own titled siblings and the elders of the subclan concerned, investigate the genealogy of the contestants, tracing their relationship to the founder of the subclan and from this founder to the point at which the subclan diverges from the body of the parent clan. These investigations, on which the award of the title depends, define for a time at least the relationship of the subclan to the senior house, at Idah, and it is by assembling each subclan's version of its title ancestry that a comprehensive picture of the clan's structure can be obtained.

But this process of genealogical co-ordination has many limitations, and does not keep the parts of the system in balance as the processes of investigation and recording do in a lineage system. Royal title disputes involve a dyadic relationship between two subclans only, and exclude members of the clan who belong to neither the ruling house nor to the subclan in which the vacancy occurs. Moreover the settlement reached in one generation is not regarded as binding upon the next, because, through the system of rotating title succession, a different lineage holds office each time the title falls vacant and the incoming lineage does not feel bound to uphold the version of a pedigree laid down for its predecessor in office. A similar lack of continuity occurs on the king's side also, if the king happens to have changed between the time when the title was last awarded and the time of the next vacancy. In this event the two lineages concerned, from the ruling subclan on the one hand and the subclan in which the vacancy exists on the other, work out their relationship afresh.

Most branches of the royal clan take Ayagba ọm Idoko as their apical ancestor, and are in this sense structurally equivalent, as subclans, with the ruling subclan based on Idah. Members of the clan are sometimes described collectively as *amọm'Ayagba,* the children of Ayagba, and royal individuals who wish to stress their genealogical identity may do so by

45

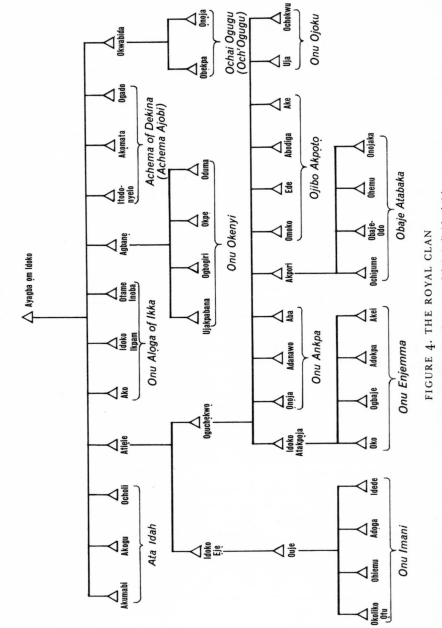

FIGURE 4. THE ROYAL CLAN

Subclans (in italic) show the names of their individual titles

46

saying *Ayagba bi wa,* 'Ayagba begot us'. The clan pedigree is, however, typical of Igala clan pedigrees in general in being so broad laterally in relation to its generation depth that the notion of common descent from Ayagba is clearly a fiction, a convenient term for the notion of common ancestry. Closer acquaintance with the pedigrees of individual lineages shows less uniformity in the structure than Igala suppose; both at Idah and in the provinces there are branches of the clan that claim descent from ancestors earlier than Ayagba, and presume equality with all the branches that stem from Ayagba himself.[1]

The most important case of dissent from the notion that Ayagba is the true apical ancestor of the royal clan occurs among the northern subclans in Igala, who tend to regard the Ankpa branch of the clan rather than the Idah one as their immediate superior. This argument turns on the status of Atiẹle, from whom the founders of these subclans are descended, and who in the commoner version of the clan pedigree is said to be a son of Ayagba. The Ankpa branch of the clan now accepts this version and gives genealogies that correspond with the one set out in figure 4 on page 46. But in 1935, administrative officers collecting historical information at Ankpa were told that:

> Atiẹle, a younger brother of the Ata Ayagba came to the Ankpa area trading. The people of Ojja who were settled there gave him a wife called Anagba who was the mother of Oguchẹ Ẹkwọ. She was a relation of a local chief called Agbaji. Oguchẹ Ẹkwọ got so strong eventually that Agbaji gave up his title and later Oguchẹ Ẹkwọ went to Idah and was given beads by the Ata.[2]

This version which places Atiẹle and Ayagba in the same generation is supported in the administrative records by the traditions of an offshoot of the Oguchẹkwo lineage, based at Okenyi. It also occurs in my own notes from the Ankpa area,

---

[1] The best known example of this is the subclan owning the Ochai Ata title. Different kings have broken the rule of succession to this title by bestowing it on their own collateral relatives, but the title strictly belongs to an independent royal subclan, forming a separate branch of the royal house.

[2] *Ankpa District Notebook,* unpublished ms.

and is clearly a major alternative in Ankpa tradition to the version that regards Atiẹle as a son of Ayagba. Which of these two accounts is dominant in any period probably depends upon the state of political relationships between Idah and Ankpa. These two branches of the royal clan have formed the focus of political opposition between the central and the north-eastern districts of the kingdom, and Ankpa has tended to regard the seniority of the Idah branch as being spiritual rather than political in character. At the turn of the century the Ankpa group rejected the Ata's authority in political matters by refusing to accept the king's choice in the succession to headship of the subclan. This led to fighting and to eventual intervention by the British Government on the king's side of the quarrel.[1] Since that period administrative changes have tended to incorporate the northern districts more closely within the framework of the kingdom. And the Ankpa subclan has finally accepted a subordinate position, as its own genealogical records now testify.[2] But the claim to equality or near equality with the Idah branch still exists in the notion that Atiẹle was a junior brother of Ayagba ọm Idoko, and not his son.

At Idah itself there are three royal descent groups that stand genealogically outside the framework of the main ruling subclan. Each of these groups has its own hereditary title, whose holder is confirmed by the Ata, and the difference in genealogical status between these lines and the main subclan reflects a degree of structural separation between their own offices and the offices that are hereditary in the Ata's subclan. The first two of these subclans, taking the title of Ochai Ata and Achenya Ata respectively, trace descent from Idoko, the

---

[1] *Ankpa District Notebook,* 1903. An expedition sent from Lokoja to uphold Oguchagi's appointment by the Ata (see figure 7, p. 80) was ambushed at Enabo on the return journey and suffered heavy casualties. A punitive expedition, which was strongly resisted, followed and a military garrison was established at Ankpa to pacify the area. A company of the West African Frontier Force was stationed in Ankpa from 1904 to 1933.

[2] In 1963 Ankpa led a movement supported by nine northern Igala Districts which aimed to establish a separate Native Authority at Ankpa, so that tax payments would be made to Ankpa and administered locally, instead of from Idah. This movement has revived Ankpa's claims to political equality with Idah.

father of Ayagba. The third group, holding the priestly title of Obajadaka, claims descent from Ọnọja Oboni, one of the protodynastic royal ancestors whose relationship to Ayagba is obscure. In the view of other members of the royal clan the first two groups are unquestionably of royal descent, but outside the mainstream of the ruling house. The third group's claims to royal ancestry are regarded as somewhat doubtful, in part because Ọnọja Oboni's own status is obscure, and there is one school of thought in the royal clan that regards him as an *ọmonobulẹ* or uterine kinsman rather than a full member by agnatic descent.

An alternative to the collective term *amọm'Ayagba* for the members of the royal clan exists in the name *amọmata* which classifies them by reference to the royal title rather than by reference to the founder. But this term is ambiguous since although in one sense it means any member of the royal clan, in another sense it describes the titled members of the royal clan and their descendants over two generations. We can conclude that there is no single term for membership of the royal clan that is without political overtones; the concept of royal descent by its very nature implies distinction of seniority and relative status, and it is only in relation to other groups of clans that these divisions disappear.

The nobility of the royal clan is a basic fact of Igala social life, maintained by a number of economic and political privileges, and expressed in these and various other customary forms of respect and deference. Basically, however, the qualities that are thought to justify this high rank are spiritual attributes, hereditary within the clan and descended in an unbroken line from its remotest ancestors. They are symbolized to the members of the clan and to the Igala as a whole by the totemic affinity that exists between the *amọmata* and the leopard, *ọmataina*, whose name combines the singular form of the clan name with the adjective *ina* meaning sacred or holy.[1]

---

[1] In one sense the term *ina* means 'the greatest' or 'supreme'. But it also suggests the notion of a spiritual or sacred counterpart of a secular reality. It occurs in the name *ọjaina* for the royal burial ground (*ọja* = group, or community), in *ọmaina*, the term for the afterbirth, and in *ọfuina*, discharge occurring in acute forms of dysentery.

49

Within the royal clan, the leopard affinity is explained by a myth that traces ultimate royal ancestry to an anthropomorphic leopard. This myth is not generally known in detail outside the royal clan, but the sacred leopard affinity is common knowledge, and knowledge of these ritual associations appears in the fact that the leopard is a quasi-sacred animal to all Igala. In hunting it is greatly feared for its ritual as well as its physical qualities. Its name must not be pronounced in the hunting field, as this act is sufficient to contaminate the hunting medicines, and if a communal hunt surprises a leopard whilst beating the bush, the hunting has to be abandoned for the day. If a leopard is killed its death is mourned in the same way as a member of the royal clan, and this obligation does not end until a member of the royal clan has been sent from Idah to collect the pelt for the Ata and supervise the ritual disposal of the leopard's body.[1]

Again, when members of the royal clan are buried their funeral ceremonies include two rites, *icholo,* that express the idea of leopard affinity. These form perhaps the commonest expression of the idea, through which everyone is reminded of the spiritual identity of the clan, and involve, as we shall see, a direct contrast with other forms of clan totemism which are expressed in the same context of burial.

In the first stage of funeral ceremonies, in which the corpse is wrapped in white cloths, *okpẹ,* brought by mourning kinsmen and friends, before the body of an *Ọmata* can be removed to the grave the shroud has to be marked down both sides of the body with spots. This is done with three pigments, white, red, and dark blue, or black. The marks are said to represent the spots of the royal leopard.[2] As the marking is

[1] These rites are referred to as *icholo,* 'funeral rites', and include the act of wrapping the pelt in white funeral cloths, *okpẹ,* in the manner of a normal burial.

[2] The pigments are made from chalk, camwood and indigo, or ashes respectively. A further instance of this rite occurs in an administrative report from Dekina where the chief, Onu Ajobi, is head of a royal subclan. The report, written in 1930, says: 'It is believed that the souls of departed Onus Ajobi can enter into the bodies of leopards. (In this connexion it is interesting to note that before burial the bodies of deceased Onus Ajobi are marked with brown and white clay in imitation of leopards' spots.)' cf. also Monckton, J. C., 'Burial Ceremonies of the Attah of Idah', *J. African*

1. Ẹkwe, the principal Igala masquerade

2. The Ata's court at Idah in 1841

3. A newly appointed chief rides in procession through his town

carried out, by the agnatic kin of the dead person, the women and other bystanders sing:

Ẹ ma dẹkọn ẹ da ama
'If you don't turn into a leopard then turn into an *ama* (hyena).'

Later, in a series associated with the second mortuary ceremony, *aku,* a bier, *abaihi* is displayed in the same manner as the shrouded corpse before the actual interment, and when this is about to be carried to the grave a rite is performed that symbolizes the snatching of the body by a leopard.[1]

One other distinctive item of royal ritual that is in use amongst the whole clan is a protective medicine called *Ejebi.* This is to be found in most ancestral shrines within the clan in the form of a small calabash filled with a black substance, stoppered, and often tied round with white cloth (*okpẹ*) strips. It has the function of an *ode ọji* (*odoji*), 'medicine of the head', that the family head applies to the foreheads of new-born babies, placing them as it were, under the protection of the ancestors from whom the medicine was inherited.

All clans use protective medicine (*Odoji*) for their children, but the variety, *Ejebi,* is specific to the royal family. Ayagba ọm Idoko is said to have appointed the Agaidoko clan, a prominent family in Idah of Igbirra extraction, to make it for himself and his successors. One intelligence report describes the medicine at Ankpa as being used especially for parturition, in cases of difficult childbirth, and the name could be interpreted literally to mean 'agree to bear children' or 'facilitating birth'. But it also has the wider functions attributed to protective medicines. As my informant said, 'It helps the royal clan in their farming, and to beget children, it brings luck their way and closes the road to witchcraft which might harm them and their families.'

Soc., Vol. XXVII, for a reference to leopard figures on the Ata's coffin, and Partridge, C., 'The Burial of the Atta of Igaraland', *Blackwood's Magazine,* Vol. CLXXVI, p. 329, for a reference to chiefs who wore a piece of leopard's skin sewn onto their gown or cap.

[1] For this rite women are driven into the houses and away from the site of the funeral, and a leather bag or similar container is beaten to represent the noise made by a leopard which is supposed to snatch the body from the bier. This rite is in fact a kind of masquerading.

The ritual qualities of royalty have negative as well as positive aspects, and there are conditions of pollution which have to be avoided. It is forbidden, *elifọ*, for an *ọmata* to eat dog's flesh, and not only the flesh is proscribed but any kind of association between the concept of a dog and the concept of royal food. So that if an *ọmata* is eating and the common term for dog, *abia,* happens to be uttered, the food should be thrown away. Negative food prohibitions are expressed in the context of death in the same way as the positive totemic association. When the titled heads of royal lineages die, one of the funeral rites, *icholo,* consists of offering a cooked meal containing dog meat.

The crises of life also contain an element capable of polluting the qualities inherent in royalty. Childbirth and new-born children are supposed to be avoided by an *ọmata*; a corpse has the same ritual significance and should not be seen for this reason. Contact with menstruating women, and the act of sexual intercourse are also contaminating and may have to be ritually cleansed. These last two forms of pollution have a wider incidence than the royal clan, and I shall try to show later which elements of royal ritual are exclusive and which are of common occurrence.

One other minor taboo associated with royalty prohibits the use of *ugbakolo* (*Ficus capensis*), a tree whose leaves are a common ingredient of native medicines for coughs and catarrh.[1] *Amọmata* may not make use of its timber for firewood, nor employ the leaves, bark, or fruits in their medicines. Again, there is a funeral *icholo* connected with this fruit which breaks the prohibition and so emphasizes the separation of the newly dead from the living.

Whereas these ritual prohibitions affect the whole clan and recur in royal burial ceremonies throughout the kingdom, other fields of ritual emphasize the clan's division into autonomous subclans. The cult of royal ancestors, for instance, is fragmented amongst the component branches of the royal clan. Each subclan has its own burial ground, similar to the Ọjaina grove at Idah, where the kings are buried, and its own set of ancestral staffs, *okwutẹ*. There is no emphasis in the ancestral ritual of the clan on genealogical continuity from

[1] It is also reputed to be an ingredient of medicines used in sorcery.

52

the period of the group's foundation, since throughout the royal group only the last nine titled ancestors of each sub-clan are remembered. When a new titleholder takes up office, the *okwute* of the earliest member of his lineage is discarded, with the result that only the last two or three ancestors of each lineage are represented in the cult. This custom is possibly related to the degree of separation between the different branches of the royal descent group.

Although the various royal subclans are ritually auto-nomous in the field of ancestral ritual, the Idah subclan occupies a special position in relation to the royal dead. Its seniority within the whole clan is unchallengeable within the framework of royal ritual which stresses the uniqueness of the Ata's position as direct descendant of Ayagba ọm Idoko, and heir to the insignia of office that are believed to have been instituted by Ayagba. In addition to these insignia, there is a physical association between the early ancestors of the royal dynasty and the capital which makes it ritually impossible for the functions of the ruling house to be transferred to any other centre in Igala.[1] At Idah in addition to maintaining the graves of the last nine kings, the royal festivals also maintain the grave of Ẹbẹlẹjonu, representing the earliest or protodynastic ancestors, and the grave of Ayagba ọm Idoko, standing for the emergence of the royal clan as a political entity. And when the festival of royal ancestors is held, it must be initiated at these graves in the capital, and the first stage be completed by the king, before the royal subclans in the provinces can perform their own ancestral rites.

The ritual, a social and political relationship of the dif-ferent branches of the royal ancestors to one another, and to the senior branch at Idah, can best be summarized by saying that the Ata is in one capacity the *ogujo olopu*, or ritual elder, of the entire clan. It is in this capacity that he confers titles within the entire royal clan, the holders of these royal titles forming, as it were, a ceremonial sibling group which reproduces the unity of the clan in the first generation of its

---

[1] Around 1950 a serious attempt was made by government to transfer the headquarters of the kingdom from Idah to a more central site, at Ochaja. But this was so strongly opposed by the Igala that the idea had to be abandoned, and work on the new site was discontinued.

foundation. When a titled member of the clan dies the king has to be informed by sending some of the title-beads cut from the dead person's wrist, together with a hat, and in return the Ata gives permission for the burial to proceed by sending a burial cloth which becomes the first of the many cloths presented at the funeral. Similarly in inheritance disputes, or in any controversy that affects royal clansmen, the king can intervene as *ogujo olopu* and give a ruling which is absolutely final, short of rebellion.

In principle, members of the royal clan are under the king's personal jurisdiction for serious offences, and cannot be punished by any other court than the king in council. *Amomata* who were condemned to death, as they might be for murder, kidnapping, or raising war against the king, were executed by the Ochai Ata, the titled head of one of the lineages in the royal subclan at Idah, instead of by the Againya or by the royal eunuchs, who executed other felons.[1] The place and method of execution were also different; it took place at the Ochai Ata's court (*okete Ochai Ata*) and was carried out by a form of strangulation.[2] It is doubtful, however, whether this judicial procedure was followed as a matter of course where the outlying subclans were concerned. The members of these groups were under the jurisdiction of their own subclan head for most misdemeanours, and there are few concrete instances of criminals being taken to Idah from the provinces for punishment because they were of royal blood. The rule was more effective in the case of members of the ruling house, but for the kingdom at large it formed part of the mythology of royalty, and of the ideal and fundamental difference between the main descent classes.

It will be obvious from this account of the royal clan that its corporate functions as a descent group are extremely re-

[1] Execution by cutting the throat and beheading took place either at *erane*, the land shrine, or at *ere Inikpi*, the shrine of the Ata's daughter, Inikpi. Kidnappers and incorrigible thieves were sometimes executed by impaling, *edunyokpa*, and this sentence was usually carried out near one of the main approaches to the capital. Offences against the king, such as adultery with a royal wife, were punished by clubbing and throwing the offender from the summit of the high cliffs overhanging the Ocheche stream.

[2] The offender was prostrated and suffocated by a stick held across the throat.

stricted, and that the bond between royal clansmen is mainly a ritual and moral one. The assumption of common descent provides this bond of unity, but the clan as a whole has no precise genealogical structure. The widest unit within which relations between clansmen are controlled by the descent model is the subclan, whose branches are inter-related as parts of a total system. The clan itself is co-ordinated geographically rather than genealogically, and although there are institutional expressions of clan unity these tend to be concentrated in the ruling house to the exclusion of the outlying branches. A major part of the contacts between the senior subclan and the other branches of the royal group are purely political in character, concerned with the spatial relationships of the different centres, and recognition of the descent tie is limited mainly to the annual festivals and to certain other formal occasions such as succession to vacant offices.

The divisions of the royal clan that I term subclans are political groupings of lineages rather than genealogical units in the strict sense of the term. If Atiele is regarded as a son of Ayagba for instance, there is no structural difference between the lineages centred at Idah and those centred at Ankpa which would justify separating them on genealogical grounds alone. The royal subclans can be regarded as descent groups only in the sense that they each monopolize the inheritance of a particular title; it is their descent from the titleholder rather than descent from the individual founder that provides the key to their unity. The members of each subclan share exclusive rights to a particular title or group of titles and it is this joint prerogative that gives the subclan the status of a hereditary corporation in its dealing with other groupings of the same order. The major titles taken by the different royal subclans are shown in the table on the following page.

In all the royal subclans there exists in addition to the major title, held by the leader of the group, a number of minor titles that are inherited within the same rotating framework as the central title. The distribution and inter-relations of these secondary titles are most significant for the structure of the subclan, whose internal segmentation can only be understood in relation to the inheritance of the whole complex of titles belonging to the subclan. To show how this system operates,

Title	Salutation	Subclan centre
Ata	Agabaidu	Idah
Onu Ankpa	Dǫga	Ankpa (Ankpa District)
Achema	Dǫga	Dekina (Dekina District)
Onu Imani	Oji, or, Dǫga	Imani (Imani District)
Onu Ojoku	Agbo, or, Dǫga	Okaba (Ojoku District)
Obaje Atabaka	Dǫga	Okpo (Olamaboro District)
Ojibo Akpǫtǫ	Dǫga	Iga (Olamaboro District)
Ochai Ogugu	Dǫga	Ogugu (Ogugu District)
Onu Alǫga	Dǫga	Ikka (Enjemma District)
Onu Okenyi	Dǫga	Okenyi (Ankpa District)

TABLE 1. TITLES HELD BY ROYAL SUBCLANS

and to analyse its structural implications, I will describe the inheritance of titles within the ruling subclan at Idah and consider in detail the distribution of these offices within one of the component lineages of the subclan, the Aju Ocholi group. It was not possible for me to spend long enough in the other subclan centres to work out their own patterns of title inheritance in similar detail. But the evidence available, which I summarize at the end of this section, suggests that the principles are the same and that a closely similar structural pattern exists within these groups.

The ruling house at Idah divides into four maximal lineages[1] that are equal to each other in the succession although they are not of the same status genealogically. As figure 5 on page 57 shows, two of the lineages have emerged from the bifurcation of the group founded by Akumabi and were at one stage of their existence major lineages within this maximal lineage. The Igala rationalize this change from a rotation of three branches to one based on four lineages by saying that Amachǫ, Akumabi's eldest son, died before his installation as Ata could be completed. The succession therefore passed to his junior brother, Itodo Aduga, and since then has alternated between the descendants of these two men and the members of the

[1] In central Igala the term olǫpu describes the segments of a clan as well as the entire descent group. Branches of this unilineal group can be distinguished loosely as 'hands', ǫwǫ, and in some eastern districts major and maximal lineages are referred to as atakpa, 'houses', or ofegbili, 'hearthstones'.

56

older maximal lineages, founded by Akogu and Ocholi. The lineages are referred to descriptively as either *olọpu Itodo Aduga*, *olọpu Amachọ*, and so on, or alternatively as *aju*, descendants, of these men.

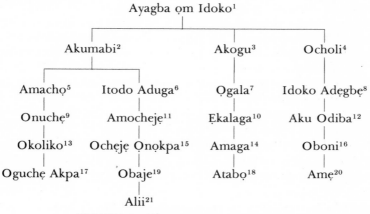

FIGURE 5. THE RULING LINEAGES

(omitting protodynastic kings, and two later rulers who left no male issue)

Politically and socially the four branches of the ruling house combine on many occasions in pairs, following the lines of the original genealogical split between Akumabi's descendants and the members of the other two lineages. The first pair, comprising the Itodo Aduga and Amachọ lineages has the collective name of Ajaku, an abbreviation of *aju Akumabi*. The second pair, comprising Aju Ocholi and Aj'akogu has no special name, but its members often describe the close connexion of the two lineages by the kinship term *ọmaiye*, which denotes children who have both parents in common. The complementary term for their relationship with the Ajaku moiety is *ọmọra*, or *ọmata*, implying that in this direction they are related through the father only. These terms are, of course, used figuratively and do not imply an actual kin relationship; there is no sense in which the two lineages could be described as forming a corporate kin group on the basis of matrifiliation.

This opposition between the two major divisions of the ruling house is a basic fact of Igala political structure and appears to have been in existence from a remote period. As Clifford first pointed out, the traditional layout of the palace area at Idah reflects this dichotomy.[1] The Itodo Aduga and Amachọ lineages build their palace in the same half of the enclosed area known as *ologbo Ata,* whilst the other two lineages, during their own tenure of office, occupy the other half of the compound. The square tower, *ọdọgọ* that forms a major landmark in the royal quarter serves as a boundary marker between these two sectors.[2]

Politically, the Ajaku branch of the ruling house tends to act in concert against the other two lineages, who regard each other as natural allies in struggles over the succession or the allocation of political power. At different times in the past the allies on either side are said to have been involved in internecine conflicts, with *aju* Itodo Aduga fighting *aju* Amachọ and *aju* Ocholi fighting *aju* Akogu. But these hostilities were limited in scale and importance, and arose mainly from local quarrels over slave-raiding and pillaging in villages that were under the protection of the allied lineage. In disputes over the succession, which turned on at least one occasion into a major war, the Akogu and Ocholi lineages traditionally fought on the same side and assisted each other against the combined strength of the Ajaku federation.

Outside the capital, the lineages of the ruling house are so widely dispersed through the metropolitan area and beyond, and their pattern of distribution changes so much from one generation to the next, that it is difficult to delimit their respective spheres of influence geographically. The Igala simplify this problem by associating each of the lineages with a centre where it is in the majority and where one or more past kings have lived before coming to the throne.

In 1907, for instance, Capt. Byng-Hall wrote that:

'The first Atta of Idah after Aiyagba settled at Akwacha. The succession now runs:
  1. Chief of Arapa.
  2. Chief of Akwacha.

---

[1] Clifford, Miles, 'A Nigerian Chiefdom . . .', *J.R.A.I.,* Vol. LXVI, 1936, pp. 415, 434.
[2] Illustrated in Allen, W., *Picturesque Views on the River Niger,* London, 1840.

3. Chief of Onupu.
4. Chief of Alo.'[1]

The villages named in this list coincide with names that are often quoted by the Igala today in describing the geographical distribution of the ruling lineages. If for the term 'chief of' in Byng-Hall's notes we substitute the phrase 'head of the lineage associated with' his list is directly comparable with one that frequently recurs in my own field notes, as follows:

Lineage	Lineage centre	District (in modern system)
Itodo Aduga	Ayangba	Okura
	Onukpo	Dekina
Amacho	Arapa	Biraidu
Akogu	Akpacha	
	Igaliuwo	Ife
Ocholi	Alo	Itobe

TABLE 2. THE GEOGRAPHICAL LOCATION OF LINEAGES IN THE RULING SUBCLAN

The actual pattern of distribution of the royal lineages is infinitely more complex than this description suggests, and there are today no moral, ritual, or political forms of leadership which make these villages predominant within the settlements of the lineages concerned. The association between the lineages and these hypothetical lineage centres is an historical one; they represent the final positions taken up by the different lineages at the end of a bitter war fought in the last century, and probably developed as the fortified sites from which each lineage conducted its own campaigns at that time.

In the early part of the nineteenth century the Ata Ẹkalaga was murdered at the end of an exceptionally long reign by members of the next lineage in the line of succession.[2] His supporters, belonging to the Akogu lineage, were expelled

[1] Byng-Hall, F. F: W., 'Notes on the Okpoto and Igara Tribes', *Journal of the African Society*, Vol. VII, no. XXV, 1907, p. 166.

[2] Amochẹjẹ came to the throne around the year 1835, and it is probable that Ẹkalaga's death occurred in this same decade. The Igala explain the assassination of Ẹkalaga by saying that his reign was excessively long and blocked the Ajaku faction's succession to the kingship and other offices. The

from the capital by the incoming Ata, Amocheje, and formed a coalition against the king with the Ocholi lineage by mobilizing the local adherents of each group throughout the metropolitan area. This coalition was defeated in a major fight near the outskirts of Idah and in other skirmishes near the capital. The Ajaku group pressed the other two lineages northwards, and consolidated its hold on the ridge of high land that runs north from Idah and debouches in the central area at Ayangba. Meanwhile the Ocholi lineage fell back on the river Niger, and took up a defensive position at Alo, about 8 miles from the left bank near Itobe. Their allies, the Akogu lineage, bore the main brunt of the fighting and were driven still further northwards into the hilly regions of what is now the Ife District, and also to the north-east of the Ocholi positions, in the Abocho area.

When peace was established the lineages dispersed from these centres, and in the following reigns continued the pattern of founding widely separated small hamlets which is more typical of the pattern of royal settlement than the pattern of concentration for defensive purposes. In Amaga's reign, when the Akogu group returned to power there were further hostilities when the king took reprisals against Ayangba for the part that its people had played in harrying the Akogu settlements throughout the metropolitan area after Ekalaga's murder. This reign re-established Akogu and Ocholi settlers in the vicinity of Idah. For instance, some of Amaga's own sons settled at Gwolawo, lying between the capital and Ayangba, and their homesteads attracted further groups of settlers from their own lineage and from the Ocholi lineage. Similarly, the area between Idah and the Anambra river came within the coalition's sphere of influence at this time, with the Ocholi lineage settling at Ogbogbo and Okoainwili and the Akogu group settling in the intervening villages of Oforachi, Achokpa, and Ikefi.

Since Amaga's reign, which ended in 1900, the need for defensive alliances within the ruling house has disappeared, and the settlements of the royal lineages have tended to

---

legends attribute Ekalaga's longevity to powerful medicine and say that it was to overcome the power of these medicines that his enemies devised a ritual manner of putting him to death by suffocation.

become so intermingled with one another that it is difficult to speak of spheres of influence in other than an historical sense. Broadly speaking, the Ocholi lineage tends to be settled along or near the left bank of the Niger, from the confluence down-stream to the southernmost reaches of the kingdom, in the Ibaji district. Akogu settlements are often found on a small scale in close proximity to the Ocholi hamlets, but the main centres of this lineage are situated along the northern margins of the metropolitan area. Ajaku settlements are most numerous on the main route north from the capital and tend to form a barrier between the outlying, and oldest, Akogu hamlets and the approaches to the capital. In the immediate vicinity of Idah homesteads of the different lineages often coexist in the same village, but the local landowning groups are traditionally oriented towards a particular branch of the ruling house.

The fluidity that characterizes the pattern of royal settle-ment outside the capital is related to the mobility of royal settlement in the capital itself. Formerly, whenever the Ata died a physical transfer of population took place in connexion with the arrival of the new king. Most of the great offices of state, which are hereditary within the royal subclan, fell vacant with the king's death, and the previous holders were expected to vacate the capital to make way for the new king's own nominees. These offices were filled mainly by members of the king's own lineage, so the royal succession involved a transfer of power from one lineage to another, and was not confined to the king and his entourage.[1]

It is clear from informants' statements and from early administrative records that the exodus from the capital that took place on the king's death was not confined to the office holders in person, but affected most of the members of the dead king's lineage who were resident at the time in the capital. In 1901 Partridge commented on this dispersal and wrote:

> The district and town (of Idah) are always occupied by the reigning family, while the other three branches, not being per-mitted to live there, retreat into the interior. At the death of an

---

[1] Hence the discontent created by Ekalaga's long reign within the next lineage in line.

Atta, then, a sort of 'double twilight' takes place—the late reigning family with all their chiefs, followers, and slaves, have to
leave the homes in which many of them have been born and
brought up, and immigrate to towns in the 'bush' which they
know only by name. At the same time the new reigning family
'come in' and their people settle in the compounds occupied by
their forefathers four reigns ago.[1]

There is no direct earlier reference to the exchange of lineages in the capital, but we can perhaps associate with this
custom the marked fluctuations in the population of Idah that
attracted the attention of the early explorers in the nineteenth century. With the advent of colonial rule royal patronage was so drastically curtailed that the exchange of lineages
was modified, and each group began to build permanent
houses in the capital. But administrative officers found it
difficult to eradicate the idea that office holders in the royal
lineage changed with the appointment of a new king, and as
late as 1929, when the Ata Atabọ died, the District Officer
found it necessary to recommend to the Resident that 'the
custom of making a clean sweep of titled officials—be no
longer followed'.

Within each of the royal lineages descent is traced by relatively exact stages through the male line from the group's
founder, and much more importance is attached to genealogical links than in the wider groupings of subclan and clan.
The sense of genealogical identity amongst members of the
group is correspondingly stronger in the lineage than in
these wider groupings. It is inconceivable to the Igala, for
instance, that members of the same lineage should fight
on opposite sides in any armed conflict. And if homicide
occurred within the lineage it would have grave ritual as well
as social consequences.[2] In the royal clan, also, the scale of its

[1] Partridge, C., 'The Burial of the Atta of Igaraland and the "Coronation"
of his Successor', *Blackwood's Magazine*, Vol. CLXXVI, 1904, p. 330.

[2] The offender would be handed over to the local district head who would
send the case to the Ata or the provincial chief for trial. But in addition
offerings would be made locally to the ancestors and to the land, to 'restore
the land', *enwochi anẹ*. An act of homicide committed by a member of the
same subclan, from a different lineage, would have similar consequences.
Igala oral traditions say that sacrifices were made to the land at the end of
the royal war that followed the murder of the Ata Ẹkalaga.

organization is so great that lineages are the widest units with an effective interest in property relations; the functions of burial and settlement of inheritance issues are performed by members of the same lineage rather than by the subclan or clan. Collateral branches of the lineage are opposed in this case in the way that collateral lineages are opposed within smaller clans.

This ideal of unity and identity amongst members of the same lineage is also expressed in several aspects of marriage regulations. The royal lineages are exogamous groups, and marriage between members is condemned as *ebita*. Sexual intercourse between agnates is less strongly condemned than a permanent liaison, but the distinction is not an easy one to make in Igala. *Ebita* marriages involve no marriage payments and there is no formal transfer of rights from the wife's group to the husband's when this kind of liaison is formed. But paternity is determined by the mother's statement, and if, as often happens, she names a lover, the child can be claimed by the progenitor's clan on payment of a fine to the legal husband's group. Sexual intercourse, therefore, potentially creates a lien on children in the same way as marriage, and in a limited sense it is equivalent to marriage because it determines the primary clan affiliation of the woman's children. And the rule of exogamy covers this case in addition to the possibility of marriage contracted in the normal way.

The same principle of lineage unity in relation to marriage underlies the Igala custom of inheriting rights over widows in the agnatic line. When a man dies his wives become *oyogwu,* 'wives of the estate' and the rights formerly held by the husband over their services are transferred to his agnatic kin. A reciprocal extension of this principle is the custom of sororal polygyny, *edunọla,* which favours marriages with classificatory sisters. The actual incidence of this type of marriage is low in Igala, amounting in my experience to three or four marriages in several hundred cases. But it is much favoured in principle for a first or senior wife to promote a second marriage for her husband within her own lineage.

The royal lineages in the ruling house subdivide genealogically into major segments that have some individual corporate functions. And these segments divide further into minor or localized lineages whose members tend to settle in one locality or in a group of related localities. This segmentation can only be understood in relation to the title system in which the major offices of state are vested. The lineages form the basic units of this system of hereditary royal offices and their own internal organization derives mainly from participation in this rotating system of authority. To show the nature of these offices I outline the composition and principal functions of the king's council before returning to the distribution of offices within a particular lineage and the question of lineage segmentation.

As the following list of titles shows, there were eighteen other royal titles besides the king's own title of Ata that were hereditary within the ruling house at Idah. These offices fell vacant when the Ata died, and formed the main source of patronage at the disposal of the new king. Appointments were made from among the Ata's siblings within his own lineage, so that succession followed the same rotating pattern as the kingship itself. But the vacant posts were not filled immediately the Ata came to office; the king created councillors gradually, throughout his reign, and it seems to have been the tendency to keep some posts in reserve so that there were often long gaps in the succession. The king could also, at his discretion, retain a few councillors from the previous reign, but it was unusual for new appointments to be made outside his own lineage.

The Ata's councillors.

Within the reigning lineage the body of royal councillors represented both the Ata's own direct line of descent and the various collateral branches. Titles were given to his own brothers, to cousins of varying degree, and, to a lesser extent, to members of the previous generation. In relation to the ruling house itself the council formed a council of elders, *abogujo olopu* drawn from one lineage. To the world at large the council was the executive body and corporate representative of the ruling house, and in a wider sense, of the royal clan as a whole. It had no other name than a set of terms that also describe membership of the clan; its members were the *amọmata,* children of the Ata. To avoid confusion with the wider use of the same term it might be necessary to refer to the councillors specifically as titled men, *amakwǫka*, 'those who tie beads', or *amajǫfę*, 'those who take title'. But the corporate

Title	Salutation	Tributary villages[1]
1. Achema Ata	Dǫga	Obofu (near Mozum)
2. Agbanata	Dǫga	Owele (Igala Mela District)
3. Agenyi Ata	Dǫga	—
4. Agenyi Ayagba	Dǫga	—
5. Amanata	Abǫ	Afa (Ibaji District)
		Emewe (Biraidu District)
		Ogbogbo (Igala Mela District)
6. Ęgeuna Ata	Dǫga	Amabo (Ibaji District)
7. Ękpa Ata	Dǫga	Agbanaka
8. Inalogu Ata	Dǫga	—
9. Ochai Ata	Kpalękǫ	Aya, Anike, Iteyi, Ogaine (Ibaji District)
10. Odokina Ata	Dǫga	Ota, Unale, Odoku, Enweli (Ibaji District)
11. Odoma Ata	Dǫga	Aburuge (Adoru District)
12. Ǫgǫhi Ata	Dǫga	Akpacha (Ife District)
13. Ohięmogbolo Ata	Dǫga	Okeku and Adegewala
14. Olimęnę Ata	Dǫga	—
15. Ǫmachi Ata	Dǫga	Adenekpa?
16. Ǫmachi Ata	Dǫga	Ayangba?
17. Ǫmakoji Ata	Badaigi	Bassa Nge area
18. Ǫmolobu	Dǫga	Itobe

TABLE 3. TITLES AND FIEFS IN THE RULING SUBCLAN

functions of the council were sufficiently well defined, and the contexts in which it was opposed to the other hereditary groups were sufficiently prominent in the life of the capital, for there to be little ambiguity in ordinary conversation.

On all occasions when the Ata holds audience or appears in public the titled *amǫmata* form a distinct and privileged group,

[1] Most of the office holders in this list were entitled to a share of the tribute paid annually by the communities subordinate to their particular title. But a few of the titles had no tributary fiefs, and derived their income from an increased share of the perquisites divided regularly by the Ata amongst the royal councillors.

which takes precedence over the royal eunuchs, *amonoji*, royal servants, *amẹdibo*, palace slaves, *amadu Ata*, and the populace at large.[1] At the annual festivals they attend the king in a body after the actual rites have been performed, bringing him back to the palace in triumph from the land shrine at the Ẹranẹ festival, and being the first to acclaim the sacrifices to the royal ancestors that are made in the palace at the Egwu festival. When the populace of Idah assembles, in the closing stages of these festivals, to congratulate the king, the *amọmata* are the first to be received by him, and the first to receive a share of the kola, beer, and food that is distributed by the king. In the daily audiences held at the palace they are similarly privileged. The *amọmata* sit to the right and left of the Ata, in close proximity, whilst the rest of the audience face the king, at a greater distance. When the Ata enters the audience chamber, the councillors rise and screen the throne momentarily by standing in a close circle around it with arms raised, so that the king can sit and arrange his robes unobserved.

In daily life the high rank of the royal councillors was symbolized and maintained by a number of privileges. Traditionally, only they, the king, and the Achadu, had the right to wear a type of bright red cloth, *ododo,* to build rectangular houses, *unyi aje,* or to ride horses in the ceremonial processions that took place during the annual festivals. Wives were frequently given to them without payment, and they claimed the nominal right to appropriate the wife or daughter of any commoner in marriage by the act of sending a messenger to place the councillor's bead insignia over the woman's head. In the provinces the councillors were treated with great deference, as the Ata's highest representatives, and whenever they went on tour, it became the duty of each village head that they visited to collect materials for their food and drink and for gifts from each section of the village. Councillors out of office still enjoyed great prestige and became centres of political influence wherever they settled in the provinces.

[1] These are the basic divisions of palace organization, and also represent the major categories into which shares of wine, kola, and other royal gifts were divided at feasts. When perquisites are being shared the senior member of each class receives the group's share and then determines the allocation to individual members on the basis of relative seniority.

4. An Igala Elder

5. Women and children singing

The high rank of the councillors was shared by their sons, and to a lesser extent by their grandsons, and in terms of rank, it is the whole group of the councillors and their children together with the king's immediate descendants that is described by the term *amọmata*. They had great influence in local politics, and, as I show later, their kinship network always constituted an avenue of communication with the central government, alternative to the formal chain of command based on territorial divisions. The daughters of councillors also share the rank of their father, and are known popularly as *amọm'ukpaihi*, 'children of power', because they frequently do not contract regular marriages, but stay with their patrikin and bring up their children as full members of their father's group. Their own children are in turn privileged and often mediate between local groups in the provinces and the central government.

Most, although not all of the titleholders in the king's council were formally responsible for collecting tribute, *enw'ire*, from a particular village or district that was traditionally linked with each title. These areas of jurisdiction are shown in the third column of the list of councillors' titles. The councillor acted as intermediary, *ohiẹgba*, between the locality concerned and the central government in judicial, political, and other matters, and derived a regular income from this connexion in the form of a share of the tribute paid by the area under his jurisdiction. In considering the significance of this administrative control it is important to remember that the councillors' closest and most influential connexions were with the localities dominated by their own major lineages. It is vital to distinguish the formal administrative network of control, whose limitations are discussed later, from the nexus of hereditary ties that formed the real basis of royal power. I discuss these hereditary aspects of royal authority later in more detail.

The titled councillors were also responsible for mobilizing the royal army in time of war, and on major expeditions accompanied the king into the field at the head of their own contingents. Descent and kinship ties were as important in this connexion as in the case of councillors' formal suzerainty over a particular locality. Councillors drew most of their support from the area in which their own major lineage was dispersed, and the political obligations of the outlying districts to assist the king in time of war were expressed to a considerable extent in terms of the kinship bonds created by marriage between the royal lineage segments and local communities.

Within the council there are six titles that are regarded as senior to the others and take precedence over them. They are:

Amanata	Odokina Ata	Ọmakoji Ata
Ochai Ata	Odoma Ata (Odomata)	Ohięmogbolo

One token of their seniority is that they formerly had traditional titled compounds, *okęte,* at fixed points in the capital,[1] whereas the other councillors were free to build on any site. The Amanata lived in the quarter known as Ukwaja, close to the Igala Mela sector; the Ochai Ata lived among some of the most important non-royal chiefs; the Odokina Ata and Ọmakoji Ata were close to the palace, among the settlement of royal eunuchs, and the Odoma Ata lived slightly further away at Idoma, between the palace and the Achadu's compound. The Ohięmogbolo's compound lay nearer the cliff, behind the residence of one of the titled eunuchs.

But seniority within the royal council was also a matter of the king's favour, and any member of the group admitted by the Ata to his circle of confidants enjoyed a status as high if not higher, than that of the nominally senior members. The corporate functions of the council were more clearly defined than the duties of individual members, and there was so little specialization of offices that the different councillors' positions were virtually interchangeable. The councillors did not spend all their time in the capital, but usually also had connexions with a rural area where they might reside for months at a time. With the exception therefore of the two or three members who were especially favoured by the king, the composition of the council changed from day to day. There was an absolute duty to attend at the annual festivals, or at the king's pleasure, but constant attendance at court was expected only of the king's favourites, and the other members seem to have been free to spend much of their time elsewhere.

[1] Their distribution coincides with the principal entrances into the royal quarter.

The history of the king's council under modern conditions illustrates the lack of any clear internal structure and the difficulty of assigning specific functions to the titled offices. In the first two decades little use seems to have been made of the traditional machinery of government, and Igala was administered directly by the divisional officers, working through professional District Heads, who were mainly non-Igala. The earliest reference to the composition of the Ata's council occurs around 1919, and says:

> The big council consisted of the Attah's brothers, nine in number:
>
> | | | |
> |---|---|---|
> | Amanata | Omalogba | Oshomakube |
> | Odomata | Inalogu | Egbena |
> | Umakoji Ata | Oshomogbolo | Ekpa |

No attempt seems to have been made by the colonial government to systematize the composition of the council until 1929, when Clifford, as District Officer, was commissioned to reorganize the administration on traditional lines. Writing of the council, Clifford said later:

> The form of government exercised by the Atas was simple and effective. At the centre was the Ata himself as Priest/King with the Achadu as chief executive—then the hereditary officers of state (kinsmen of the reigning Ata) and a Council composed of the nine Igala chieftains . . .[1]

The reorganized council included five royal titleholders and three Igala Mela members, who were all assigned departmental duties.[2] Elsewhere Clifford described the council on

---

[1] *Igala Divisional Report,* 1931.

[2] The duties were:

Achadu	Vice-President
Ochai Ata	Justice and Titles
Odomata	District Affairs and Tax
Amanata	Departmental
Ẹtẹmaihi	A co-opted member
Egena Ata	Supernumerary member, for missions to province
Odokina Ata	Supernumerary member, for missions to province
Abaigbo	Supernumerary member, for missions to province

The Egena Ata and Odokina Ata were later stationed permanently in the provinces, as Resident Councillors at Ankpa and Dekina, whilst the other councillors without specific duties were employed as Touring Councillors.

his arrival as 'an unwieldy and nondescript body with no specific duties assigned to it'.[1] But his own reconstituted council did not work smoothly, in spite of various later changes. Its composition was changed so that eight of the members came from the ruling lineage, and only the Achadu represented the Igala Mela. But the division of functions became increasingly blurred, and H. C. Gill, who was sent to report on the efficiency of the reorganized system wrote in 1943 that the councillors no longer had definite spheres of authority, but took their cue from the Ata.[2] Three traditional members were withdrawn from the council as a result of Gill's criticisms, and following his recommendations the council was put on a professional basis over the next 5 years. By 1949 only one titled member of the ruling house, the Odomata, was retained on the council; four posts were held by salaried councillors representing different administrative departments, three by judicial members, one was allocated to education and native affairs, and two others were held by titled chiefs from the provinces, the Onu Ogugu and the Onu Dekina.[3]

It is clear from the balance of power in the traditional council and from the failure of attempts to develop the council into a system of specialized offices that the traditional titles were relatively undifferentiated. In so far as the council was hierarchical in its organization it reproduced the pattern of seniority that characterizes sibling groups in Igala. The council itself was in a sense a model sibling group, and is so regarded by the Igala themselves. But the question of seniority within the council, apart from a purely ceremonial ranking, turned on the king's favour so that the roles of senior and junior sibling which the Igala assign to the different titles are in the last resort nominal positions, and not predetermined. But it is also a feature of this system that the difference in status between the various titles was not great. The titled offices were the key links in the complex chains of descent and kinship ties that oriented outlying villages towards the centre. And the essential duty of a titled *omata* was to act as spokesman for his own major lineage and for the wide kin group that

[1] *The Administration of Igala N.A. 1943–48,* ms. file.
[2] ibid.
[3] *Notes on Procedure, 1949. Igala Division,* ms. file.

centred upon this segment of the reigning group. The titled councillors commanded and mobilized the support of the villages in which their own agnatic kin were settled and with which this lineage group had hereditary connexions from the past. So that in the last resort any analysis of the workings of the traditional council is essentially concerned with the distribution of power and offices between the various major segments of the maximal royal lineage.

In appointing councillors from his own lineage the Ata chooses a fairly high proportion of his own siblings, not more distantly related than through a common grandfather or great-grandfather. Collateral branches are usually allocated around half the total number of offices available, so that the senior branch, of those in the direct line of succession, receives a larger share than any other lineage segment. To illustrate this point, figure 6 on pp. 72–3 gives an outline genealogy of the Ocholi lineage, showing succession to titles. The record is not complete, because knowledge of the succession was scanty, and the facts had to be pieced together from widely scattered sources. But this reconstruction does show that the senior branch has a share in most of the titles, and shows also that offices could be transferred from one line to another or from the line in which they were usually hereditary to the senior branch of the lineage. Table 4 summarizes the number of turns taken by each of the five major lineage segments in respect of the different titles.

Although they are not hereditary in an exclusive sense, titles nevertheless tend to be regarded as the hereditary property of major segments, or major lineages. Allegiance to the title-holder, and his descendants, creates an important bond of unity within the lineage segment, and gives a focus to corporate activity which would otherwise be lacking. The title-holder mediates between the segment members and the central government, and his house at Idah serves as an unofficial meeting place for the group. In Ocholi lineage, for instance, the late Odomata, Agọnọ Okenyi, was the undisputed head of the lineage segment founded by Ohiẹmini Gadagu; its members were sometimes described, by the rest of the lineage, as *abo Odomata*, the Odomata's people. At the annual royal festivals, the descendants of Ohiẹmini Gadagu were reunited

FIGURE 6. SUCCESSION TO TITLES IN THE OCHOLI LINEAGE

(see table 4 for key)

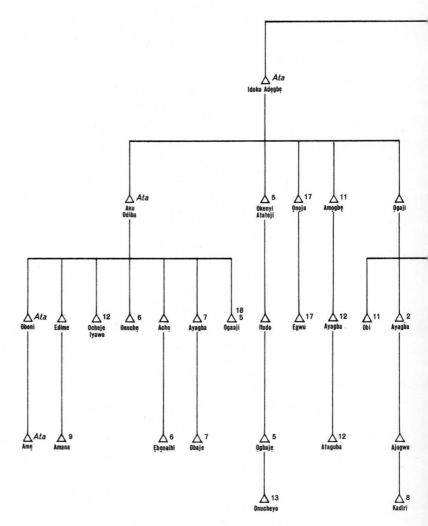

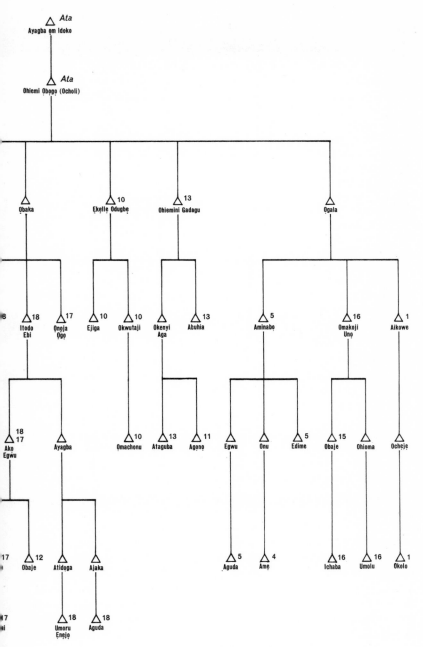

73

in the Odomata's compound before returning to their scattered homesteads, and throughout the year it formed the main centre for members of this group to meet or obtain news of each other.

Title	Aju Idoko Adegbe	Aju Obaka	Aju Ekelle Odugbe	Aju Ohiemini Gadagu	Aju Ogala
1. Achema Ata					2
2. Agbanata	1				
3. Agenyi Ata					
4. Agenyi Ayagba	1				
5. Amanata	3				
6. Egeuna Ata	2				
7. Ekpa Ata	2				
8. Inalogu	1				
9. Ochai Ata	1				
10. Odokina Ata			4		
11. Odoma Ata	2			1	
12. Ogohi Ata	1				
13. Ohiemogbolo	1			3	
14. Olimene					
15. Omachi Oma					4
16. Omachi Ata					
17. Omakoji Ata	2	4			
18. Omolobu	1	5			

TABLE 4. KEY TO FIGURE 6

The lineage segments regard themselves as the basic units of the royal title system, and describe changes in the distribution of titles in terms of the success or failure of individual segments. For instance, before Agono Okenyi, no member of the Ohiemini segment had taken the Odomata title, and his kinsmen regarded the appointment as an advance in status on the title of Ohiemogbolo that had been inherited previously. Unrelated groups in Idah described the Ohiemini group as having 'taken over', emugba, the new title from two groups in the major lineage of Idoko Adegbe that had previously shared the office. A similar situation occurred over the title of Omakoji Ata which went from father to son twice in the line of

74

Idoko Adẹgbẹ before transferring to Obaka's descendants, who had previously monopolized the title of Ọmọlọbu.

These transfers of office from one segment to another are sometimes made for personal reasons, when a segment's candidate is unsuitable. But they also used to be influenced by the wealth and standing of the parties concerned. It is claimed for instance, that *aju* Ọgala, in Ocholi lineage, resisted strongly when the title of Amanata was withdrawn from them and given to Ogbaje Itodo, whose own grandfather, Idoko Adẹgbẹ's son had previously held the office. Being wealthy, and already in possession of one councillor's office (Ọmachi Ọma) they were able to persuade the Ata to rescind the appointment and award it to the son of the previous titleholder, in their own segment.

Although the distribution of titles within the reigning lineage underlines the social ascendancy of the senior branch, it also reflects a certain lack of political cohesion in this group. By comparison with the other collateral branches, the senior line tends to split into a number of smaller segments, of about three generations depth, and although these are co-ordinated by their specially close relationship with the Ata, they nevertheless tend to be autonomous with regard to titles and the activities that centre on a councillor's office. Because of the multiple representation at the capital there is considerable rivalry within the major segment over the handling of provincial business, and members are sometimes found supporting opposite sides of the same issue in a way that does not seem to occur within collateral branches.

Political offices are the mainspring of segmentary opposition within the ruling lineages, and although members of each major segment are bound together by a strong sense of kin solidarity there are virtually no corporate functions of a non-political character. There is usually some continuity in residence between the titled head of the group and its founder, but the segment as a whole is widely dispersed and has no clearly defined territorial unity. The Ohiẹmini segment, for instance, has settlements at Oguma and Opada in Igala Mela District, and also at Gwolawo and Ofenya, about 12 miles away, with further scattered homesteads in the direction of Itobe. The major lineage founded by Idoko Adẹgbẹ is

75

dispersed between Itobe and Idah. The lineage founded by Ogala has associations with Shintaku and Adenekpa, near the Niger–Benue confluence. But its members are also settled in the metropolitan area and the Ibaji District. The other major lineages are similarly widely scattered, and can only be located spatially by referring to the homes of the reigning or the most recent titleholder from that particular group.

Within the major lineage the settlements of the titleholders give rise in time to smaller, localized groupings that can appropriately be termed localized lineages. I give examples of this type of grouping in discussing local communities and need only say here that in structure they are shallow agnatic groups structured around the descendants of a titleholder. Under modern conditions these units frequently have a small section based in the capital in addition to the parent body situated in an outlying district. Leadership within them tends to be inherited by the titleholder's children in order of seniority and then by their own eldest children in turn. But the groups are so shortlived that they tend to disintegrate before the third generation is reached; the sons of the founder inherit something of his high political status but this impetus is lost by the next generation unless a new political office is achieved.

Localized lineages do not form part of a total system of segmentation in the same way as major lineages within the maximal lineages or as maximal lineages within the subclan. They are as it were the nuclei into which the major lineages contract in the period when the maximal lineage is out of office, and from which the corporate organization of the major lineage can grow again when the whole lineage resumes office. But relations between localized lineages are competitive in the long term to the extent that different groups may be favoured when a new king is appointed from the maximal lineage to which they belong. For instance, within the Ohiemini major lineage in the Ocholi group the whole major segment was in Oboni's reign oriented towards the Oguma group which held the title of Ohiemogbolo. But when the Ocholi lineage next came to the throne, in Ame's reign, a rival minor lineage, led by Okenyi Aga's son at Ofenya, 'took over' a new title, Odomata, and became the leaders of the Ohiemini segment. The localized lineage centred on Oguma was given no title in this reign, but still retains the prestige of having supplied two holders of the Ohiẹmogbolo title in previous reigns. There are other groups of similar scale within this major lineage, but the struggle for leadership of the segment has become focused on the relations of these two titled groups, and the other units have not attained the same degree of corporate organization or corporate status. They would be better described as extended families rather than localized lineages, since their unity is domestic and not political in character. But, potentially, they are capable of taking on the same functions, i.e. of achieving the same degree of cohesion if their leaders manage to achieve royal favour at any time in the future.

The royal subclans centred in outlying districts of the kingdom divide in the same way as the Idah group into maximal lineages that are the basic units of a rotating title system. These maximal lineages are exogamous groups and show the same kind of unity in relation to marriage as the equivalent segments of the ruling subclan at Idah. They are likewise associated with different centres, so that the genealogical relationship between the different segments can be represented by a spatial model. But as in the metropolitan area this association with different centres is mainly an historical one, and the maximal lineages are in fact widely dispersed. In the following table the segmentation of the different subclans is summarized by showing the number of maximal lineages into which each group divides. The last two columns show the names of the lineages and their respective centres.

Subclan (Title in brackets)	No. of lineages	Lineage names	Lineage centres
Ankpa (Onu Ankpa)	4	Onoja Ikoja Aba Ojogobi	Abacẹ Acẹrane Ofugo Ojogobi
Dekina (Achema Ajobi)	2	Akomata Ọgadọ	

77

Subclan (Title in brackets)	No. of lineages	Lineage names	Lineage centres
Imani (Onu Imani)	4	Ohimu Okorikoto Onyuke Adede	Agariga Ẹkẹkpe Abo (Imaniabo) Ogẹnẹ Ago
Ojoku (Onu Ojoku)	8 (in two groups of four)	Ẹkẹlẹ Anawo Oko Enyikwọle Ẹkẹlẹ Onegelegu Eje Agbane Oboni	Bagele Ọgwọwala Okaba Onupi Utalu Ojoko Ojẹjẹ Inyologu Abodọ
Okpo (Obaje Atabaka)	5	Obaje-odo Odemu Ochiguma Onojaka Ote	Agbaduma Okpe Ocheku Etutẹkpẹ Okpo
Iga (Ojibo Akpọtọ)	4	Omoko Ede Abodiga Ake	Ogẹnẹ Ocheba Agala Ocheba
Ogugu (Ochogugu)	2	Onoja Obekpa	Omagaba Okegbi
Ikka (Onu Alọga)	4	Ame-Alebe Idoko Okpano Idagba Ogilijaja	
Okenyi (Onu Okenyi)	4	Ujakpabana Ogbogiri Okpe Oduma	

TABLE 5. SUBDIVISIONS OF THE PROVINCIAL
ROYAL SUBCLANS

In some cases maximal lineages that participate in the title succession have been assimilated into the subclan from elsewhere, and are not members of the descent group in the strict

78

genealogical sense. For instance, four out of the five lineages making up the Okpo subclan trace their descent from Oguchẹ Ẹkwọ, who also founded the Ankpa subclan. But the fifth lineage in the succession, named after its founder, Obaje Ote, traces its descent to the Ajaku branch of the Idah subclan. In this instance the assimilated lineage belongs ultimately to the same clan, but in other cases of assimilation the immigrants are of alien clan origin. For instance one of the four lineages in the Ikka subclan is of Ibo origin and claims that its founder was rescued from slavery by the founder of one of the other lineages. In another case, in the Imani group, the Onyuka lineage was founded by a daughter of the first chief, and its members are technically uterine kin, ọmonobulẹ, and not agnates. They nevertheless take an equal share in the rotation, and qualify politically for full membership of the descent group. It is in cases of this kind that the fiction of common descent is used by classifying members as children of the title rather than as children of a particular person. The category amọmonu 'children of the chief', assumes a different kind of unity from that obtaining within the maximal lineage, and adapts the descent model to refer to a kind of positional succession.

Maximal lineages can also arise in these outlying subclans from fission of an existing group, in the same way that the Ajaku branch of the ruling subclan at Idah has bifurcated. As the following genealogy of the Ankpa subclan shows, the Ikoja and Ojogobi lineages are genealogically major rather than maximal lineages and both belong to one lineage, Adanawo which is equivalent in order of segmentation to the other two maximal lineages, Ọnoja and Aba. But the four groups have become equivalent politically, and the two divisions of the Anawo lineage rank as maximal lineages in the title succession. There is moreover within the same segment a third lineage, Ẹkẹlẹ Onugbajẹ, that claims equal rights in the succession, and if this claim is allowed in future it will expand the existing rotation into a system of five lineages.

On being appointed, the heads of the provincial royal subclans select councillors from the members of their own maximal lineage and appoint them to a range of minor titles that are hereditary within the subclan concerned. This system of

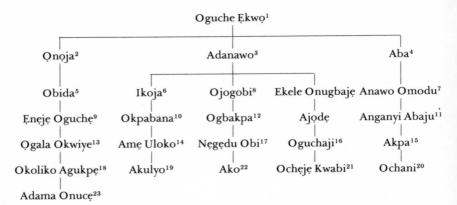

FIGURE 7. SUCCESSION TO CHIEFTAINCY IN THE
ROYAL SUBCLAN AT ANKPA

subordinate posts is clearly modelled on the Idah pattern, and
many of the titles have the same names as the offices found in
the Idah system. I summarize below the titles that are hereditary within each of the subclans.

Ankpa	Ojoku
Onu Ankpa	Onu Ojoku
Abọkkọ Onu Ankpa	Ochai Onu Ojoku
Onu Megwa	Ochẹjẹ Onu Ojoku
Agenyi Onu Ankpa	
Odoma Onu Ankpa	
Ochai Onu Ankpa	
Ohionugba	

Ogugu	Imani
Och'Ogugu	Onu Imani (Ọdda Imani)
Ochai Onu Ojoku	Ochai Ọdda
Ochẹjẹ Onu Ojoku	Ogala Ọdda
	Arune Ọdda
	Amana Ọdda
	Oche Ọdda
	Ọmachi Ọdda

Okpo	Iga
Obaje Atabaka	Ojibo Akpọtọ
Ochai Obaje	Odoma Ojibo Akpọtọ
Odoma Obaje	Ochai Ojibo Akpọtọ

	Iga
	Amana Ojibo Akpọtọ
	Abọkkọ Ojibo Akpọtọ
Ikka	*Okenyi*
Onu Aloga	Onu Okenyi
Ochai Onu Aloga	Ochai Onu Okenyi

TABLE 6. TITLES IN THE PROVINCIAL ROYAL SUBCLANS

One important difference between the pattern of royal titles in the capital and in the provinces is that in the northern districts the Ochai title tends to be used to denote the heir apparent. It is therefore given to a member of the next lineage in line, and not, as the other titles are, to members of the reigning maximal lineage. The heir apparent is chosen by the subclan head acting in consultation with the elders of the next lineage in line, and is then given beads and duties at the provincial court in the same way as the other titled councillors. This practice is, however, explicitly rejected at present by the Ata at Idah, since it cuts across the king's rights to appoint the heads of all the royal subclans. Subclan heads continue to appoint to the Ochai title in their own subclans, but the king refuses to be bound by this indication of an heir apparent, and awards titles on the basis of his own investigation of the claims of rival contestants.

The kingmakers.

Through the heads of the outlying royal subclans the king controlled a sufficient number of the traditional provinces to give the royal clan an overwhelming preponderance in the geographical distribution of power. The areas controlled from these royal provincial centres were relatively smaller than the metropolitan area, representing the sphere of influence of the Idah subclan. But including this central region the royal clan governed at least half of the total area of the kingdom directly through the heads of its different subclans. They were the highest administrative and judicial authorities in the areas concerned, with the right to receive tribute, settle disputes, and try all serious criminal offences that threatened the peace of the districts under their jurisdiction.

The authority exercised by the king as head of the royal clan

81

was limited by the segmentary nature of the clan organization, which opposed units of similar scale to one another at different levels on a descending scale. Within the clan as a whole the king's political functions were paralleled by those of the other subclan heads who were to a considerable extent independent of his authority. Similarly, within each subclan the division into maximal lineages tended to restrict the effective administrative authority of the subclan head to the area controlled by his own lineage. At each level of segmentation the units were defined by contraposition to units of similar scale and functions, their mutual relations were competitive and often hostile, and the units merged only in relation to the pattern of division existing in the order above them.

The Igala descent system is, however, unlike a segmentary lineage system in the emphasis that it places on relative seniority within the system. In each order of segmentation the units that emerge are ranked in a pattern of seniority. At the highest level of division this pattern is fixed so that the royal house of *amajata* is permanently in the ascendant. But in the lower orders of segmentation the principle of seniority is applied on a rotating basis or on the basis of age so that the locus of authority shifts in each generation, and the units take it in turn to exercise rights that are vested ultimately in the whole group.

The balance of power between the major segments of the royal clan is maintained ultimately by the groups that control the succession to their principal corporate offices. The king exercises this control over appointments to the headship of the provincial royal subclans, but his own office is subject in this respect to the authority of the kingmakers at Idah, who control the election of a new king and umpire the rotation of authority amongst the four maximal lineages of the ruling house. In the royal provinces there are non-royal clans whose functions are analogous to those of the kingmakers at Idah, and who hold a similar range of titles. But their authority over the provincial chiefs is ritual and moral in character rather than political, since succession to these provincial offices is determined within the hierarchical structure of authority running through the royal clan as a whole. To illustrate the kingmakers' functions in the political system I follow the same pattern as before of considering the metropolitan area in detail, followed by a brief comparison of this system with the provincial pattern.

Igala oral tradition explains the role of the kingmakers in the state system by postulating a transfer of political sovereignty from the original landowners at Idah to the immigrant founders of the royal clan. As we saw earlier, this transfer created a contractual relationship between the one group of clans and the royal descent group. But the modification of this primeval arrangement is acknowledged by the assimilation of another immigrant group which consolidated the indigenous landowning clans under the authority of its own head, the Achadu. The two stages of this myth summarize the powers that are hereditary in the federation of kingmaking clans, and validate the dominance of the Achadu's descent group within the federation.

The Igala Mela clans are nominally nine in number, and, in principle also, the descendants of the autochthonous population of Idah. In practice neither the group's composition nor its membership are as rigidly exclusive as these ideals imply. At least eleven clans lay claim to the status of belonging to this group. And again, the rule of indigenous origin is sufficiently flexible to allow one clan with traditions of immigrant origin to be regarded by all Igala as a full member of the federation.

One of the reasons for this discrepancy between the norm and the reality is that the term, 'Igala Mela', refers to spatial as well as to structural arrangements. It describes a sector of the capital lying between the inner and the outer defences of the old city, occupied by a cluster of homesteads belonging to the Igala Mela clan heads.[1] Any titleholder whose family has lived for more than one generation on this low ridge of land lying between Igalogwa and Ukwaja tends to be classed by the people of Idah as belonging to the Igala Mela. The Aleji clan, for instance, which was originally of Igbirra stock, has become fully assimilated through long residence. The Ochijenu clan, on the other hand, claims to have been physically established there for several generations, and is regarded by members of other clan groups as Igala Mela, but is not yet fully accepted by the Igala Mela themselves. Finally, there is the example of

[1] See map on p. 121.

83

a clan, taking the title of Achadu Kịkịlị Ukwaja, which has moved from the quarter and is in the process of losing its Igala Mela affiliation, although it is still regarded as a full member in connexion with the kingmakers' ceremonial duties. A list of the eleven clans claiming Igala Mela status, is given in the table on pp. 84–5. This table also summarizes the salutations that are used in greeting the men and women of each clan, and shows, in the last column, the *elifọ olopu* that has to be observed by all members of the clan in each case. With the addition of the Achadu's own clan, which is shown separately at the foot of the table, the clans listed comprise the complete federation of kingmakers.

The clans in the Igala Mela are individually much smaller in scale than the royal house at Idah to which they are opposed politically. This is true of their genealogical span and depth, as can be seen from the following summary of the number of generations and maximal lineages, in each of the clans.

Clan	Number of maximal lineages	Generations	Protodynastic ancestors
Ẹtẹmaihi	5	4	3
Onubiogbo	2	4	3
Okwẹjẹ	2	6	—
Unana	4 (?)	5	—
Agbẹnyọ	2	6	—
Obajadaka	2	4	5
Achadu Kịkịlị Ukwaja	4	6	4
Ochijenu	3	9	2
Onẹde	3	5	—

TABLE 7. LINEAGE DEPTH AND SPAN IN THE KINGMAKERS' CLANS

Clan title		Clan salutations		Ritual prohibitions
	Title	Men	Women	
Ẹtẹmaihi	Takida	Ohiọwa	Ugodo	Flesh of monitor lizard, *abaji*
Onubiogbo	Aguba	Onu Igala	Onu Igala	Flesh of crocodile, *ọnyẹ*

84

Clan title	Clan salutations			Ritual prohibitions
	Title	Men	Women	
Onẹde	Ojogobi	Onu Igala	Onu Igala	Use of *ugbakolo* or *ikpokpo* wood for firewood
Aleji	Ebije	Ahiebu	Anyebu	Forbidden for a needle, *olẹ*, to be brought in contact with food, or named when a member of the clan is eating
Okweje	Ẹde	Ahiebu	Anyebu	Flesh of the ground-squirrel, *okwejẹ*
Unana	Onu Igala	Ahiebu	Anyebu	Flesh of palm civet, *ewọlọ*
Agbẹnyọ	Onu Igala	Ọyọwọ	Ọyọwọ	Forbidden to use palm leaf fans, *utowo ẹkpẹ*. Also forbidden to use three-forked sticks as pot supports
Achanyuwọ	Ẹde	Ahiebu	Anyebu	Flesh of palm civet, *ewọlọ*, and wood of *ugbakolo* tree
Obajadaka	Dọga	Ọyọ	Ọyọ	Forbidden to touch food with an unhafted knife, *ukpakẹllẹ ọbẹ*
Ochijenu	Udẹ	Oohi	Onyẹtẹ	Forbidden to use palm fronds, *akpaga*, for firewood
Achadu Kịkịlị Ukwaja	Agukili	Ohiukwa	Aina	A leaf vegetable, *ọrọ dudu*, and flesh of *ouwẹ* fish
Achadu	Anu	Ọmanu	Ugodo	The *ouwẹ* fish

TABLE 8. THE FEDERATION OF KINGMAKERS

85

The corresponding numbers for the ruling subclan are four maximal lineages, seven generations, and at least four proto-dynastic ancestors.

The difference in scale between this group and the royal house is also reflected in the fact that the clan as a whole is exogamous in each case, instead of the maximal lineages. Finally, there is an associated difference in the numerical size of the Igala Mela clans which individually contain no more than a few hundred adults each. One can conclude that the Igala Mela clans, in size and scale, are more closely comparable with the maximal or major lineages of the ruling house than with the whole subclan. But they are distinct descent groups in each case, with the same corporate functions and tokens of identity as the royal clan itself. They have no traditions of common origin in the genealogical sense, but form a closely united federation whose members are bound together by a strong sense of historical unity and common political opposition to the reigning royal subclan.

Within the federation of kingmakers' clans there is a marked discrepancy of size and scale between the Igala Mela clans and the Achadu's own descent group, which is closely comparable with the ruling house. In the same way that the royal descent group, in virtue of its size and dispersal co-ordinates the corporate activities of small localized clans throughout the kingdom into a unified system, so the Achadu's clan performs a co-ordinating role within the much more restricted field of kingmakers' activities. The Achadu's dominance and leadership of the kingmakers is a function of his clan's preponderance within this group of clans, which ultimately provides the Achadu with a greater command of human and physical resources than the heads of the Igala Mela descent groups.

The Achadu's title is hereditary, as figure 8 shows, within a group of four lineages who trace their descent from a common male ancestor, Omẹppa. As in the case of the Idah and Ankpa subclans in the royal descent group, two of the lineages have been created by a process of segmentation within a unit of the same order as the other two major branches. They now form maximal lineages with the same functions as the older branches in the rotation, and can inter-marry with one another or with either of the older branches. All four lineages

86

are widely dispersed in the modern districts of Adoru, Igala Mela, and Igalǫgwa. But they have individual historical associations with different villages, and their settlements are to some extent concentrated around the following centres.

Lineage	Centres
Onogu	Ojuwo (Adoru District)
	Alaba (Gwolawo District)
Abutu Ejibo	Adoru (Adoru District)
	Alloma (Alloma, Igalǫgwa District)
Atikǫ	Okula (Igalǫgwa District)
	Akpadǫdǫ (Igalǫgwa District)
Inedu Otubi	Igoti (Igalǫgwa District)
	Gbamaka (Igalǫgwa District)
	Agojeju (Igalǫgwa District)
	Mamęrębǫ (Igalǫgwa District)

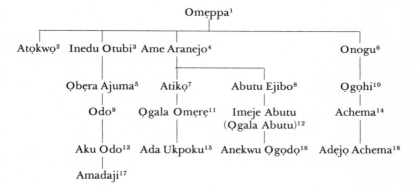

FIGURE 8. SUCCESSION TO THE ACHADU'S TITLE

The Achadu's powers of office include the right to appoint members of his own maximal lineage to a range of hereditary titles similar in name and function to the groups of secondary titles in the royal clan. But these offices are different from their royal counterparts in being held for life, and not for the period in which the clan head is in office. In the Achadu's clan there is an overlapping of lineages in the tenure of these secondary titles so that at present, for instance, a few appointments have been made by the reigning Achadu, but the majority of existing appointments date from the previous

Achadu's reign with a few also from the reign of the last but one Achadu. Each of the offices has a small fief or tribute area, anẹ ọfẹ, associated with it: in some cases the association is not hereditary but is a purely administrative arrangement specific to the titleholder concerned and may be altered by the grant of a new fief when the office becomes vacant. The titles and their traditional tributary areas in 1963 were as follows:

Title	Fief
Ochai Achadu	Allọma (Igalọgwa District)
Achema Achadu	Adoru (Adọru District)
Ẹgẹuna Achadu	Alakwa (Adọru District)
Odokina Achadu	Amaka (Adọru District)
Odoma Achadu	Ojuwo (Adòru District)
Amana Achadu	Anẹkẹ (Adòru District)
Agenyi Achadu	Igoti (Igalọgwa District)
Egwu Achadu	Egwubi (Adọru District)
Ode Achadu	Gwolawo (Gwolawo District)
Ashikala Achadu	Akpachala (Igala Mela District)
Achenya Achadu	Okotikpa (Igala Mela District)
Ọkpala Achadu	Okopo
Ọgọhi Achadu	Ajiya
Ohioma Achadu	subsidiary to Achema Achadu

TABLE 9. TITLES AND FIEFS IN THE ACHADU'S CLAN

In addition to controlling these offices within his own clan, the Achadu appoints the titled heads of certain other clans in the Adoru area, as listed below:

Title	Clan centre
Abaigbọ	Akpanya
Atakubi	Ukpabioko
Ochai Atẹkpa	Oyo
Oche	Ugbokiti
Onuilo	Akolo

These clans claim a kin connexion with the Achadu's clan by saying that they are ọm Achadu, children of the Achadu. But as descent groups they are independent of the main clan, and have no known ancestor in the parent group. Nor have they been assimilated politically by integration of their own functions with those of the Achadu's clan as a whole. Their title rotation is entirely separate from the transfer of titles within the Achadu's descent group and they have no structural connexion with the latter.

The local political connexions of the other kingmakers at Idah are extremely limited by comparison with the far-reaching ties maintained by the Achadu through the settlements of his own clan and through those of the satellite clans that take their titles from him. Individually, the Igala Mela clans' jurisdiction is limited to small groups of villages, making up single districts. These settlements are dotted in a narrow circle around the capital, whereas the Achadu's corresponding sphere of influence sweeps in a broad arc outside this inner ring from Alloma, north-east of Idah, to the border with Ibo territory in the east and south-east. The Igala Mela tributary areas are as follows:

Title	Tributary villages
Etemaihi	Ufoloko Etutu Ukpo Ajire (Igala Mela District) Ojuwo Okpoogodo
Onubiogbo	Emachi (Igala Mela District)
Onede	Ojiagba Ajire (Igala Mela District) Etutu
Aleji	Odogwu (Ibaji District)
Okweje	Alade (Igala Mela District)
Unana	Okpachala Obagwukolo Obajeli Apata Ala Ogwajiadu
Agbenyo	—
Achanyuwo	Ogbojogbo (Ibaji District)
Obajadaka	Obagukolo (Igala Mela District)
Ochijenu	Alaba (Gwolawo District)
Achadu Kikili Ukwaja	Alokoina (Ibaji District)

TABLE 10. THE KINGMAKERS' FIEFS

As head of a clan second in rank only to the royal descent group, and as leader of the kingmakers at Idah, the Achadu was permitted to maintain an impressive court in the capital, at Igalǫgwa, the traditional seat of every Achadu. In many features of layout and organization this court mirrored the royal palace. Igalǫgwa was surrounded by a high wall, with official entrances, and its buildings were on a scale found elsewhere only in the royal palace. Like the Ata, the Achadu was attended by a large following and met regularly with his titled councillors to settle disputes arising within the area under his jurisdiction. In addition to controlling an extensive fief directly, the Achadu was the *ohięgba* or intermediary for all titleholders in the Ibo border area who were not directly related to the king. All petitions for titles and judicial investigations in the border area beyond the Anambra river were channelled through the Achadu's court before they reached the king, and in most cases petitioners resided with the Achadu's followers during their stay in Idah rather than in the royal quarter or with any of the other officials.

The Achadu, like the Ata, had his own *ędibo*, or palace retainers, and a considerable following of slaves, *amadu*. As we shall see, his office was counterpoised ceremonially and ritually to that of the king. The Achadu carried out the same kinds of daily ritual as the Ata, and at the great annual festivals acted as ritual custodian of the land shrine, *ęranę*, which in a political sense belongs to the Ata.

Earlier writers sum up the Achadu's position in central government by describing him as a kind of Prime Minister, or by comparing his role with that of the Waziri in the Muslim emirates of Northern Nigeria. Partridge, for instance, wrote:

> The older race is represented by the Asadu, a title signifying Prime Minister. The Asadu calls himself 'the Atta's Wife', and is a great landowner, having as much power as, if not more than, the Atta himself.[1]

But the Achadu played a much less direct role in government than these interpretations suggest. The Achadu had the

---

[1] Partridge, C., 'The Burial of the Atta of Igaraland and the "Coronation" of his Successor', *Blackwood's Magazine*, Vol. CLXXVI, 1904, p. 329.

same right as the king's titled siblings to be consulted on matters of peace or war and on major changes of policy. But his relations with the king were more formal than theirs. The Achadu did not attend the council regularly, but spent most of the time in his own court at Igalogwa; the areas administered by the king and the kingmakers were separate administratively although they overlapped and interlocked with one another geographically. The Achadu's position is, therefore, more closely analogous to that of the quasi-autonomous provincial heads than it is to the office of a deputy or adjutant. But even this analogy can be misleading, since the Achadu's office belongs to, and is representative of, a group of clans that are opposed to the royal descent group. It is the supreme expression of a different principle of sovereignty and does not merely complement the functions of the royal clan as a sovereign group

By comparison with the importance attaching to the Achadu's office the other kingmakers seem insignificant both in the state system and in the social and political arrangements of the capital. Until 1930, when Clifford began his researches, their corporate functions had not come to the notice of the administration, and although the kingmakers' titles are mentioned individually, the term Igala Mela does not appear in the early administrative records.

When Clifford became aware of the kingmakers' duties, and investigated the position of the Igala Mela, he found that most of the Igala Mela chiefs were living outside the capital, and had no obvious administrative functions in the central government at Idah. In order to reconcile this appearance of weakness with the traditional conception of the Igala Mela's relationship with the king, Clifford postulated a successful intrigue by the royal councillors to exclude the Igala Mela from power and force them out of the capital. He supposed that they had initially held offices of the highest importance politically and administratively, and that they had formed 'a sort of advisory council to the Ata—and further acted as a kind of check on the activities of an over-oppressive Ata'. Their fall from office was, he believed, due to their connivance in the murder of the Ata Ekalaga, which led subsequent kings to attack their privileges.

91

Ekalaga's successor—fearing a like fate perhaps, contrived with the support of his own nobles and councillors to elbow the Igala Tara (Igala Mela) out of their lawful position and thereafter their status continued to decline so that by the close of the nineteenth century they had ceased to exist as a corporate body, while retaining however their hereditary offices in various rituals.[1]

There is, however, no evidence that the Igala Mela were more directly involved in government in the past than they were in Clifford's time; the early administrative records do not suggest this, nor do the oral traditions of the clans centred at Idah. Moreover, the argument that Igala hold the Igala Mela responsible for Ekalaga's murder is incorrect. The story of his assassination is quoted by Igala today as an instance of the power to make and unmake kings vested in the Achadu as head of the kingmakers, and the whole tenor of Igala thought on this subject is that the Achadu is the one primarily responsible for the collective actions of the kingmakers. The opposition between the royal clan and the kingmakers has tended to become concentrated on these two offices, which are almost equal in rank and use parallel symbolism and notions of power. This development may in turn be related to the internal logic of the clan system of which the offices are an expression. The royal clan tends to assimilate members of other clans within its own sphere of influence, through a number of mechanisms which I describe later. Similarly, the kingmakers' clans tends towards a unified descent structure in which one clan monopolizes a wide range of hereditary offices. But as the kingmakers' clans form the archetype of descent groups that are locally sovereign and ritually autonomous the process of assimilation cannot proceed towards the emergence of a single clan. By the nature of their duties and offices the kingmakers stand for the federal principle, and although the logic of the wider political system is towards an opposition of units that are genealogically and structurally equal, this is modified by the identification of the nine clans with the principle of individual local sovereignty.

The kingmakers' official duties in the capital fall into two major categories, one centring on succession to the kingship

[1] Clifford, Miles, ms. letter, *The Igala Tara* (Igala Mela), Nov. 1931. cf. also Clifford, 'A Nigerian Chiefdom . . .', *J.R.A.I.*, Vol. LXVI, 1936, p. 403.

and the other on ritual connected with the land shrine, *ẹranẹ*. Symbolically, the ceremonies and ritual through which these duties are discharged express in two different forms a basic-ally similar notion of ultimate sovereignty over the land. They are a ritual continuation and consummation of the original role of the Igala Mela as landowners in their own right, and in performing these duties the Igala Mela represent, at a national level, the landowning clans who, throughout the kingdom, have accepted the sovereignty of the royal clan and pay tribute to it. The transfer of sovereignty that is supposed to have been made to the royal group was irrevocable, so that the two classes of royal and non-royal are permanently in a position of superordination and subordination. But ritual control of the land cannot be permanently alienated; the royal group therefore need to have their position confirmed at the accession of each new Ata, and also annually in the festival of *Ẹrane*.

When the Igala king dies, an interregnum is avoided by synchronizing the funeral rites of the dead king, which create a formal vacancy in the kingship, with the accession ceremonies of his successor. The absolute continuity of government is symbolized by the postponement of the official announcement of the king's death until an occasion when the new ruler could be proclaimed in the same utterance; in theory it was even forbidden for the herald to draw breath in the middle of this announcement. Unofficially, the news of the death had already been made public by breaking down the roof of the palace tower, *ọdọgọ*, and by changing the site of a small market held outside the palace. The death could therefore be referred to euphemistically, but not in terms that would imply a vacancy in the kingship and the consequent suspension of government.

Although there was some overlapping between the two spheres, responsibility for the funeral rites was on the whole separated from responsibility for the accession ceremonies. The former devolved on the royal eunuchs, in conjunction with some of the Igala titleholders, whilst the Igala Mela took the initiative in preparing the new king for his office, and were the chief actors in the accession ceremonies proper. It was the Achadu's duty to send for the chosen candidate for the throne,

93

and to bestow on him the interim title of *Adukainya* (salutation, *Todo*). On arriving at Idah from the provinces the candidate spent several days in the Achadu's compound, where his ears were pierced by the Achadu's wife, and he also made a formal payment to the Achadu for his right to the Ata's title. This stage, which coincided with the funeral ceremonies of the previous king, ended when the king left the Achadu's compound and went to spend 9 days with Eguọla the keeper of the royal graves at Ọjaina. From here the Adokainya begins his formal entry to the capital by crossing the Inachalo stream to Ofukolo, where he is ritually reborn by the Onẹde, an Igala Mela chief, with the Onubiogbo, from the same group, acting as the king's father. This is the definitive rite of passage from the status of Adokainya to that of Ata, although the new Ata still has to be clothed in the king's ceremonial garments, and invested with the insignia of office. When this has been done, at the same site, the Ata mounts a horse and rides towards the palace. On the way he stops at the land shrine, *ẹranẹ*, and offers a tortoise and kola nuts; the act of sacrifice being performed by the *Atẹbọ*, an Igala chief, whilst the actual invocation to the land is made by the Achadu.[1] From *ẹranẹ* the Ata passes through the Igala Mela quarter to his palace, receiving his first acclamation as king from the people of Idah.

In this ceremonial transition from the status of royal heir to that of king there are five main stages. In the first the candidate becomes the 'wife' of the Achadu and is prepared for the office. In the second the Adukainya visits several shrines and remains at the last one visited, the royal burial ground. Next he is reborn, as Ata, and invested with the royal regalia. Fourthly, he makes an offering at the land shrine before entering the palace. And, finally, he offers to the royal ancestral shrine within the palace, and also sends offerings to various other royal shrines that were not among those visited at the Adukainya stage.

The accession ceremonies are not conducted wholly by the

---

[1] On this occasion the Achadu represents the other kingmakers, but on other occasions their responsibility for the land shrine is expressed. For instance Ẹtẹmaihi, according to oral tradition, led the Igala Mela before the first Achadu was appointed and can claim any criminal condemned to die at *ẹranẹ* and save him from execution by making him his own slave.

Igala Mela, and only three of the chiefs in this group have actual duties to perform on this occasion. But the Igala Mela initiate three of the stages, and make a major contribution to the underlying symbolism. In the course of the accession the king goes through the whole gamut of his ritual responsibilities, and the ceremonies define his position in relation to various social groups and to the spiritual agencies with which they are associated. The Igala Mela have some duties in connexion with the royal funeral ceremonies and the king's eventual transition to ancestral status. But their main duties are connected with the land, and we can relate the notion of their authority over the king, which is expressed in the accession ceremonies, to this basic role. The act of rebirth symbolizes the delegation of political sovereignty to the royal line, but also, in conjunction with the offering made at the land shrine, emphasizes the continuance of the kingmakers' ritual sovereignty over the land.

The annual land festival, in which the king and the Achadu are chiefly concerned, is called *Ocho*, and used to be held towards the end of the dry season. To understand its procedure and symbolism fully the festival needs to be related to the festivals performed annually by the heads of local landowning clans. At this stage it will be enough to say of this connexion that the king represents the head of a hunting group, whilst the Achadu represents the indigenous landowners, *amọmọnuane*. For the festival, a ceremonial hunting camp is established by erecting a tent at a spot in the bush selected by divination. The king sleeps one night in the camp, and on the next day symbolically burns the savannah grass and carries out a successful hunt. At the end of the day the hunting party moves to the permanent land shrine, *ẹranẹ*, where the king makes an offering through the Achadu and is blessed by him. He then receives the homage of the titled *amọmata*, followed by that of the Igala Mela, led by Ẹtẹmaihi, and the whole party returns in triumph to the palace. As the following diagram shows, this order of proceedings and the situation of the land shrine in relation to the palace emphasizes the opposition of the kingmakers to the royal descent group, and of the Achadu to the king within this wider dichotomy.

The kingmakers' right to determine the royal succession,

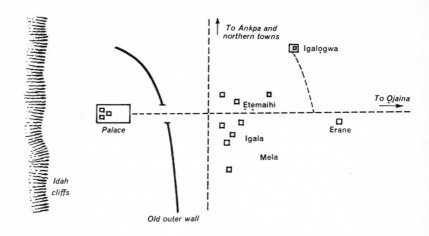

FIGURE 9. THE PALACE, KINGMAKERS' QUARTER AND
EARTH SHRINE

which is the last of their duties to be considered, is so circumscribed by precedent that they have little scope for varying the
rotation of lineages or of departing from the rule that the
eldest surviving son of the last ruler in the lineage is the one
to inherit the title. Igala accept only two instances, one in the
order of lineages and one in the eldest son rule, as definite
evidence of change made by the kingmakers, although they
sometimes tell stories in which it is claimed that a junior
brother took precedence over a senior brother in becoming
king.[1] Nevertheless it is universally accepted that the kingmakers do hold the right to change the order of lineage
succession in exceptional circumstances, and to reject any
candidate for the throne, regardless of seniority, if he seems
personally incapable of discharging the duties of kingship.
The legends that support these rights also claim that the kingmakers can sanction the Ata's deposition if his rule goes
against the established principles, although it is likewise clear
from the examples that this involves bringing about the Ata's
death since the throne does not become vacant until this
occurs.

[1] See appendix.

The first deviation from the regular pattern of royal succession occurred when Amachǫ, who, chosen by the Igala Mela to succeed the Ata Ohiemi Ǫbǫgǫ, failed to complete the accession ceremonies and was replaced by his brother Itodo Aduga. Informants from opposite sides of the royal house give different versions of the event. The Ajaku branch of the subclan argues that Amachǫ died at Igalǫgwa as Adukainya and that the Igala Mela therefore took the next candidate from this lineage, who was the next eldest son of Itodo Aduga. This version is more widely accepted than a variant told in the Ocholi and Akogu lineages which says that Amachǫ was found unsuitable and dismissed by the Igala Mela during the Adukainya stage. Amachǫ's children are said to have become unbearably arrogant during the interregnum, and a quarrel with the kingmakers was precipitated when the Adukainya's eldest son rode down a child from their quarter.[1] Disregarding these differences, which reflect the major political division running through the royal subclan, the point of the story is that the kingmakers have power to vary the order of succession between branches of the royal lineage. Since by accepting two candidates from the Ajaku lineage they established a precedent which was later followed in allowing Ajaku to segment in relation to the succession and to take two turns on equal terms with the other maximal lineages.

The other incident concerns the kingmakers' power to depose an unpopular king, and centres on the death of the Ata Ekalaga. Here again there are two versions of the event, from opposite sides of the royal subclan. The Ajaku branch maintain that Ekalaga allowed his sons to terrorize the countryside around Idah, by selling people into slavery, plundering traders, and making extortionate demands on village heads. The climax was reached when one of the sons abused the Achadu in public, and as the king failed to punish the offender, the Igala Mela met and invited Amocheje to take over the throne. The Ocholi version of the deposition is that Ajaku

---

[1] This explanation of Amacho's failure to complete the Adukainya period was associated by my informant with the proverb:

anya defu foti ǫka lǫ
'The horse that was pregnant ate a whole bundle of corn.'

97

were incensed by the great length of Ekalaga's reign, which kept them out of office, and therefore conspired against him with the kingmakers. In the first version Ekalaga is said to have been killed openly in the course of an armed rebellion; whereas in the second he is described as being murdered with the connivance of his palace eunuchs, who had been bribed by the kingmakers and by members of the Ajaku lineage. Again, disregarding the political bias of these narratives, there is agreement between them on the fact that the king could only be deposed by the kingmakers; without their consent, even though the king were to be killed, the council would continue to function, and the succession would be formally blocked as though the king were still alive.

In the provinces succession to the major political offices is controlled by the senior branch of the royal subclan at Idah, and no group can emerge with functions exactly like those of the kingmakers at Idah. But there are in each province a group of titles, usually headed by an Achadu, whose holders are responsible for the land shrine of the provincial capital, and also symbolically recognize the new provincial head on his return from investiture at Idah. In the provinces succession is bound up with responsibility for funeral ritual, and these opposed groups exercise a measure of control over the succession through their right to control the *icholo* that are performed for the previous titleholder when a new provincial head takes up office. Until the incoming titleholder is ready to carry out the Aku ceremony of his predecessor he cannot formally take up residence in the provincial court, but must stay in temporary accommodation elsewhere.[1]

Responsibility for the funeral ritual connected with accession and for the land cult maintained at the provincial court is sometimes divided. At Ankpa, for instance, the clan holding the title of Onu Ejegbo is responsible for the *erane* shrine, whilst three other clans are in charge of the final burial ceremonies, *icholo*, of the previous chief. The head of the senior clan in this last group, the Achadu Onu Ankpa, sewed a leopard's skin around each dead Onu Ankpa's coffin, *oko*, which was then carried to the grave by members of two other

---

[1] Ideally with a sister's son, *omonobule*. See p. 137.

clans, Ọlọbu Onu Ankpa and Achadu Agukịlị. But elsewhere the two duties were closely integrated. At Ojoku, for instance, the chief s land shrine is in the charge of the Achadu. But the burial ceremonies are performed jointly by the Achadu and another clan head, the Inegbulu. In their own words:

> The traditional duties and rituals performed by us (are): We both knock at the door where the deceased Onu ·Ojoku lies. We dress the corpse, other relatives do the actual burial. We keep the regalia which we produce at the final day of ceremonial burial.

I list below the titles held in various royal provinces by these guardians of the land and of the traditional rites of royal accession.

Ankpa

Achadu Onu Ankpa
Achadu Agukịlị
Ọlọbu Onu Ankpa
Anawo Onu Ankpa
  (Onu Ẹjẹgbo)

Ojoku

Achadu Onu Ojoku
Onu Odogum
Inegbulu

Ogugu

Achadu Och'Ogugu
Odu
Ogbedaliga
Auchi of Ikelegu

Imani

Achadu Ọdda
Otoku Ọdda

Okpo

Achadu Obaje
Adọja

Iga

Achadu Ojibo Akpọtọ
Adọga
Okpoju Ọmachi

It was not possible, in the time available, to study provincial government in sufficient detail to discover whether clans in this position have ever interfered with the appointment of provincial chiefs by blocking their accession. But it is obvious from the nature of their duties, and from the fact that each clan has a district directly under its control, that these clans are in a position to exercise the same kind of restraining influence on the ruling group as the kingmakers do collectively at Idah. The succession depends so much upon their co-operation and acceptance of the new chief that they are able, potentially, to hold the balance of power between lineages or individuals competing for this right.

Subsidiary clans.

One aspect of the kingmakers' role which can scarcely be over-emphasized is the fact that they are formally representative as a group of the whole class of non-royal clans in Igala. This is evident from the nature of their duties, which centre upon their responsibility for the ritual condition of the land. It appears also in the terminology of the clan groupings. Non-royal elements of the population are opposed linguistically to the royal element, the *amọmata*, by describing them as *abo Igala*, 'Igala people', or *olọpu Igala*, 'Igala clans'. Within this class the kingmakers are distinguished by referring to them collectively as *Igala Mela*. We can conclude therefore that they are identified with this wider class, and with its members in their opposition to the royal group, and that the difference between them and the other non-royal clans is one of degree only turning on their greater seniority and their unique geographical position.

The duties performed by the Igala Mela, and the symbolism of their offices, are an expression of the local sovereign rights that are vested in non-royal clans throughout the kingdom. Virtually all the non-royal clans possess rights in land and exercise certain political functions as the 'landowners' or 'chiefs of the land' in the areas where they are centred. It is by dramatizing the inalienable nature of this class of rights, and by opposing their own local sovereignty over the land to the principle of royal or national sovereignty that the king-makers set limits to the king's power, which would otherwise be absolute. But the compromise that is built into the framework of the central government at Idah runs through the clan system as a whole, and forms the basis of local administrative arrangements as well as of the system of succession in the capital. At every level of political organization the principle of ritual or local sovereignty is opposed to that of the royal or national sovereignty. There is thus a basic interdependence of both groups of clans within the political system, of the royal group who monopolize policy-making, certain types of judicial decision, and the right to organize military coercion, and the non-royal groups whose primary control of local communities is symbolized and validated by the notion of ritual custody of the land. To some extent both sets of functions are expressed in the same idiom, since the king is the source of all political power and is ultimately responsible for the aspects of government symbolized by the well-being of the land as well as for those aspects that are symbolized by the integrity of his own position in relation to the founding royal ancestors. But when this idiom is employed, to assert for example, that the king owns the land, *Ata nanę*, or that the kingdom is the 'land of Ayagba', *an'Ayagba*, these statements are always qualified by the fact that the royal clan does not 'own land', *enanę*, in the same sense as the true 'chief of the land', *onu anę*. As I show in a later section, its members are subject, in a ritual sense, to the local 'chiefs of the land', and cannot entirely usurp the juridical and administrative functions that are summed up in this ritual image.

In addition to acting as administrative heads in the districts where their clans are centred, some of the non-royal titleholders exercise other functions. The duties place them politically in an intermediate position between the royal group and those non-royal clans whose duties are limited to the basic function of administering a local district. But although the degree of specialization of the clan office forms the basis of distinction of rank in Igala, there is no formal linguistic recognition of any difference between clans holding these more specialized offices and those whose heads belong only to the category of land chiefs. Some distinction of this kind is, however, useful for analytical purposes, and I employ the term 'subsidiary clans' for those descent groups holding titles which combine the function of land chief with the duty of assisting the king of the central government in some more specialized capacity. In the metropolitan area there is an important group of clans falling into this category, whose offices form a third major division in the structure of central government. To describe this type of clan and its functions, I shall proceed as before in drawing most of my examples from the arrangement at the centre, before going on to consider the variants that occur in the provinces.

101

In the metropolitan area there are about twenty subsidiary clans, whose titled heads hold office in the central government at Idah and form a class opposed to the royal councillors and to the kingmakers. In some cases the hereditary duties of the title are mainly ritual whilst in others they are mainly administrative, and the group could be subdivided on this basis into two grades of specialists. But the Igala do not make this distinction, possibly because almost all the clan heads participate to some extent in the succession ritual, and partly also because of the unity imposed on this class of clans by its being in an intermediate position between the royal group and the kingmakers.

In sharp contrast to the Igala Mela, the clans in this division are Igala by assimilation and not by origin. The majority of them, according to their own traditions of origin, are of immigrant stock, and their founders are said to have come from other tribal groups. The greater part of the settlers who founded the clans are from one or other of the three major divisions of the Igbirra tribe, from Panda on the Benue, Koton Kerifi (Igu) on the left bank of the Niger above the confluence, or from the Hima group whose settlements run inland from Ajokuta on the right bank of the Niger. The points of origin mentioned in the legends cannot always be identified and in some cases the reference is simply to Ojukpali, the hilly north, which could mean either Igbirra, Nupe, or the country further beyond.

To a smaller extent the Edọ-speaking peoples across the Niger (Kukuruku) are also represented amongst these immigrant groups, together with the Ibo and Hausa.

The list of subsidiary clans (table 11) shows their origins, as related by the present clan heads. The clan names are those of the title taken by each clan; in this group as among the Igala Mela, a clan is typically a federation of lineages that takes a common title in rotation and explains its unity by the hypothesis of common ancestry. In the same table I include, in separate columns, details of the greetings used towards members of the clan, and of the hereditary ritual prohibitions, ẹlifọ olọpu observed in each clan.

Some of the clans in this list are grouped in pairs as hereditary allies, and present a common front in their political

Clan title	Title	Clan salutations		Ritual prohibition	Tribe of origin (and place of origin)
		Men	Women		
Abọkọ Onukwu Ata	Ebije	Onyimọ	Onyimọ	Ouwẹ fish. Breaking firewood over one's knee	Igbirra (Ohimọjọ)
Abọkọ Ochẹjẹ	Ebije	Ohiẹda	Ugodo		Inẹlẹ (Kukuruku Division)
Adọkpulu	Agẹnapoje	Ohiọwa	Aje	Wood or leaves of *ugbakolo* and *ikpokpo*	Igala (Idah)
Agaidoko	Ẹdẹ	Ohieda	Ugodo		Igbirra (Panda)
Atẹbọ	Oduma	Onu Igala	Onu Igala	Wood or leaves of *ugbakolo* and *udogu* and *ugbakolo*	Igala (Ankpa area)
Eguọla	Ọchu	Ahiebu	Anyebu		Igala (Idah)
Ẹwọ	Iyesi	Ẹyẹdẹ	Ẹyẹdẹ		Ojukpali (common origin with Omọgbaje clan)
Onu Idokoliko	Awuhi	Ọyọ	Ọyọ		Igala (Idah)
Ogelinya	Adogbo	Ohiẹdẹ	Ugodo	Ouwẹ fish; *udogu* and *ugbakolo* trees	Igbirra (Igu)
Ohiemogbo Obiga (*and* Ochada)	Ẹdẹ	Oyikwa	Oyina	Ouwẹ fish; *ugbakolo* tree	Igbirra
Ohiuga	Ẹdẹ	Ohietẹ Ahiebu	Onyetẹ Anyebu	*Ikpokpo* or *ugbakolo* trees; *ouwẹ* fish	Igbirra (Acadachi)
Omọgbajẹ	Ọga	Obewa	Onyọnwa	Ouwẹ fish	
Onupia	Onuwo	Ohieda	Ugodo	Ouwẹ fish	
Onu Ohiiji	Ebije	Inọmẹ	Inọmẹ	Placing iron utensil in the fire below a cooking pot	Igbirra (Ohimọjọ) Inẹlẹ (Kukuruku Division)
Uchalla Angwa	Uwodi	Ọna	Ọna	A Moslem title, associated with the usual Islamic avoidance of pork, monkey flesh, etc.	Kano
Ulimam Ata	Uwodi	Ọna	Ọna	A Moslem title, associated with the usual Islamic avoidance of pork, monkey flesh, etc.	Kano
Okpayigebẹ	Udẹ				Ibo
Akaihiama					Ibo

TABLE 11. SUBSIDIARY CLANS IN THE METROPOLITAN AREA

103

dealings with the other clans in this system. At Idah, the homesteads of the two titleholders making up such a partnership are usually situated close together, and there is a continual exchange of views between them on political and other matters which is in marked contrast to the competitive or merely negative relations that tend to occur between clan heads outside this pattern. The alliance is asymmetrical in the sense that one title is formally senior to the second one. Abokko Onukwu Ata, for instance, is senior to the linked title of Onupia, and similarly Omogbaje is senior to its partner, Ewo. The partnerships tend to be described, as do most hereditary political links in Igala in a kinship idiom. The last two clans, for instance, claim that their founders were related as brothers before they migrated to Idah, and that Ewo, who came to Igala first, sent for his junior brother, who became the founder of the second clan. The second group in time won more favour at Idah than the first, and so, as its name implies,[1] took over the senior role and came to wield authority over the first group.

All the subsidiary clans in the metropolitan area claim to be contemporary in origin with Ayagba om Idoko, and believe that their offices were created either by Ayagba himself or by Akumabi. This tradition symbolizes the equivalence, within the political system, of the Igala clans to the other major divisions of government. With the exception of the Ata's office and the Achadu's the actual posts held by the amomata and Igala Mela chiefs are similarly said to have been created in the first reigns and there is no historical order of seniority among the different offices. The tradition also symbolizes the complete assimilation of these immigrant groups into the fabric of Igala social life. Apart from their traditions of origin, and in some cases their geographical association with the riverain area, there are no distinctively alien features in their corporate character. They have adopted both the Igala language and Igala forms of ceremony and ritual.

Some of the immigrant groups among the Igala clans claim that their founders were of high rank in their country of

---

[1] *Oma gba je*—'the child ate first', referring to a legend in which the junior brother snatched his elder brother's share of gifts made by the Ata.

origin. A typical legend, describing the origin of the Agaidoko clan, says:

We are descended from Anda, who was an Igbirra man and came from Opanda to Idah.[1] Anda's father, Ahangaji, was the ruler of Opanda, and had power there in the same way as the Ata is powerful at Idah. He alone had the right to use trumpets, *kakatsi*, and there were nine trumpet-players in his retinue. Anda himself and Akumabi, the Ata's son, were kinsmen on the mother's side (*ǫmaiye*). Their mothers were sisters, the children of Oji. Anda was senior to Ayagba (older than?) and was titled in his own father's area at the time when Ayagba was reigning. When Ayagba died, Akumabi sent for his kinsmen to help him with the burial ceremonies of his own father, and Anda came to Idah. After the funeral, Akumabi begged him to stay and offered him a choice of titles to compensate for the loss of his own high position in Igbirra.

The legend goes on to say that Anda rejected the post of councillor because the councillor's access to the king was supervised by the palace eunuchs. So he took over, as his nominal duty, the task of leading the king's horse on cere-monial occasions, a post which had previously been filled by a slave and was therefore not subject to the procedure of approaching the king through an intermediary.

This kind of claim to a special kinship connexion with the royal clan frequently recurs in Igala, and is usually found in situations where the group in question is interposed between two clans or clan segments of high rank and with similar political functions. In this case the riverain clans use this type of tradition to counterbalance the high status of the other two major divisions of government in Idah. They are poised be-tween the royal clan, with its traditions of an inherent right to rule, and the kingmakers, who represent the rights of the non-royal population, both ritually and politically. In this division the riverain groups align themselves with the royal faction, and claim a degree of equality with the royal group through the idiom of kinship and royal ancestry. A similar situation occurs among some of the northern clans who are

[1] Panda was the capital of an Igbirra kingdom located north of the Benue, which was destroyed by the Fulani in 1850.

non-royal in origin and interposed politically between competing subclans of the royal group.

The Igala clans at Idah vary in genealogical depth in the same way and to about the same extent as the Igala Mela clans. In scale they are generally much smaller than the royal clan. The summary of ten genealogies set out below shows that only one group is equivalent in depth to the royal group, and that the majority count either four or five generations from the apical ancestor to the present clan head, or his deputy. In span they are likewise smaller in scale; three of the clans in the sample have no regular pattern of segmentation in the title succession, and a further four have only two branches. The Agaidoko clan, one of the leading clans in the group, has five branches. The assimilated status of the group as a whole is reflected in the relative absence of pre-apical ancestors; the Agaidoko group is exceptional in retaining the name of a wholly alien forbear.

Clan	No. of maximal lineages	Depth	Pre-apical ancestors
Adọkpulu	3	4	—
Agaidoko	5	5	1
Akaihiama	1	5	—
Eguọla	4	4	1
Ẹwọ	2	5	—
Ohiuga	2	6	—
Ogẹlinya	2	4	—
Okpayigẹbẹ	1	5	—
Ohiiji	1	6	—
Ọmọgbajẹ	2	7	—
Ohiomogbo Obiga	2	6	—
Onupia	2	5	—

TABLE 12. LINEAGE DEPTH AND SPAN IN THE
SUBSIDIARY CLANS

Within the Igala group of titles there is a dual division of offices, one group being administrative in character and the other ritual. But this distinction is not an absolute one, most of the clans have some ritual duty to perform in connexion with royal mortuary ceremonies, and the divisions merge in relation to the royal succession. Conversely, the holders of major priestly offices are also the heads of important territorial segments outside the capital, and are involved to some extent in the secular hierarchy of authority. The Igala clans as a group are associated with the riverain area of the kingdom, where their main settlements are located and where they also collect tribute. And their historical and geographical orientation towards the river is such an important principle of unity that their ritual and political functions in government should be regarded as complementary and not mutually exclusive.

The titleholders with mainly ritual duties are:

Ohiuga	Adokpulu	Uchalla Angwa
Atebo	Onu Idokoliko	Ulimam
Eguola		

The Ohiuga, or royal diviner, is a specialist in the *Ifa* system of divination, employing four strings of seed pods. *Ifa* was traditionally consulted before any major decision of state was put into effect, and also in any crisis affecting the king; Ohiuga's role therefore was that of priest to a state oracle.

The Atebo's office is associated with the collective authority of the royal ancestors, symbolized by the staff, *Otutubatu*, of which he is the guardian. This staff completed the royal insignia of kinship, and had to be present whenever the Ata performed an important ritual in public. It complements the nine ritual staffs, *okwute*, that represent the ruling dynasty from Ayagba onwards, and stands for the royal ancestors as a group, notably for the predynastic members and the kings who are no longer worshipped as individuals. This collective authority is immanent in the Atebo's office, and empowers the Atebo to rebuke the king publicly for any ritual offences. Like the senior councillors, the Atebo does not prostrate in greeting the Ata, but greets him as an equal. Again, when the king dies, the Atebo is summoned to make the first offering, and puts on the dead king's robes. He ritually impersonates the king until, towards the end of the mortuary ceremonies, the masquerades *okolo* and *ilo* perform to symbolize the king's transition to ancestral status.

Eguola and Adokpulu are jointly responsible for the royal burial ground, Ojaina, and the former is also in charge of a set of nine *okwute* representing dead kings. Eguola and Atebo were jointly responsible for the offerings made to the royal ancestors during the annual Egu festival; they also officiated at different stages of the royal mortuary rites. And, as we have seen, the latter were integrated with the accession ceremonies in such a way that the Adukainya spent nine days in Eguola's house immediately after the completion of the funeral. During this stay the Adukainya visited the royal grave, and selected a site for his own eventual interment. He also brought red cloth that was used by Eguola to swathe the *okwute* of his predecessor. On the last day, the Adukainya was given the wrist beads of office by the Eguola, and also made to choose, blindfold, his own father's staff from among the ancestral *okwute*.

Onu Idokoliko is the custodian of a shrine dedicated to a nature spirit, Idokoliko, that is believed to inhabit the deep stream, Ocheche, flowing under the face of the cliffs on which the capital is situated. The spirit belongs to a class of tutelary deities, *eb'oji Ata*, whose functions I describe more fully later. Close to this shrine, where the Ocheche flows into the Niger, is the site of another shrine dedicated to the king's daughter, Inikpi, and although there is no direct connexion between the two sites, they are closely associated with the defence of Idah against attack from the river, and have the common function of protecting the king against witchcraft and sorcery that might be employed by members of the local community at Idah and its waterside villages.

The Uchalla Angwa and the Ulimam are both Islamic priests, and leaders of rival sections of the Moslem community at Idah. In the past, under the pagan régime, they acted as scribes to the court, as assistant judges, and as charm makers. The Angwa community led by Uchalla also performed an annual ceremony, the *Ogane*, which ritually cleansed the palace of evil.

The clans to whom these ritual duties are allocated are in many ways in a position similar to that of the Igala Mela. Potentially they can exercise a restraining influence on the king and his councillors through their ritual authority over

108

the king's office. But in practice they tend to be overshadowed politically by the other subordinate clans who have no permanent ritual duties, but derive their strength from control of riverain affairs. The position of this dominant group is in turn analogous to that of the Achadu's clan within the federation of kingmakers. Its members are dispersed along one of the main frontiers of the kingdom and mediate between the central government and the alien groups with whom the Igala come into contact in this direction. They do not participate to the same extent as the Achadu in the corporate ritual activities of the clan division to which they belong. But this is counterbalanced by the greater strategic importance of their sphere of influence. Control of the riverain markets was one of the economic mainstays of the traditional system of kingship, and the river was also relatively more significant at the military and political level than the border areas inland. It is perhaps this difference in economic and military potential that accounts for the differences in organization between the subsidiary clans and the kingmakers. Riverain politics are basically more dynamic than the power situation associated with control of the inland borders and the relatively greater scope for competition has prevented the dominant subsidiary clans from achieving the level of consolidation and political unity represented by the federation of clans and lineages within and around the Achadu's descent group.

Control of the riverain area was vested traditionally in a group of titles, revolving around the three major offices of Abokko Onukwu Ata, Agaidoko, and Omogbaje. The other clans in this constellation were linked with one or other of these major titles and need not be considered apart from their alignment within this tripartite division of power.

Relations between the three leading riverain clans were intensely competitive and the division of functions between them represents a balance of power rather than an institutional delegation of responsibility. At present each of the three clans' heads claims that it was the prerogative of his own title to be the Ata's chief lieutenant in the Niger both above and below Idah, with the duty of keeping the peace, of providing canoes for the Ata's service, and of acting as intermediary between the king and the alien groups that used the river for trade.

In practice their spheres of influence are to some extent regionalized, with Agaidoko controlling the river downstream from Idah, Ọmọgbajẹ presiding over the waterside area at Idah, and the Abọkkọ clan governing the upper districts of the river. But each clan claims a wider jurisdiction than this, and this division of interest represents only the most recent phase of a long period of adjustment characterized by intense political and economic competition. We are fortunate in possessing historical records which document part of this process, and which throw light not only on the mutual relations of the clans concerned, but also on their relationship with the central government and the extent of the king's control over them.

When the Lander brothers made their voyage of discovery down the Niger in 1832, they were befriended by one of the Abọkkọ family, then living in exile at Adamugu, on an island in the river below Idah. Subsequent expeditions followed up this connexion, and conducted much of their business with the court at Idah through the Abọkkọ clan head. The Abọkkọ office holder claimed the exclusive right to negotiate with the Europeans, who in turn regarded him as 'Superintendent of the Board of Trade in this river'. There was, however, chronic rivalry between Abọkkọ and Agaidoko, whom Crowther described as 'the war chief of the river'. In the course of the 1834 expedition, Abọkkọ reported to the commander that Agaidoko was trying to persuade the Ata to allow him to attack and loot the ships, and although this was not proved beyond doubt, the accusations created such tension at Idah that the expedition's stay there was cut short.[1] In 1854, the third Niger expedition found the two clans at war with one another, following a clash at the market of Asaba, in Ibo country.[2] In the long term, the Agaidoko clan gained from this struggle, since the Abọkkọ group withdrew from their older centre at Adamagu, and moved upstream to a new site above Idah, called

[1] Laird, MacGregor, and Oldfield, R. A. K., *Narrative of an Expedition into the Interior of Africa*, 1837, Vol. 2, pp. 256–8 and 262–3.

[2] Baikie, W. B., *Narrative of an Exploring Voyage up the Rivers Kwora and Benue in 1854*, 1856, p. 54. cf. also Crowther, Samuel, and Schön, J. F., *Journal of an Expedition up the Niger and Tshadda Rivers . . . in 1854*, 1855, pp. 34–5.

Oko Okeyin (Okokenyi) after the son of the earlier Abọkkọ met by Lander.[1] Baikie's exploring party heard this news whilst they were still in the Benue river, and when returning downstream they met the clan head in his new settlement. Baikie also noted, as he sailed further down the river, that the market set up by Abọkkọ near Adamagu had closed, and that Ibo traders from Aboh who were friendly with the clan were going further upstream to exchange their goods, to the detriment of trade at Idah.[2]

The changes that occurred in the Abọkkọ's political fortunes cannot be explained entirely by the factor of rivalry with the other riverain chiefs; they also turned upon the degree of royal favour that he enjoyed. After losing his foothold in the southern districts of the river, Abọkkọ's position deteriorated still further and his clan's friendship with the European expeditions ended in a bitter denouement as a result of this decline. Following the quarrel with Agaidoko and the move to Okokenyi the clan head and his followers returned to Idah, but became involved in a dispute over the Anaja title at Igbobe, an important town on the left bank near the confluence. Okeyin's elder brother Amẹ Abọkkọ held this office, at Igbobe, his mother's town, until 1863.[3] But when he died, the Ata appointed a candidate unacceptable to the Abọkkọ clan as a whole, and the clan head once again went into exile with his followers. Bishop Crowther noted in 1864 that many of Abọkkọ's supporters had left the capital, and in 1867 he wrote that both Abọkkọ and Agaidoko had left the capital:

> Abọkkọ has removed to his farm Oko-Okein about 14 miles above Idah, and Agaidoko about 12 miles above Onitsha—no one can call them to account. The Atta has no power at all out of Idah, no sooner they quitted the town into the river, they are out of his reach and defy him. He has no fleet of canoes in his service.[4]

Shortly after this, in the same year, Crowther himself was seized by Abọkkọ and kept at Oko-kein with the aim of

[1] Baikie, ibid., p. 268 and pp. 281–2.
[2] ibid., pp. 290–1.
[3] Crowther, Samuel, ms. letter to Rev. H. Venn, 1863.
[4] ibid., ms. *Report on Idda Station*, 1867.

obtaining a ransom.[1] As a result of this act of piracy Abọkkọ was not allowed to return to Idah until 1872, but by then he had lost his former importance, and was in Crowther's words 'reduced to beggary for his daily bread'.[2] His act also cost the Igala the goodwill of the British government, who lost a vice-consul in rescuing Crowther, and the favour of the Anglican Mission, who closed down their station at Idah.

The changes in royal favour which punctuated Abọkkọ's decline suggest that the riverain chiefs were more or less permanently allied with one or other side of the major lineages in the royal subclan. The Abọkkọ clan was aligned with the Ajaku branch in this division and enjoyed most favour when either the Itodo Aduga or the Amachọ lineages were in power. They were correspondingly depressed in status when the other two lineages came to the throne. When the first expedition arrived, during Ẹkalaga's reign (Akogu lineage) Abọkkọ was out of favour, and had been in exile for seven years.[3] Lander exerted himself to get Abọkkọ reinstated at the

[1] Bishop Crowther was detained on 19 September 1867 and released on 28 September by the Vice-Consul, W. Fell, Esq. cf. Bishop Crowther's Narrative of his detention by the Chief Abọkkọ, *Church Missionary Intelligencer*, Vol. IV (new series), pp. 9–12 and 19–20.

The reasons that Abọkkọ gave Crowther for this act of piracy reflect Abọkkọ's resentment against his loss of influence at court. Abọkkọ complained: 'That he, although superintendent of the board of trade in this part of the river was not recognized by the English merchants; that he was slighted by being made only small and paltry presents, . . . neither would the ships open trade with him. That the ships had visited the river this year (taking the Thomas Beazley's two trips to be by two different ships) yet none would recognize him. Although the small ship stopped at Idah and gave handsome presents to the Atta, yet he, who owns the river and all the Oibos (Europeans) who travel on it, was contemptuously overlooked,' ibid., p. 10. At about the same time that Bishop Crowther was held to ransom by Abọkkọ in 1876, the mission again at Idah had received a message from the Atta 'to say that he would afford them protection no longer than the arrival of the next steamer, i.e. that they must look to Abọkkọ as their protector because he is the superintendent of all the matters arising in the river, and all the Oibos (Europeans) are in his jurisdiction'. Crowther ms. *Report on Idda Station, 1867*.

[2] Crowther, Samuel, *Report of the Annual Visit to the Niger Mission in 1873*, ms. and *Church Missionary Intelligencer*, 1868, pp. 9–13 and 19–20. cf. also Laird and Oldfield, op. cit., 1857.

[3] Laird and Oldfield, op. cit., Vol. 1, p. 402.

court, and it was from then on, during Amocheje's reign, that Abokko was most useful to the expeditions and seems to have enjoyed most favour from the king. The war with Agaidoko, towards the end of Amocheje's reign, seems to have resulted from the latter's intense jealousy at Abokko's increasing prestige and his invasion of the southern area, in Ibo country which Agaidoko claimed as his own sphere of influence.

When the next king, Aku Odiba (Ocholi lineage), came to the throne, in 1856, his first act was to challenge the Abokko clan by appointing an unpopular candidate to the Anaja title, which had been vacant since 1853.[1] This quarrel degenerated into a war between the Abokko clan and the Ocholi lineage, fought out in the area of Agbenema, adjacent to Okokenyi. The Abokko people killed two of the king's chief eunuchs in this war, and were ordered to pay an indemnity of nine slaves before peace was made. But it was not until the pendulum swung back again, with the death of Aku Odiba and the succession of Okoliko from the Ajaku side that Abokko was able to return to Idah. The Anaja title quarrel, which had kept the wider dispute alive was also settled temporarily in this reign, by persuading Aku Odiba's candidate to submit to the candidate approved by the clan. But in the following reign again, Amaga found fault with the Anaja approved by Okoliko, and commissioned the Ocholi lineage at Agbenema to attack him, and drive him across the river. The feud between these two groups was then cut short by the extension of company rule along the Niger, and the establishment of government in 1900.

The Abokko clan's alliance with the Ajaku branch of the royal subclan was shared by the Agaidoko clan, which, as we have seen, also left Idah during the reign of Aku Odiba, when the Ocholi lineage controlled patronage at Idah. Agaidoko fought on Abokko's side in the war precipitated by the Anaja title dispute, and Crowther records that in 1867 Agaidoko and Abaje, with one other person unsuccessfully besieged Lokoja for eight months.[2] This Abaje is almost certainly the same as

[1] Paul, Rev. Charles, ms. *Journal for the year ending September 30th, 1866.* Crowther, Samuel, ms. reports and letter, 1866.

[2] Crowther ms. 1867. cf. also Geary, Sir William Nevil, *Nigeria under British Rule, 1927*, p. 169, who says that the blockade was carried on by the Chiefs who had taken Bishop Crowther captive, Semiberiga, Abeye, and Agabedoho.

the Abaje who was supported by the Abọkkọ clan in the Anaja title dispute, and who had attacked Igbobe, downstream from Lokoja, in the previous year. Agaidoko's and Abaje's opposition to Aku Odiba also took the form of raids on canoes and settlements in the upper section of the river, within the Anaja's area of jurisdiction. Crowther wrote of their operation in this area:

> These pirates are roving characters, being rebels against the Atta—they remain in no settled town, occupying the banks of the river with their slaves in frail grass huts which they can easily remove from one place to another three or four times in a year.

We can conclude from this evidence that although Abọkkọ and Agaidoko were rivals for power in the river, and clashed over their respective spheres of influence, they were united by their alignment with the Ajaku branch of the ruling house, and by their common opposition, deriving from this, to the Ocholi and Akogu lineages. The Ocholi lineage, which held the throne for a long reign in the period covered by the records bore the brunt of this opposition, which was tacitly but not actively supported by the descendants of Ajaku.

In its conflict with the Abọkkọ–Agaidoko coalition the Ocholi lineage found allies among the other riverain chiefs, including the Ohiuga clan as well as some of those with purely political offices. This does not appear in the contemporary records, partly because they were based mainly on information from the Abọkkọ clan, and partly because the observers thought of the struggle only in terms of rebellion against the king. But the Igala concerned think of events as a contest between opposed groups of riverain clans centring on the

---

A = Abọkkọ Ochẹjẹ clan
B = Ohiuga clan
C = Ocholi lineage of royal house
D = Ọmọgbajẹ clan
E = Akogu lineage of royal house
F = Ewọ clan

Amana—holds Ochai Ata title
Agbonika—holds Ewọ title
Abaro—holds Ohiuga title
Kutẹnọ—a strong candidate for the vacant title of Ọmọgbajẹ

114

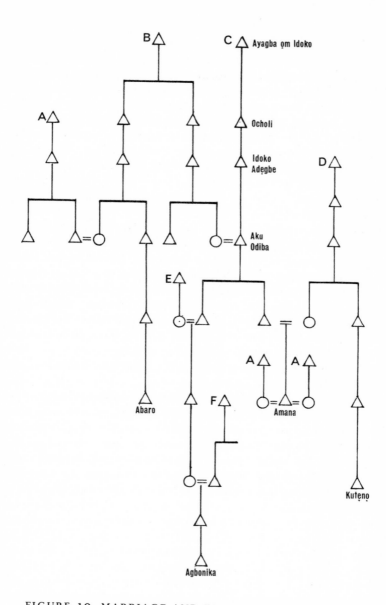

FIGURE 10. MARRIAGE AND KINSHIP TIES BETWEEN THE
OCHOLI LINEAGE AND SOME RIVERAIN CLANS

major opposition of the two branches of the royal house. The friendly political relations between allies were consolidated by marriage, and their alliances with one another have been perpetuated down to the present day through the kinship ties generated by these earlier marriages. Thus, the Ohiuga clan, which originally gave land to the Abokko group for their new settlement at Oko-Okein, was drawn into the conflict on Aku Odiba's side through a marriage with the king. The son of this marriage, Edime, settled at Agbenema, on his mother's land, and directed the attempts made by the royal group to destroy Abokko's base at Oko-Okein. Through the marriage with Ohiuga, the royal group also gained support from the Abokko Ocheje clan, closely intermarried with the former. It also allied itself by marriage with the Omogbaje clan, and its satellite, Ewo, which monopolized the valuable salt trade carried on by river with the Jukun. The heads of these groups today maintain close relations with one another on account of the kin connexions resulting from their earlier alliance, and although the area of political conflict between clans has been diminished by modern changes, they form a united group in their political relations with the other riverain clans. Figure 10 on page 115 outlines the kinship constellation that underlies this political grouping.

We can conclude from this historical evidence that the development of the riverain titles as administrative offices is conditioned by the rivalry existing within the royal house at Idah. Whereas the kingmakers, through their control of the succession, are independent of this rivalry, the leading subsidiary clans are dependent upon the favour of one or other branch of the ruling house, and tend to gain or diminish in power according to the fortunes of their royal patrons. The division of power between a number of different clans is also related to the pattern of segmentation in the royal house, which formerly kept in being an intense competition for control or trade and markets on the Niger, and of dealings with the merchants from overseas and from other parts of the river who were in contact with Idah. This again contrasts with the tendency towards a unified administration that was evolved in the Ibo border area, where similar political and commercial problems arose.

To conclude this sketch of the subsidiary clans it will be useful to refer briefly to their part in the succession procedure, which complements that of the kingmakers. As the following brief summary shows, the former are mainly responsible for the burial ceremonies of the dead king, whilst the kingmakers take the initiative and perform most of the ritual in the accession ceremonies. It is worth noting that the competitive relationship of the leading riverain clans is symbolized in acts of ceremonial hostility towards each other that accompany the performance of their duties. The Agaidoko and Abọkkọ clans are responsible for carrying the Ata's coffin over different stages of its journey to the burial ground. Traditionally they quarrel over this division of labour, with members of each clan abusing the other group and threatening to fight. This relationship of stylized hostility contrasts sharply with the behaviour pattern ascribed to the other clans in these ceremonies, and underlines the absence of an agreed order of seniority between the clans concerned.

| Stage | Participation by: | |
	Igala chiefs	Igala Mela chiefs
Temporary burial in palace	Atẹbọ (ritually represents the Ata)	Achadu is informed
Successor summoned to Idah		Achadu, after consulting the other kingmakers
Adukainya's ears pierced, and other preparation		Achadu and Achadu's wife
Coffin made ready. Grave at Ọjaina dug and plastered	Onu Ohiiji (iron trestles), Uchalla Angwa (plastering)	Achadu Kikili Ukwaja (coffin), Aleji (brass plates on coffin)
Disinterment and removal to Ọjaina (by night)	Atẹbọ, Abọkkọ Onukwu Ata, Abọkkọ Ochẹjẹ, Agaidoko	
Burial at Ọjaina (by night)	Eguọla, Adọkpulu, Uchada	

117

| | Participation by: | |
Stage	Igala chiefs	Igala Mela chiefs
Ceremonial funeral (repeats last two stages, by day, using dummy coffin, *abaihi*)	As for the actual burial	
Adukainya leaves the Achadu's house, for Ojaina	Adokpulu, Eguola	
Unfinished grave left for eight days	Atebo (secluded in Ojaina grove), Ohimogbo and Uchada (perform Ilo masquerade daily)	Obajadaka brings late king's bed to Ojaina, Okweje (performs Okolo masquerade)
Closing of grave	Eguola and Adokpulu, Atebo ends seclusion	
Adukainya leaves Ojaina, and is invested		Onubiogbo and Onede (birth of Ata)
Offering at land shrine	Atebo	Achadu
The new king enters the capital	All Igala chiefs wait near palace	Igala Mela chiefs acclaim the king in their own quarter

TABLE 13. THE MAIN STAGES OF THE IGALA
SUCCESSION CEREMONY

In the royal provinces outside the metropolitan area the distinction between subsidiary titles and offices in control of the succession tends to disappear, and the two kinds of office form an undivided class. The Igala express this terminologically by including the land priests in the provincial capitals with those who perform the burial and accession ceremonies. They are, collectively, the chief's titleholders with ritual duties, *amajofe ki achicholo nwonu*. Their administrative role is not specialized in the same way as the subsidiary titles at Idah,

118

and their jurisdiction and authority is limited to the district on which each clan is based.

The boundaries of the royal provinces in Igala are not sharply defined territorially, and in the past were continually subject to alteration through changes of allegiance at the district level. To some extent the different royal subclans compete with one another for the loyalty of the local landowning clans, and provinces were in the past not so much territorial entities as networks of influence, consolidated by hereditary ties of allegiance and orientation. The senior royal subclan at Idah participated in this struggle for power, and consistently extended its own sphere of influence at the expense of the other royal subclans by granting titles to clans in outlying districts. In this way provincial non-royal descent groups could transfer their allegiance from junior branches of the royal clan to the senior branch at Idah, and were placed in a special relationship analogous to that of the subsidiary clans in the metropolitan area. I term such groups subsidiary provincial clans, and distinguish them from the provincial kingmakers and other non-royal clans in the provinces who owed allegiance and paid tribute to one or other of the junior branches of the royal clan.

In some cases the territories controlled by these subsidiary provincial clans formed privileged enclaves within the sphere of influence of one of the junior branches of the royal clan. For instance, in the Ankpa onuate there are three districts whose heads take title from the Ata at Idah, and regard themselves as independent of the Onu Ankpa. In the Okpo and Iga areas there are two titles that are appointed in the same way by the king, and not by the local provincial chief.[1]

In other cases the subsidiary provincial clans are not merely independent of the local royal chiefs, but compete with them politically. By favouring the local rivals of the royal centres in the provinces, the king is able to isolate his own titled clansmen and limit the spread of their influence in the surrounding

[1] The districts concerned in these provinces are:

Ankpa province	Okpo and Iga province
Ejinya	Inyelle
Emekutu	Ade
Emanyi	

districts. Dekina, for instance, has never been able to achieve the importance of the royal onuates in the north-east because the jurisdiction of the chief there clashes with that of three subsidiary clans centred at Oddu, Ojokiti, and Iyale, who take titles from Idah and have been closely allied with the central government at Idah. The Iyale clan for instance, holds a major title, Onu Iyale, that has certain ritual duties permanently delegated to it by the crown. The titleholder is the custodian of an ẹbọ shrine that is regarded as having belonged originally to the royal subclan at Idah, and as having been transferred to this area from Idah on the advice of the Ifa oracle. This origin myth validates the clan's direct relationship with the ruling house, and justifies its claim to equality of political status with the junior branch of the royal clan that is situated near by at Dekina. The Oddu clan claims a similar status on account of its responsibility for a local ẹbọ shrine, and regards its own title as a specialized ritual office that integrates ultimately with the system of priestly titles in the metropolitan area.

KEY TO MAP: IGALA CLAN CENTRES

Non-royal provincial clans	*Royal subclans*	*Non-royal metropolitan clans*
1. Ife	1. Idah	1. Abọkkọ Onukwu Ata
2. Abocho	2. Dekina	2. Adọkpulu
3. Ojokiti	3. Ankpa	3. Agaidoko
4. Oddu	4. Ikka	4. Atẹbọ
5. Iyale	5. Ẹnjẹmma	5. Eguọla
6. Egume	6. Ojoku	6. Ewọ
	7. Imani	7. Onu Idokoliko
Igala Mela	8. Iga	8. Ohiemogbo Obiga
1. Ẹtẹmaihi	9. Okpo	9. Ohiuga
2. Onubiogbo		10. Onu Ohiiji
3. Onẹde	*Achadu*	11. Uchala Angwa
4. Aleji	1. Ochai Achadu	12. Ulimam Ata
5. Okweje	2. Achenya Achadu	13. Ọkpayigẹbẹ
6. Unana	3. Ẹgeuna Achadu	14. Akahiama
7. Achanyuwọ	4. Odoma Achadu	
8. Obajadaka	5. Abaigbọ Achadu	
9. Ochijenu	6. Odokina Achadu	
10. Achadu Kikili Ukwaja	7. Achema Achadu	

■ *Royal subclans*
△ *Non-royal provincial clans*
▲ *Non-royal metropolitan clans*
● *Achadu clans*
○ *Igala Mela clans*

0 4 8 12 *Miles*

FIGURE 11. IGALA CLAN CENTRES

121

In competing with the junior branches of the royal clan the subsidiary clans extend their influence through the same mechanisms as the royal group, and tend to reproduce the political functions of the latter almost exactly. Under sufficiently favourable conditions the natural outcome of this competition is the emergence of non-royal provinces that are identical in organization and political functions with the spheres of influence of the royal groups. The three onuates already considered, Oddu, Iyale, and Ojokiti, represent intermediate stages in this process of evolution and have evolved all the features of provincial organization but on such a small scale that they form only minor provinces. But there are three other non-royal clans, centred at Ife, Ęnjęmma, and Egume, whose area of jurisdiction is fully equivalent, both geographically and structurally, to the most extensive of the royal provinces.

The titled heads of these six non-royal subsidiary clans have the same judicial powers as the royal provincial chiefs, and also perform the same administrative functions of maintaining order and collecting tribute within the districts under their jurisdiction. Their administration is based, like that of the royal subclan heads, on the award of titles. I list below the hereditary offices that existed formerly in four of these non-royal provinces. As the list shows, these offices can be divided into titles hereditary within the dominant clan and titles held by the local landowning clans, in charge of districts. The second class subdivides through the fact that some of the local district heads performed ritual duties in addition to their administrative functions. These more specialized titles are senior to the other offices in this class, and their holders to a limited extent monitored the rotation of lineages within the dominant clan through their control of the accession ritual.

IFE PROVINCE

| Dominant clan | Subordinate clans | |
	Senior	Junior
Onu Ife	Owǫ Onu Ife	Onu Ihiakpę
Odoma Onu Ife	Obisaya	Onu Ikęm
Ęgęuna Onu Ife	Adeni Onu Ife	
Ǫmachi Onu Ife	Achadu Onu Ife	

Dominant clan	Subordinate clans	
	Senior	Junior
Onu Enjemma	Achadu Onu Enjemma	Onu Egbuila
Ochai Onu Enjemma	Egbulu Onu Enjemma	Onu Egba
Onu Ohioma	Imeje Onu Enjemma	Enekoja
Odoma Onu Enjemma	Ochibonu	
Agenyi Onu Enjemma		

EGUME PROVINCE

Dominant clan	Subordinate clans	
	Senior	Junior
Onu Egume	Achadu Ina	Orego
	Achadu Kikili	Achimere
		Onumama

IYALE ONUATE

Dominant clan	Subordinate clans	
	Senior	Junior
Onu Iyale	Owo Onu Iyale	Ochomocho
Odoma Onu Iyale	Achadu Onu Iyale	Achakpali
Amana Onu Iyale		Achaku
Agenyi Onu Iyale		

In the early stages of growth the subsidiary clans in the provinces are so dependent on the favour and support of the ruling house at Idah that they form the natural allies of the latter in their own competition for power with the junior branches of the royal subclan. This is reflected in the history of the Oddu and Iyale clans, which have a long tradition of intermarriage with the royal maximal lineages at Idah, and have provided the leading members of these royal groups with a refuge in the period when their descent groups were out of office at Idah. Ife, similarly, has a long tradition of close co-operation with the ruling house at Idah, culminating in the establishment of many settlements of the Akogu lineage in this province during the wars of succession that occurred after the Ata Ekalaga was murdered.

Some of the sudsidiary clans in the provinces claim a special kin connexion with the royal clan as a whole, and it is possible that this use of the idiom of perpetual kinship represents an attempt to justify and institutionalize political equivalence of these non-royal groups to the royal subclans. The members of the Onu Ife clan, for instance, claim that their founder, Aba, was related to Ayagba ọm Idoko as *ọmaiye* in having the same mother but not the same father. The Ẹnjẹmma group, on the other hand, claim to be *ọmonobulẹ* or uterine kin, of the royal clan through the genealogical link shown below:

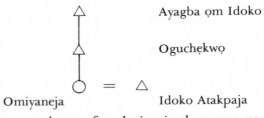

Omiyaneja   Idoko Atakpaja

The ultimate tendency of evolution in these non-royal provinces seems to lie towards assimilation into the structure of the royal clan; the subsidiary clans eventually become full members of the royal descent group and form junior subclans tracing their descent from one of the major branches of the clan. In many political contexts the special relationship that exists between the subsidiary provincial clans and the ruling house is represented as an agnatic connexion with the clan as a whole. The autonomy of the non-royal provinces is thus ultimately guaranteed against the senior branch of the royal clan as well as against the junior branches, but this can only be achieved by claiming full membership of the royal descent group.

The Ẹnjẹmma clan genealogy provides a good instance of this type of assimilation. In the diagram above I have shown a widely accepted version of their special connexion with the royal clan, which uses the paradigm of uterine kinship. But the present District Head improved this earlier version of his clan's position in relation to the royal clan by claiming full membership, as follows:

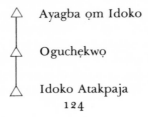

This claim has not been fully accepted by the other members of the royal clan. But the transition from uterine kinship status to agnatic descent is an easy one in political contexts, and members of the Enjẹmma group are already regarded as kin *efu*, in contrast to the heads of lesser subsidiary clans, who are unrelated. As I show in more detail later, the identification of cognatic, and especially of uterine, kin with nuclear agnatic lines is the most important of the various processes through which assimilation into descent groups takes place. And this process of assimilation occurs at all levels of structure, ranging from the individual to entire descent groups.

To conclude this outline of the clan system we can say that although clans are the structural units of the Igala political system, they are not static either individually or in their relations with other clans. There is a major division of political functions between small-scale clans whose territorial interests are narrow and spatially circumscribed, and large-scale clans with wider interests who play a co-ordinating role and whose inter-action creates a wider system of political relations. This division of functions is controlled by the unilineal descent principle, and the fixed and hereditary aspect of the system is expressed politically and socially in differences of rank and title. But the system as a whole is segmentary, and competition between equivalent units at the different levels of political organization creates a situation of mobility and change within the clan network. The aristocratic clans and subclans recruit members from groups lower in the scale of rank, and their external rivalry makes it possible for new units to emerge within the system. But competition, and the associated processes of change and growth, are kept within bounds by the rule of seniority that is elaborated in connexion with the principle of unilineal descent. The segmentary tendencies of unilineal descent systems can lead to such a fragmentation of corporate functions and so elaborate a division of labour that there is no effective corporate representation at the higher levels of organization. But in Igala this is checked by the institution of rotating succession, itself a special application of the general rule of seniority. This pattern of succession vests the full corporate authority of the descent group in one segment at a time. Furthermore through the descent group there is a pattern of seniority which subordinates the equivalence of individuals or of lineal segments to the principle of hierarchy and delegation of authority. The whole notion of descent in Igala is bound up with the existence of single offices that condense the authority and corporate functions which are nominally vested in the entire membership of corporate unilineal descent groups. And it is through these offices that the whole structure of the clan network can be represented and maintained by the pattern of seniority existing within the title system.

One class of non-hereditary political offices remains to be considered, and until this has been described it will be in a sense premature to generalize about the nature of the Igala administrative hierarchy. Anticipating this later section, however, it can be said that compared with the bureaucratic organization of other large kingdoms in Africa, the Igala system is relatively weak in administrative offices. The hereditary titles through which the central government exercises its authority have comparatively few specialized administrative duties, and there is little differentiation within the title system, either between individual offices or between the major groupings of titles. This characteristic can perhaps be related to the proliferation of kinship ties through the kingdom, which to some extent take the place of a more formal administrative network. The clan system is highly developed as a total system in the sense that clanship embraces every aspect of political relations, and also that ties of kinship and marriage are correspondingly developed to maintain and express subtle modes of alliance and deployment of human resources within the framework of the descent system. Segmentation, for instance, can be seen as occurring through the contraposition of lineal segments of different clans as much through a process of internal differentiation within a single unilineal group.

The poor development of administrative institutions in this kingdom may also be related to the fluidity of territorial groupings within the political system, which in turn is correlated with the dynamic state of equilibrium existing within individual clans and within the clan system as a whole. In the short term each set of clan, subclan, or lineage oppositions has a territorial basis, and involves a corresponding set of spatial oppositions between communities of different orders of magnitude. But in the long term these territorial groupings change as the structure of the descent groups is redefined, with the result that continuity is provided ultimately by the descent system rather than by division into provinces and districts.

CHAPTER FOUR

THE FRAMEWORK OF LOCAL
GOVERNMENT

Kinship and the local community.

The basic unit of settlement in Igala is the hamlet, *aja*,[1] forming a small self-contained community whose homesteads are traditionally clustered together and separated from those of neighbouring hamlets by tracts of intervening woodland or farmland. A group of hamlets sharing one farming area and other common facilities such as water, a main path or road, and groves of secondary forest, make up a village, *ewo*. Formerly hamlets were scattered through the area of a village and only loosely united by a network of interconnecting paths. But with the construction of modern roads, settlements tend to congregate around convenient points of access to the road system, and hamlets are increasingly becoming contiguous within the village. This development is paralleled by an increase in village solidarity, and by the emergence of new or intensified forms of village co-operation. But the hamlet remains the basic unit of social life and village organization is still dominated by the traditional pattern of relations between hamlets. The contrast between social and spatial distance in village relationships is often extremely marked even in the more compact type of settlement and in general the communal life of the village is poorly developed by comparison with the wealth of ceremonial, ritual, and social activities that occur at hamlet level.

In a typical hamlet the compound of the group's founder dominates the other homesteads by its size and central position,

---

[1] This term rarely occurs on its own, because it is habitual to identify hamlets by suffixing the name of the founder or that of the hamlet to it, as in *aj'Odaudu*, Odaudu's hamlet, or *aj'Itanyi*, Itanyi's hamlet. Hamlets may also have geographical names, commonly derived from local ecological features, or be identified locally by relation to village topography as 'the people above', *abo ate*, or below, *abo ǫganę*. But the commonest reference is to the person in authority over the hamlet.

128

and to some extent the entire network of paths and buildings that makes up the hamlet is co-ordinated topographically by the main axes of this primary homestead. The high ridged roof of the reception house, *atakpa*, that fronts this central compound is visible from most points of the hamlet, and forms an important symbol of the group's spatial and social identity. It is in this hut that visitors are received formally by the head of the settlement, and here also that any major disputes or other issues affecting all members of the group are discussed and settled. The *atakpa* and its site are also symbols of the ritual identity of the group and of the spiritual welfare of the whole community. Near the entrance to the *atakpa*, on the main path used by persons entering the hamlet, stand small shelters that house various protective medicines, *ode*, and spirit shrines, *unyi ẹbọ*. And the *atakpa* itself guards an inner courtyard, *anuku*, whose wall encloses domestic buildings and a collection of ancestor shrines, *unyi ibegwu*, graves, *ojinoji*, and protective fetishes, *ode*.

Each hamlet is connected with the public highway, and so with the outside world, by a long, straight, and well-maintained entrance path, *ojïkpologu*, which debouches into the heart of the settlement opposite the *atakpa* of its founder. For ritual, ceremonial, and some political purposes the Igala disregard the existence of the numerous minor back ways, *okpa ubi oko*, that fan out from the settlement and think of the hamlet as having only one entrance and exit. This cul-de-sac layout symbolizes the separation of the hamlet from the rest of the village and creates a physically self-contained community. It also has a defensive purpose,[1] advertising the coming of strangers before they reach the *atakpa*, and giving the elders of the hamlet a chance to withdraw if they do not wish to encounter them at once. In line with this purpose, compounds are often built with a grinding house *odo okuta* in front of the *atakpa*, so that the women and children, who spend much of

---

[1] The traditional preference for a degree of isolation and immunity reflects the Igala's belief in the action of sorcery and witchcraft. But it also has political and social implications, and more than once the Igala have explained the purpose of the long, straight entrance path to me by saying that in the past it protected them against the depredations of the *amọmata*, by giving the men of the hamlet a chance to escape unwelcome visitors.

their time working there, can be aware of people entering and leaving the hamlet.

Hamlets that form the centres of clan segments or lineages may possess an additional ancestral shrine in the form of a separate grove, *an'okula*. In plan this grove constitutes a symbolic model of the hamlet itself, being a circular clearing with a tree in the centre at whose foot pots or pot necks are sunk into the ground to receive offerings to the group's ancestors. The grove has its own *ojikpologu* which often continues the line of the main entrance to the hamlet itself in such a way that the grove and the hamlet are like mirror images of one another, separated by the main highway.

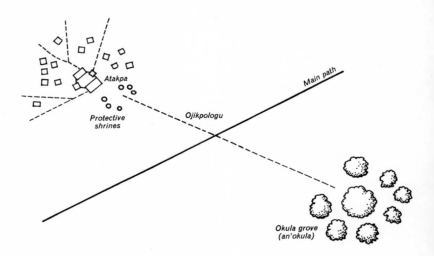

FIGURE 12. DIAGRAMMATIC SKETCH OF HAMLET LAYOUT

On the day of the annual Okula festival the two communities of the living and the dead are reunited and the patrilineal nucleus of the hamlet asserts its membership of a wider agnatic grouping. Offerings of cocks are made collectively and individually in the morning, followed by a communal meal in

6. Masquerades representing clan ancestors in the Okula festival

7. A typical homestead

8. An *Ọmọnobulẹ* in a funeral procession

which all the men of the hamlet and the collateral agnatic relatives of the hamlet head take part. Then, in the evening, masquerades, Egwu Afia, are brought out in the grove, and go in procession to the hamlet itself. They spend one or more nights in the *atakpa* of the hamlet's founder and speak to the members of the group through the Egwu Afia of the founder or his son, before disappearing for another year.

In most cases, though not all, the hamlet is a community of kinship, whose members are related to one another by birth or by marriage. Figure 13 on page 132 shows the composition of a typical hamlet, whose members comprise two distinct but related extended families. The oldest and largest of these two groups is descended from Odaudu Itodo, the founder of the hamlet. The second group has grown up around a series of marriages with the first, and most of its members are in the position of in-laws, *ana*, to Odaudu. Spatially the hamlet is grouped around the compound of the founder, Odaudu, with the affinal group's houses lying, on the whole, further away from the centre than the homes of Odaudu's own sons and other agnatic relatives.

The domestic aspect of the kinship pattern does not concern us here, but since kinship terms and their associated principles of behaviour have such a wide currency in Igala society it will be useful to analyse the major categories within the comparatively restricted context of hamlet organization, in order to show the oppositions that run through the system of terminology and differentiate the various classes of relatives from one another.[1]

The most extensive category of relationship in this localized kinship configuration is the cognatic tie of common blood, *efu* (pl. *amefu*). The importance of this tie is reflected in the fact that the terms distinguishing sex and generation membership within the kin group are cognatic in application. Kinsmen in this relationship co-operate in a wide range of activities, in farming, trading, hunting, housebuilding, in preparing for festivals and ceremonies and in providing hospitality for

[1] This approach to kinship follows the example set by my former teacher, L. Dumont, in his study of Dravidian kinship. cf. Dumont, L., 'The Dravidian Kinship Terminology as an Expression of Marriage', *Man*, 54, Vol. LIII, 1953.

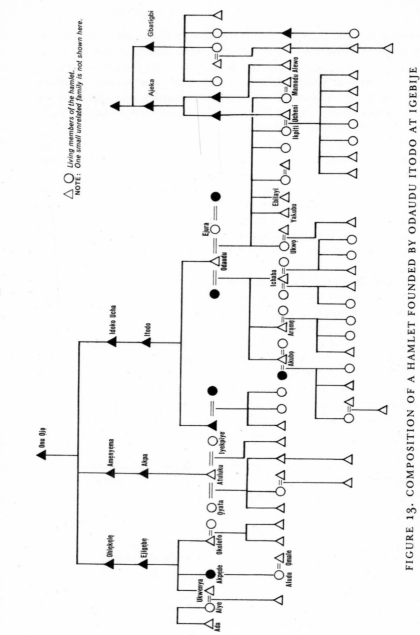

FIGURE 13. COMPOSITION OF A HAMLET FOUNDED BY ODAUDU ITODO AT IGEBIJE

132

strangers. They also exchange small personal services, sending children to assist with domestic work, sharing food in the famine season, and eating and drinking together regularly. A kinsman is fully committed to maintaining the corporate life of the hamlet, and has an absolute right to know all its business and to be called in to share any distribution of food or drink. Conversely, kinsmen have a positive duty to answer calls on their time and assistance, and forms of co-operation that are optional between unrelated men, at village level, are obligatory within the kinship network of the hamlet.

The class of cognatic kin, *amefu*, is opposed to another major grouping, of affines, *ana*. There is a marked difference in status between the two groups within the hamlet, and this contrast in status forms a major bond of unity between blood kin on either side of the marriage tie. *Ana* within the hamlet are, typically, the husbands of young women in the group, who reside with their wife's kin for a period of from 5 to 7 years to complete the farming and other labour services on which recognition of the marriage depends. Their subordination to the kin group is most marked in relation to the wife's patrikin, but it is also noticeable in their relations with the kin group as a whole. *Ana* perform the most difficult or most menial tasks in hamlet activities, puddling the clay for house-building, carrying the heaviest timber, and being expected to work harder than any other group. They provide the labour force for unwelcome tasks such as grave-digging, carrying messages to distant places, or public works to which the kin group has to send representatives. Their attitude towards members of the kin group should always be respectful, even submissive, the sanction for repeated breaches of this rule being expulsion from the hamlet and dissolution of the marriage.

The group of blood kinsmen that maintains the social and economic life of the hamlet has, at its centre, a smaller group of agnatic kin who are either descended from the founder, or are patrilineally related to him. In the hamlet illustrated by figure 13 on page 132 this nucleus comprises the founder and his own sons, together with four of his clansmen and their male offspring. In the three other hamlets in the same village the founder was represented only by his sons, there being no other fellow clansmen living in the same hamlet. This difference is correlated with size, the first example being larger than the other three. And the same pattern occurs in surrounding villages, larger hamlets having a nucleus of an extended family wide enough to include clansmen, whereas smaller hamlets are structured around a single genealogical segment. The larger type seems to be a natural stage in the evolution of these local communities.

Through the tie of clanship, the members of the agnatic nucleus share in the authority over hamlet affairs that is vested in its founder. The political, public, and ritual life of the hamlet coincides to a considerable extent with the corporate life of the clan segment associated with the community's inception. And because of this the bond between the founder, or his representative, and their fellow clansmen in the hamlet has a political content which distinguishes their relationships from the other kinds of kinship bond within the hamlet grouping. They are the natural representatives of the hamlet head in his lifetime, his 'second men' *amękejiwn*, who can deputize in his absence and who also execute the policy decisions that he makes. After his death they are the rightful heirs to his position, and are eligible in order of seniority.

Relationships within the agnatic nucleus of the hamlet follow the general pattern of clan relations. But they intensify the emphasis on seniority that characterizes this wider pattern. Between fellow clansmen living in the same hamlet much attention is paid to formal etiquette in eating and drinking, and relative status is also expressed in manner of address, sitting positions, and other minute details of behaviour. Economic competition between clansmen in this position is limited by the formal order of precedence, so that a junior brother would not, for instance, build a larger or better house than a senior brother unless the latter gave his full consent and seemed to have no reservations in the matter. The junior members of this nuclear group also accept the senior members' authority in matters of ritual, by maintaining relatively few shrines of their own, and by avoiding any appearance of ostentation or of desire for independence in ritual matters. Their submission to the will of the senior patrikin ultimately creates a standard of obedience to the hamlet head which affects all other kin relations and lays the foundation of the latter's political authority within the hamlet.

One other category of relationship is distinguished within the broad group of blood kin who make up the bulk of the hamlet's population. All the descendants in the male line of the female members of the agnatic nucleus are classed together as *ọmọnobulẹ* and occupy a special position in the affairs of the hamlet. Structurally this class complements the class of patrikin, and the two are so closely linked that the rights and privileges of each class are defined to a large extent by reference to the other, through a process of opposition and contraposition. Terminologically also the two categories are natural counterparts of one another. Uterine kin are described as *ọmọnobulẹ*, 'child (of) woman', and agnates as *ọmẹnẹkẹlẹ*, 'child (of) man'. Both of these terms are abstractions from a particular set of genealogical relationships, and do not specify actual kinship positions. In the same way that the latter term ramifies indefinitely through male links, so the link of matrifiliation is transmitted from one generation to the next, and includes not only sisters' sons but daughters' sons and fathers' sisters' sons together with the descendants of these relatives in the male line.

In analysing the structural aspects of this connexion it is essential first to consider the pattern of co-operation between agnatic and uterine kin in relation to the Igala rules of residence after marriage. Igalas regard their own system of residence after marriage as being a virilocal one, but there is in fact an element of uxorilocal residence and of co-operation with matrifilial kin which vitally affects the development of the uterine kinship tie.

In the traditional system of marriage, as we have seen, the husband resides initially with his wife's kin for a period varying from 5 to 7 years. Completion of the bridewealth services in this period entitles him to take his wife and her children to his own natal group, and marriage is regarded as changing at this stage from an uxorilocal to a virilocal residential pattern. In practice, residence with or near the bride's group is frequently protracted beyond the minimum period. At the completion of the bridewealth period the husband ceases to farm for his father-in-law, and may also symbolize his independence by building a new house away from the latter's compound, sometimes moving to another hamlet in the village for this purpose. But the link with the wife's kin is maintained, and the husband still belongs to the category of *ana* in his relationship with the local community. If this pattern persists until the husband acquires a position of seniority among the affines residing in the hamlet his settlement may attract junior clansmen and other kinsmen to it, so that it becomes in time the nucleus of an extended family, opposed by marriage to the wife's own kin group. The second group in Odaudu's hamlet evolved in this way, around the uxorilocal marriage of Ucheni with Odaudu's daughter, Ikpiti.

In the five hamlets making up the village of Igebije, approximately half of the men who had completed their marriage services were living virilocally, with their own patrikin or with fellow clansmen. Uxorilocal marriages accounted for approximately a third of the total, and the remainder were divided amongst men living with cognatic kin, or with friends. The totals for each of the five hamlets are as follows:

Hamlet	Total	Virilocal	Uxorilocal	Cognatic	Friends, etc.
Ofagba Ebutu	4	—	1	2	1
Okweje	25	12	10	3	—
Odoma Obo	13	7	5	1	—
Itanyi	25	11	7	6	1
Ada	12	7	3	1	1
Totals	79	37	26	13	3
Percentage	100%	47%	33%	16%	4%

TABLE 14. RESIDENCE AFTER MARRIAGE IN IGEBIJE

This summary shows that a high proportion of completed marriages in a typical hamlet are uxorilocal, and suggests that the virilocal rule of residence has only a symbolic value where these exceptions are concerned. In terms of kinship connexions, the residential pattern creates a close tie with the mother's natal group, and often confers membership of this group on individuals rather than membership of the group of patrikin to which they are bound ritually, politically, and jurally. Within the group of virilocal marriages, this tie with the mother's group is still strong. Most marriages are between kin groups that are within easy walking distance of one another, and the children keep up close relations with their mothers' groups as well as with the patrilineal clan segment to which they are affiliated. Again, it is common for a woman to send one of her sons, often the eldest, to live with her brother, and to receive in return one of the man's daughters to bring up. It is from these norms of close association between agnatic and uterine kin that the polarity of their ideal relationship flows.

The duties and privileges of *ǫmonobule* define the status of uterine kin in relation to their mother's patrilineal group, and separate their participation in its corporate activities from the jural interest in property and offices that is transmitted in the male line. Their contribution to the life of the matrifilial group is primarily a ritual and spiritual one. The principal formal duty of *ǫmonobule* is to officiate at the ancestral shrine of their mother's patrilineal kin, where they act as spokesmen for the full members of the group. Sacrifices can be offered to the ancestors, *abegwu*, without their intervention, but the full procedure of ancestral sacrifice which is followed at funerals, at the annual festivals, and on any other occasion of special importance, demands the presence of a uterine kinsman. This relative mediates physically between the ancestral cult symbols and the head of the lineage or family group owning the shrine. When offerings are made at the ancestral shrine, *unyi ibegwu*, the *ǫmonobule* kneels inside the hut and performs the oblation whilst the *ǫmęnękęlę* sits outside. Each ritual act and invocation is initiated by the latter, and then repeated by the *ǫmonobule* who is, as it were, in the actual presence of the ancestors. The Igala explain this arrangement simply by saying that the ancestors prefer the invocation and sacrifice to be made by a uterine kinsman, and that the offering is less likely to be rejected by them if this procedure is followed. They say:

abegwu agbǫla amomonobule teyi amǫmęnękęlęli.
'The ancestors understand (lit.: hear) the uterine kin better than they understand the agnates.'

Ọmonobulẹ also mediate between the living and the dead members of the patrikin group in the situation of death, immunizing the dead man's descendants from the ritual dangers that attend the transition of a member from the status of elder to that of ancestor. They play an important part in washing and preparing the body for burial, and in watching over the grave until the burial ceremonies have been completed. The dead man's widows, who are most affected by the contaminating influence of death and by the ambivalent status of the deceased, depend on ọmonobulẹ for their release from this condition. The first stage of widows' mourning ends when an ọmonobulẹ leads the widow from her own room and places her hand on the grinding stones and other domestic utensils that she has been forbidden to touch. Some months later, ọmonobulẹ perform the final ritual of mourning which includes offering a goat, cooked food, and beer to the former husband. They then shave the widow's head and formally burn the clippings together with some of the clothes worn during the mourning period.

This association of uterine kin with the ritual of mourning and burial reaches its highest development in the funerals of titled ọmata. At certain stages of these ceremonies an ọmonobulẹ takes the part of the dead man by putting on the clothes that he formerly wore, and by taking his seat on the mud couch, ẹde, in the reception house. Informants say that in this capacity the uterine kinsman could speak with the authority of the dead man himself, and settle any disputes that arose between agnates over the funeral procedure or over the settlement of inheritance. This custom seems to have died out, but I witnessed a ceremony in the capital in which an ọmonobulẹ rode at the head of a funeral procession, sitting on the dead man's own horse, and wearing his full court dress. In the royal provinces ọmonobulẹ were responsible for preserving the body of a dead subclan head until the next incumbent had been appointed and was ready to perform the last funeral rites. This gave them a quasi-judicial authority over the funeral and the inheritance settlement, since agnates were prohibited from entering the area where the body was kept, and could not carry out the funeral rituals without the consent and active co-operation of the uterine kin.

The second major ritual duty performed by *ǫmonobulę* is the purification ceremony, *erǫla*, whose procedure was described earlier. As with ancestor ritual, this can be carried out by the individual concerned without becoming invalid, but on formal occasions, or in cases of grave pollution, a uterine kinsman is summoned to perform the rite. If a wife confesses adultery, for instance, the *ǫmonobulę* hears the confession and touches the walls of the house with a chicken to ritually cleanse it. He then offers a cock to the husband's ancestor shrine, and, as a final act of re-establishment, takes food cooked by the woman and gives it to her husband. Similarly before a family head performs any major ancestral ritual he may call upon an *ǫmonobulę* to perform a rite of personal lustration over him, to cleanse himself of all pollution, *ębię*.

Uterine kin also have authority over certain aspects of the corporate life of their matrifilial group, particularly those that concern reproduction and the biological continuity of the group. The wives of the men in the group are subject to their authority on all occasions, and it is often said that if an *ǫmonobulę* disapproves of the behaviour of a particular wife, he can divorce her from the husband without the latter's consent. In ordinary divorce, the broken kola nut that symbolizes separation is given to the wife by a uterine kinsman, and kin in this category are so intimately concerned with the spiritual welfare of the matrifilial group that they are credited with the power to perform this separation on their own authority.[1]

In ordinary social life if wives quarrel with one another, uterine kin can intervene and fine any of them by appropriating their personal belongings and compelling them to buy them back. Or again, if in quarrelling with her husband a wife gravely insults him, an *ǫmonobulę* may punish her by killing the first cock that comes to hand, naming the woman responsible so that the owner of the bird looks to her for recompense.

The final sanction underlying the *ǫmonobulę's* authority over the wives of his maternal kin is the power of cursing them

---

[1] Conversely a wife is not free to marry again after her husband's death until she has been formally released by an *ǫmonobulę*. A widow who takes a lover during the mourning period may be cursed by a relative in this class saying *okǫ wę ki kwo tęketa*—'may your husband become a third person' (between you).

ritually. An informant described this as follows:

> Uterine kin are greatly respected by the members of their mother's group, and even feared by them (*ma che nẹgaihi*). When a man kills an animal in the hunt or has any other windfall he sends a portion to the *ọmonobulẹ* so that their hearts will be cool. If *ọmonobulẹ* are angered they go to the *ibegwu* shrine of their maternal kin and call the names of the woman from whom they are descended, of her own father and of his lineal ancestors. They invoke them (*gule*) and ritually spray saliva (*fichẹ*) over the shrine. From then on the wives of the men in that group will bear only female children, and this will continue until their stock becomes extinct (*ugbẹ ma ala*).

The curse must be ritually removed by persuading the *ọmonobulẹ* to return to the shrine and to make another invocation in which absolute forgiveness is expressed. This is also symbolized, and the *efichẹ* neutralized, by allowing cold water to trickle from the kinsman's mouth on to the shrine, *efalura*.

Agnates have no comparable privileges in relation to *ọmonobulẹ*. Uterine kin are outside the structure of authority that governs the conduct of the mother's patrilineal group and have the right to discipline its members without being themselves subordinate in any way. The Igala explain their ritual duties and privileged position by saying that *ọmonobulẹ nẹlifọ unyi iyenw*, 'the uterine kinsman is not bound by the ritual prohibitions of his mother's place'. The notion of ritual prohibitions in this context stands for the conventions of respect and avoidance that surround the authority of the patrilineal group and differentiate its members in a rigid order of seniority. In contrast to the agnatic members of this group, uterine kin have complete freedom of access and movement within the hamlet. They are not bound, for instance, by the rules limiting access to the shrines within the *anuku*, or inner courtyard, to the head of the compound. Similarly they can sit on the householder's couch without showing disrespect, eat food before he takes his own share, consume portions of foods that are proscribed[1] to members of the male line, and so on.

---

[1] All ancestral offerings fall into this category, and can only be consumed by uterine kin, after the ancestors' token portion has been detached. Food offerings taken into the *unyi ibegwu* become the property of *ọmonobulẹ*, and it is this rule which underlies the joking behaviour described here.

The privileged position of uterine kin and their freedom from the restraints imposed on agnatic kin is dramatized on formal occasions, and especially at funeral ceremonies, where their ritual role is also prominent. They can interrupt the funeral presentations of cloth, food, and drink offerings by snatching some of the gifts offered and consuming or hiding them without waiting for the formal distribution of shares that follows each presentation. This snatching interposes an irresponsible element between the sets of agnatic groups formally opposed by the pattern of funeral offerings. There is a marked contrast between the hierarchic ordering of the groups principally concerned in these exchanges, and the freedom accorded to junior members of the uterine kin group to make away with valuable portions of the gifts presented.

In some typical instances of this right of 'ritual snatching' that took place at a royal funeral, the *ǫmonobulę* stole mainly from the gifts brought by the affines of the dead man's lineage. They began by stealing a pot of beer brought by a brother-in-law, and then raided a line of tethered goats, waiting to be presented, and led away seven out of about twenty animals. Finally, one of the uterine kin, who had been appointed to carry out the ceremony of shaving the widows' hair, demanded and got for carrying out this service a payment that was far in excess of the rate fixed by the *ajiegwu*. On each occasion the elders of the dead man's lineage complained at the flouting of their authority by the uterine kin. But this was largely a formal protest, since it was clear that the uterine kin were acting within their rights; moreover this act of teasing the elders by a group of young men greatly delighted the crowd. When the goats were stolen, the dead man's eldest brother threatened to present the remaining animals to the uterine kin, and ordered them to kill and consume the beasts before they left the compound. But this was at best an attempt to shame the *ǫmǫnobulę* into returning some of the goats, and as a sanction it was entirely ineffective.[1]

This outline of kinship terms and behaviour deals with only one, localized, aspect of the total system. And it must be emphasized again that the basic principles analysed here have a

---

[1] The uterine kin ignored this command and eventually sold the animals in a neighbouring market, dividing the money amongst their group.

wide currency and provide a flexible idiom in which many different kinds of political and social connexions can be expressed. The terms of relationship, moreover, derive their meaning from the entire range of their application and are not in any sense derived from their concentrated use in the localized context of the hamlet. But the hamlet situation forms a useful paradigm of the wider system, since the small scale of the setting makes it easier to discern the basic identifications and oppositions of the whole complex. In particular it demonstrates the inter-relatedness of the different classes as parts of a common structure. The different kinship categories modify one another in such a way that each class of relationship is defined as much by exclusion of and contrast with the other classes as it is by its internal characteristics. The concept of descent, for instance, is complemented by the concept of uterine filiation, and these two categories modify the wider opposition of cognatic kinship to affinity.

The clan system, with its mechanisms for maintaining perpetual succession to corporate offices, provides the framework within which ties of kinship and marriage are extended to their widest limits. But although descent is highly developed as an institution to sustain this structure, it does not function entirely in isolation from the other principles of relationship. Ties of affinity play an important part in the definition of unilineal segments within the clan, and uterine ties similarly serve corporate ends by opposing lineal groupings in a relation of perpetual kinship. This principle of complementary structural relationships is so important in the Igala descent system that segmentation within clans and within lineages could be said to be governed as much by extra-lineal factors as by factors arising from the inter-action of segments within the same unilineal descent group. This characteristic of the descent system as a whole is possibly related to the marked differences of rank that exist in the clan system. Kinship and marriage bonds modify these differences by creating special links between the segments of the major descent units, and also facilitate assimilation into the higher ranking units from the lower orders.

Terminologically marriage opposes entire clans or subclans to one another, since the reciprocal category, *ana*, is used classificatorily across the full width of these groupings. But responsibility for marriage arrangements is in fact vested in the localized lineage, or maximal lineage in small-scale clans, and the opposition of such groups in marriage is a major factor in maintaining the corporate solidarity of each group on either side of the marriage tie. At funerals, for instance, the formal presentations that accompany the rituals oppose all the clansmen of the deceased to his in-laws, *ana*. But this formal exchange of gifts and courtesies centres in fact on the relations of the deceased's own lineage with the lineages of his affines. When the *ana* offer gifts in the shape of funeral cloths, *okpẹ*, food, and beer, the *ajiegwu* can publicly review the relationship of the two lineal groups and reject the offering if any member of the dead person's group has a complaint against the way in which the opposed lineage has discharged its duties as affines. This opposition of lineages reaches its most developed form in the final burial ceremonies, *aku*, for which the affinal groups build shelters and camp in the deceased's homestead for several days. Men who have taken wives from the deceased's own lineage bring masquerades on the last night of the funeral ceremonies to dance in honour of the dead, and to represent the attendance of the ancestors upon the new entrant to their society.

Uterine kinship ties have a similar potential, and in addition to uniting entire descent groups in a relation of perpetual kinship they oppose unilineal segments of the same order as those concerned with the arrangement of marriage. In this case the relationship is asymmetrical. Each single unilineal group of *ọmonobulẹ* represents a new segment in process of formation on the periphery of the lineage or clan to which it belongs. And again, as other writers have commented,[1] the strongest lineal emphasis in this situation is on the unity of the central group to which the links of matrifiliation is traced. The group is defined as it were residually, by tracing some of its boundaries. For instance, in the royal funeral mentioned earlier, the deceased belonged to the major lineage founded by Ohiemini Gadagu within the Ocholi maximal lineage. In the agnatic grouping that emerged in connexion with the funeral arrangements this major lineage submerged its own

[1] cf. Beattie, J., 'Nyoro Kinship', *Africa*, Vol. XXVII, 1957; also by the same author, 'Nyoro Marriage and Affinity', *Africa*, Vol. XXVIII, 1958.

143

identity, and its leading members were ranked as junior siblings in a pattern of seniority that spanned the full width of the Ocholi group. But the *ǫmonobulẹ* who carried out the funeral rituals on behalf of this group were related to it through the women of the Ohiemini Gadagu segment, as figure 14 on page 145 shows. So the major lineage was defined by contraposition to a special class of kin within the broad category of relatives by marriage and was represented in relation to the ancestors by the uterine kin rather than by the agnates themselves.[1]

In the traditional political system hamlets were sufficiently self-contained and sufficiently isolated from other hamlets in their neighbourhood to be regarded as units of political organization in their own right. The identity of interest that characterized the tight kinship network of the hamlet was expressed politically in the recognition of a hamlet head whose authority covered a wide field of social arrangements. Land disputes, divorce cases, criminal accusations, and other matters in which members of the hamlet were involved affected the hamlet as a whole and were subject in the first case to the jurisdiction of the hamlet head. When, for instance, a farmer at Igebije was accused of starting a fire which spread to a neighbouring district and spoiled the reserve hunting area there, the case was taken up by the head of the farmer's own hamlet and eventually settled by negotiations between him and the head of the district affected.

Hamlets are grouped loosely together in villages, *ewo*, and are bound to one another within these groupings mainly by ties of economic interest. The members of each hamlet obtain land through the village grouping since the clan that holds sovereign rights in land in each district usually delegates its right to apportion land to the head of the senior hamlet in each village. As it comes into being, each hamlet is given enough farming land for its members' needs, together with rights over tree crops in certain areas of secondary forest and

---

[1] A major weakness of the English structuralist school is the tendency to regard kinship and descent as mutually exclusive categories. The French approach with its emphasis on the external aspect of lineage organization and the inter-action of separate descent groups through marriage forms a most useful corrective.

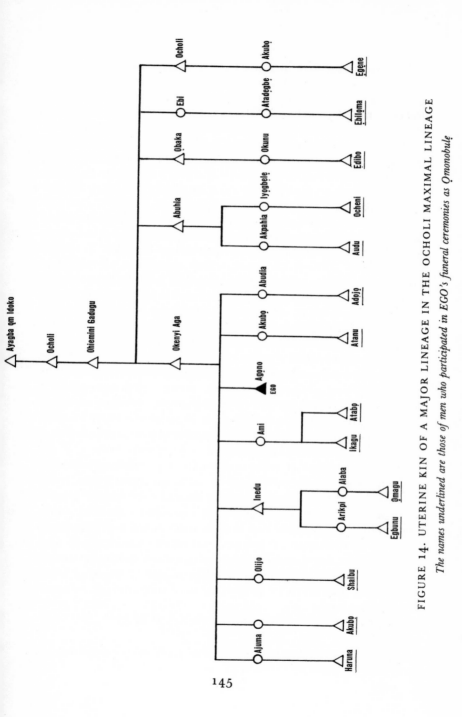

FIGURE 14. UTERINE KIN OF A MAJOR LINEAGE IN THE OCHOLI MAXIMAL LINEAGE

The names underlined are those of men who participated in EGO's funeral ceremonies as Ọmọnobulẹ

145

grass woodland. For instance, rights in oil palms that stand on uncultivated land are allocated to hamlets individually. Hamlets thus share a common tract of farming land and woodland and accept the jurisdiction of the most senior hamlet head over these areas in the same way that they accept the principle of village control over other communal resources, such as water, markets, paths, and the dense bush that fringes most villages.

The system of arable farming practised over most of Igala also encourages permanent co-operation between hamlets, since the combination of savannah and forest crops demands, at certain periods, intensive cultivation by a labour force usually larger than that which the average hamlet can muster on its own. Yam cultivation, which the Igala value highly, involves extensive clearing of secondary bush, and hoeing operations. And because this is combined with large-scale cultivation of maize, the whole operation of planting yams has to be completed in the dry season, leaving the farmer free to concentrate on maize and other savannah crops in the relatively short rainy season.

This demand for intensive labour is met by co-operation on a village basis. There are several forms of traditional co-operation between members of adjoining hamlets, of which the most important are *ailo*, or co-operation between a few individuals, and *ọwẹ*, or co-operation within a much larger group that usually corresponds to a local community. In the former a group of friends undertakes to work together once only for each of the members in turn, on any task that may be appointed for the group at the time. In the second type of co-operation the association is open to all the members of the local community, and the task is usually clearly defined. It may be an exchange of services connected with clearing, hoeing, and planting yams, or this cycle combined with a secondary one of preparing the ground for a maize crop. In the first type of co-operation there is often no outlay on food or drink for the working party, in the second, the host provides a pot of corn gruel, *ubiọlọ*, at the farm and a pot of beer, *ọtẹ*, at his own house for consumption in the evening.

From co-operation in agriculture flow other forms of mutual assistance which are also organized on a village basis. Con-

9. An *owe* group hoeing yam mounds

10. Invocation to an earth shrine

tribution groups are one common form, in which members of the same village meet regularly and contribute fixed amounts to a common pool. The total collected at each meeting, or the major part of it, is taken by different hamlets in turn, and allocated within the hamlet to one of the members, in order of seniority. The fund can be used, by advancing him out of turn, to help any member who is in trouble and needs capital urgently. There may also be a small reserve fund, financed by a levy on the total at each meeting, used to entertain guests or to buy beer for other special occasions.

Co-operative activities in the village tend to be organized on an informal age-grade basis. In Igebije, for instance, there were three contribution clubs whose membership was open to the young boys, *abimọtọ*, the young men, *abokolabia*, and the elders or adult men, *abogujo*, respectively. The membership of these groups roughly coincided with the division of farming co-operation into three major *ọwẹ* groups. Two of these groups took their names from the day of the week on which they met for contribution purposes, being known as *uchẹ alade*, the Sunday farmers, and *uchẹ ajuma*, the Friday farmers. The junior group's activities extended beyond farming and contributions to dancing and singing. They had their own masquerade and drumming group, and at one stage began to learn a type of singing, *ugwolo*, which had not previously been performed in the village.

In those activities in which the whole village participates, leaders are elected on the basis of merit, and loosely co-ordinate village co-operation. In Igebije one of the best farmers was recognized as *agboji ọwẹ* or head of the collective farming arrangements. Similarly there was an *agboji ukọlọ*, a 'head of work', who directed the communal labour that the village undertook voluntarily on roads and school sites in the hope of attracting government capital for their improvement schemes. Again, one of the elders who had been a famous hunter in his youth was appointed *agboji ọdẹ* or chief hunter by the adult men of the village. Finally, there was in the same village an *agboji abokolobia*, 'head of the young men', who supervised the work of harvesting palm fruit in connexion with payment of tribute to the village head. All these posts are elective, and carry little real authority.

The most senior hamlet in each village community mediates between the other hamlets and the head of the district on whose land the village is situated. On account of this special position the head of the senior hamlet has some of the functions of an administrative village head, and may be termed *onu ewo*, chief of the village, or *onu oja*, chief of the group. The *onu ewo* is ultimately responsible for the collection of tribute and for the maintenance of law and order in the village. But real authority in administrative matters lies with the head of the hamlet, and the village head governs only with the consent of the heads of these residential groupings. Igala say of group organization in general that *onu noja koja nonu*, 'the chief owns the group and the group owns the chief'. And this is especially true of the pattern of village authority, which, traditionally, was based on consultation with hamlet heads.

In the last resort in the traditional system a village head whose subordinate elders refuse to implement his decisions has no way of enforcing his will on them. The collection of palm tribute, for instance, is primarily carried out by the young men of each hamlet, and only loosely co-ordinated by the village-wide organization. At Igebije two hamlets defaulted in the payment of this tribute during the year of my stay there, because the heads of these settlements were apathetic in enforcing the rule that their young men should cut fruit and take a fixed number of fruit bunches per household to the village head.

Attempts by any village head to overcome the limitations on his authority tend to be regarded by the other members of the village as oppression, and lead in the long run to depopulation of the village through emigration. In popular opinion the effectiveness of a village head's government is measured largely by reference to the size of the community.[1] An expanding village, filled with houses and people, is by definition well governed, and a contracting one is correspondingly either neglected or ruled oppressively. For instance, when an inquiry was held at Dekina in 1917 into the causes of an armed rising against an unpopular District Head, several village heads said in evidence that they condoned the

[1] The same standards are used of royal government and a king may be praised or condemned according to the size of the capital in his reign.

Miles

0 2½ 5

○ Traditional centres of local government
● Modern centres of local government

FIGURE 15. PART OF THE METROPOLITAN AREA

showing traditional district centres and centres of modern village areas

rising because their own villages were becoming depopulated as a result of the arbitrary taxation and other exactions that they had been compelled to enforce.

Within the traditional system of local government villages that are also district centres form a special class, with more highly developed administrative and political functions than the villages that are immediately subordinate to them. These functions are vested in the single office of *onu anẹ* which I describe fully in the next section. The administrative authority of the *onu anẹ* over his own village reflected his status as district head, and was supported by ritual sanctions that have no direct counterpart in the position of the heads of subordinate villages. Villages in this class also have a strong sense of historical continuity and of corporate solidarity through their association with the landowning clan. The history of individual districts in the metropolitan area suggests that in the distant past these district centres were the only permanent villages in the system of local government. And that they were opposed to and dominant over hamlets rather than villages, which were scattered through the territory of the various districts. But the modern trend of settlement, as I indicated earlier, is towards consolidation of hamlets in separate villages. And the older distinction between villages at the centre of each district and hamlets in a satellite position is gradually breaking down.

Local sovereignty.

Districts were small and closely integrated in the traditional political system, usually less than 20 square miles in extent with their population distributed among a relatively small number of hamlets and villages. In the modern political system these units have been grouped together to create a wider system of district organization. But they retain their administrative functions in many cases as subdivisions of the modern district, with the status of village areas in the new administrative hierarchy. In the metropolitan area today village areas have an average population of about 1,700 persons, and although their boundaries do not exactly coincide with those of the traditional districts there is sufficient continuity for this total to be accepted as an approximation to the traditional district's maximum size.[1]

In the traditional system authority over this administrative unit is vested in the office of *onu anẹ*, 'chief of the land'. The term *onu* has a wide range of applications in Igala, and can describe the chief or master of any type of assembly or community of people. Legends, for instance, contrast the world of the dead with that of the living by referring to *onu ọj'egwu*, the chief of the dead, and *onu ọj'ile*, the chief of the world.[2] Other instances of its use occur in the terms *onu ọja* and *onu ewo*, and in the offices of market master, *onu aja*, and of chief of the waterside at Idah, *onu ega*. In association with the term for land, *anẹ*, used here to mean a district, it describes one of the basic orientations of Igala political life, towards the head of the widest local community.

The authority of the traditional district head is hereditary within a clan whose members are known collectively as the *amọmonuanẹ*. They claim sovereign rights over the area in which the clan is centred, and justify this claim by traditions of origin that describe the clan as being descended from the first persons to settle in that particular are?

The clan's sovereignty is acknowledged by members of other descent groups in the area in a number of ways, but principally by paying tribute in kind to the *onu anẹ*. The form which this tribute takes varies according to local economic factors. In the riverain areas of Ibaji, for instance, which specialize in fishing and yam farming, tribute was paid mainly in these commodities. But inland it was commonly paid in palm produce and other tree crops, and in wild game. In these areas if yams or other produce were included they were regarded as additional gifts rather than as substitutes for the other commodities.

The payment of palm produce is associated with a closed season for cutting palm fruit which ends with an abundant harvest and payment of tribute at the rate from one to three

[1] The map on p. 149 shows that the modern village areas frequently merge a number of smaller traditional districts into a larger unit. But they also cut across traditional boundaries to some extent, so that the modern units often represent a new grouping and are not invariably formed by consolidating a group of traditional districts.

[2] Literally 'master of the community of the dead' and 'master of the community of the world' respectively.

fruit bunches per household, according to the yield. This prohibition on cutting, *ẹkpe elaba*, is imposed by the *onu anẹ*, and applies to all the oil palms that grow in fallow land, woodland, secondary forest, and any other kind of uncultivated grove. Oil palms grown on cultivated land or in the immediate area of the homestead are exempt, since they are allocated to the individual owners of the farms or buildings and remain exclusively under their control as long as they either farm or live in these particular spots. Authority over the remaining palms is vested in the *onu anẹ*, who allocates them by areas to individual hamlets or villages in the district. All residents have an equal right to use the communal palms in the groves allocated to their community. Even though an individual goes regularly to a particular tree and clears a path to it, this does not establish an exclusive right to its produce.

The duration of the prohibition on cutting palm fruits is decided by the *onu anẹ* in consultation with the other village heads, and with the heads of hamlets in his own village. Its ending, *ẹkpe elaba*, is announced publicly and harvesting is then carried out by the young men, *abokolobia*, of each hamlet under the supervision of the village head of their age group. The fruits set aside as tribute are collected at the house of the hamlet head, and handed over formally to the *onu anẹ*, who usually sells them to women living in the neighbourhood. If the distances involved are great, tins or pots of expressed palm oil may be offered to the *onu anẹ* in lieu of fruit bunches.

The tribute of palm produce concerns mainly the men of each community, and forms a kind of tax on male householders, which is collected through the usual channels of masculine organization in the hamlet and the village. Women pay a separate tribute, also in tree crops but not in palm fruit. They contribute two fruits that play an important role in the Igala diet, and also form a small but valuable export crop, the seeds of *okpwiyẹ* (*Prosopis Africana*) and of *ọrọ aikpẹllẹ* (*Irvingia sp.*). In some areas there is a third alternative, *ugba* (*Parkia Filicoidea*), but it is not a typical form of women's tribute, possibly because the harvesting of this variety was not exclusively women's work.

Women pay tribute less frequently and more sporadically than men; they are not under the same obligation to pay regularly, nor are they bound by any formal rules of harvesting. It seems to have been customary for each household to give a bowl or two of fruits to the *onu anẹ* in a good year, as a thanksgiving for the good harvest and prosperity. But in bad years, or what the women consider to be bad years, this is not given or expected. The tribute from men may be similarly forgone in a year when the oil palms yield badly. But there is less latitude in this arrangement, and the right to control fruit cutting is relatively more important among the land chief's prerogatives than the right to expect occasional gifts of tree crops from the women of the community.

Rights over hunting spoils also form an important part of the land chief's economic privileges, and the transfer of portions of game animals that traditionally belong to him is classed as payment of tribute in the same way as the transfer of food crops. The *onu anẹ* of each district is traditionally entitled to the hind leg, *uta (ut'ela)*, of any large animal killed on his land, nominally from the side that first touches the ground when the beast falls. Animals classed as large game, *ọkela*, for this purpose include elephant, bushcow, wild pig, and various species of large antelope. In addition to these portions the land chief was entitled to portions of smaller animals on the opening day of the communal hunts, *ọdẹ ọdọ*, for which he was responsible.

As an administrator the *onu anẹ* was responsible to the central government for maintaining law and order in the district under his jurisdiction, and was a major witness in any major dispute forwarded to the provincial court or to the royal court at Idah for settlement. Judicial powers were to some extent divided between these central courts and the local district head. But the king in the metropolitan area and the provincial chiefs in the provinces claimed the right to transfer any case from the lower courts, and plaintiffs could also initiate court action in their courts without going to a lower court first. Subject to this condition, the land chief had jurisdiction over all classes of delict except homicide, kidnapping, repeated felonies, and offences of a political character. The exceptions came directly under the authority of the provincial chiefs, and of the Ata at Idah.

The administrative responsibilities of the *onu anẹ* included fiscal duties, and a portion of the tribute that he collected locally was supposed to be forwarded to the central government. I describe the machinery for enforcing this arrangement later, and need only say at this stage that payment was often irregular. The web of kinship ties between the royal clan and locally sovereign descent groups provided so many alternative channels of communication with the central government that the formal system of command, based on territorial divisions, frequently lapsed to be revived a few years later by the payment of an exceptionally large annual tribute.

The economic activities of each community within the district were regulated primarily by the hamlet and secondarily by the associations formed in co-operation at the village level. Farming, harvesting tree crops, fishing, and other aspects of land use were ultimately, however, under the jurisdiction of the *onu anẹ*, who settled disputes and was the final arbiter[1] of boundaries within the district. In addition, the land chief controlled directly the best areas of hunting land in his district, and set these aside as reserved lands on which farming was prohibited and hunting was strictly controlled. The reserved area formed a refuge for the wild game in the district as the hunting season advanced and burning of the savannah grass in surrounding areas progressively reduced the natural cover in which they sheltered. And the burning and beating of this great reserve formed the climax of the hunting year. The *odẹ odọ* or hunt of the year, as this battue was called, was the responsibility of the *onu anẹ* who mobilized the whole adult male population of his district for this purpose and also invited the heads of adjoining districts to send their best hunters and beaters to the hunt.

The office of land chief is not purely a secular administrative position, but has ritual duties and religious associations that identify the *onu anẹ* with the ritual welfare of the whole district community. The primary symbol of this identification

---

[1] To this day most of the land disputes that go to court concern inter-district quarrels and only rarely involve members of the same district. Informants say that appeals from the *onu anẹ*'s jurisdiction in a local dispute, though technically possible, were rare in practice. We can associate this with the strong ritual sanctions that upheld the *onu anẹ*'s jurisdiction over the land.

is the district land shrine, *erane*, which belongs to the land-owning clan, and is maintained by occasional offerings, and by a major annual ceremony. Every year, in the early part of the dry season, the head of each hamlet in the district brings small gifts of yams, beer, kola, and a few ears of guineacorn and millet to the land chief to be offered in the *erane* festival. These are taken to the shrine and laid there whilst the land chief invokes his clan ancestors to ward off witchcraft and sickness in the following year, to let the women of the village be fertile and the land yield abundantly.

This land festival is also a hunting festival, and in a ritual sense inaugurates the hunting season that is later terminated by the ritual performed during the period in which the reserved hunting land is thrown open by the *onu ane*. On this occasion the hunt is a smaller affair, covering the area in the vicinity of the land shrine and lasting only a few hours. Its main purpose is to obtain a few animals to make a second offering at the land shrine before the elders of the district disperse for the day. But it is significant that the land chief's ritual functions centre equally on hunting and arable farming.

The ritual association between the office of *onu ane* and the well-being of the district community is also expressed in his control of a masquerade, *abule*, in the power of ritual cursing in the name of the land, and in the concept of the pollution that is caused when death in the community results from certain kinds of sickness that are regarded as evil in themselves.

The masquerade *abule* belongs to the class of noise-making masquerades who come out by night and are, in principle, not seen by members of the community. They are in a sense *egwu* or ancestors, and speak with the shrill, stylized voices that are associated especially with the ancestors. But they are not the ancestors of a particular clan or lineage, as *egwu afia* are. Although they are associated with the clan of the *omonuane*, and are controlled by the *onu ane*, they are entirely separate from the concept of former members of this group, or of any other clan represented in the community. *Abule* symbolize rather the collective authority of the dead, and the association between former members of the community and the land that supported them. This association of the collectivity of ancestors with the land is one of the basic

155

notions of Igala religion, and the *abule* masquerade is one of the few forms in which this notion is translated into a form of social control.

The *abule* come out from time to time in connexion with the land festival to warn householders to be ready or to punish any man whose behaviour during the year consistently falls short of the standards set for a member of the community. At Igebije they appeared first during my stay, to announce that every household should contribute a pot of beer for the next land festival. After the festival they came out again, to fine those who had not complied. And in the course of this second appearance they publicly ridiculed one householder who took little part in village affairs and was suspected of sorcery and other anti-social practices. In extreme cases of this nature the *onu anẹ* could order a person to leave his land, and employ the *abule* to expel him if he refused to leave.

Abule also come out on special occasions if a succession of accidents or crop failures indicate that the land is ritually polluted, *biẹ*. If this occurs a black hen and a black she-goat are offered at the land shrine by the *onu anẹ*, and the goat's body is then dragged around the outskirts of the village at night by the *abule*. In Igebije the last occasion on which this had occurred was the sudden death of the *onu anẹ* himself, who fell from a palm tree and died afterwards. His death was attributed to harmful ritual, *inacha*, and the *abule* appeared to cleanse the land and avert any further misfortune to the community. Of this instance my informants said, *abule fanẹ nwochi*, 'the *abule* restored (or repaired) the land'. In a neighbouring district the same rite was performed after a leading farmer had collapsed and died whilst farming.

This association between the land, the ancestors, and the office of *onu anẹ* also appears in the latter's right to pronounce a ritual curse upon certain classes of offender. The Igala distinguish two degrees or stages in pronouncing such a curse; to caution solemnly or conditionally, *ehiunọ*, is different from the final pronouncement implied by the verb *egbaru*. These categories apply mainly to cursing in the name of the land and to curses pronounced in the names of the ancestors, although other classes of spiritual agency may also be invoked in the same curse. In connexion with the land a ritual curse is the prerogative of the *onu ane*, and in connexion with the ancestors it is the prerogative of the elders, *abogujo*.

This power of cursing had little direct connexion with the administrative and judicial responsibilities of the *onu ane*. It was not employed as a sanction for political offences, felonies, or secular misdemeanours. A ritual curse by the *onu ane* was directed rather at spiritual forms of wrongdoing, at witchcraft, *ochu*, sorcery, *ogwu bibi*, and at the combination of malice and evil magic that Igala describe by the term *inacha*. It identified the *onu ane* with the spiritual protection of the community, and in so doing defined the district, *ane*, as the basic community of Igala social life, within which the positive aspects of human co-operation were ultimately superior to the negative and destructive tendencies that co-operation also inevitably engendered.

As ritual guardian of the land, the *onu ane* is also responsible for the cleansing ceremonies that have to be performed when a death occurring in the community is recognized to be an 'evil death', *ukwu bibi*. Death resulting from any condition in which the patient's stomach swells up belongs to this category, together with death from leprosy, which is classed as an 'evil sickness', *oga bibi*. The same burial ritual has to be followed for a man suffering from elephantiasis of the scrotum, or for a pregnant woman who dies before her child is delivered. Similarly, death attributed to an *ebo* may be regarded as *ukwu bibi* if the sufferer confesses to being a witch and regards the sickness as a punishment sent by the *ebo*.

In all these cases the death creates a situation of ritual pollution which has to be removed by specialists. The pollution of the immediate homestead and its members is treated by specialists who know the medicine appropriate to the sickness or the condition of the sufferer. Burial of the corpse prevents the contagion from spreading through the community at large. But this has to be accompanied by ritual which the *onu ane* performs to symbolically limit the contagion. In these special circumstances burial takes place in the bush and not in the homestead. And before the interment can proceed, the *onu ane*, or someone sent by him, offers palm oil, *ekpo*, sheanut butter, *okume*, and a black hen to the land. The invocation accompanying this offering prays the land not to take offence,

157

and to carry away the sickness so that it will not come back to strike the descendants and relatives of the dead person. No fee is charged for this ritual service, but the *onu anẹ* is allowed to keep the hen in some cases, without sacrificing it.

The ritual duties of the *onu anẹ* that concern the community as a whole cannot be delegated, and the holder of the office alone is responsible for the annual festivals, for the land ritual connected with hunting, for curses pronounced in the name of the land, and for the removal of pollution associated with 'bad deaths'. Individual householders may, however, request the *onu anẹ* to establish a branch of the *ẹranẹ* shrine in their own homesteads. This is done by offering a black hen, beer, millet and guineacorn, and cooked yam to the land at a spot in the main clearing before the man's house. The site is then covered with two or three large stones, and a stick cut from one of a fast-growing species of tree is thrust into the ground. If this does not take root, the householder goes on planting shoots until one becomes established. The household land shrine may be set up in response to a direction from the *ifa* oracle. But it also symbolizes a stage in the growth of a homestead, and indicates that the owner is farming on his own account and is head of an independent household. The household land shrine of the founder of a hamlet in time serves the whole hamlet and is an important focus of ritual unity. But there is no corresponding shrine for the village, and village heads have no ritual authority delegated to them from the *onu anẹ* other than that which they possess in relation to their own hamlet, as successor to its founder.

Transmission of the economic, political, and ritual privileges of the land chief has a catalytic effect on clan structure and the internal segmentation of descent groups is affected at several different levels simultaneously when the land chief dies and his successor has to be appointed. The pattern of succession varies with clan scale, and is less formal and less systematic in the small-scale, low-ranking descent groups, than in the larger clans of intermediate or aristocratic rank. These differences centre on the fact that most clans in the latter group are titled, whereas many of the smaller clans are untitled. In titled clans the succession is monitored by the head of another clan, to which the clan taking the title is politically subordinate.

Whereas in untitled groups, the appointment is determined within the clan itself and concerns the outside world only in so far as it may give rise to disputes that are settled through the normal machinery of central government.

In titled clans the privileges and duties of the land chief are vested in a formal title, *ofẹ*, which combines the two offices of *onu anẹ* and *ogujo olọpu*. The titleholder, *ajofẹ*, is during his tenure of office in charge of every aspect of the clan's corporate activities. He receives the tribute that is paid by all residents on the clan land, settles disputes, and carries out the ritual of the land and hunting. He is also in charge of the clan's ancestral cults, centring on the *Egwu Afia* or upon *okwutẹ*, ritual staffs, and *unyi ibegwu*, ancestral shrines. The first set of duties correspond to those vested in the office of *onu anẹ*, and the second to those that are vested in the position of *ogujo olọpu*.

In discussing the genealogical aspect of succession to clan titles the Igala tend to describe the number of maximal lineages in the rotation as an unvarying total, that was fixed permanently in the period of the clan's foundation. But in practice the total can vary, either through the recognition of new maximal lineages, or by 'closing the mouth', *ekpalu*, of an earlier lineage so that it no longer takes a separate turn in the rotation but is merged with other maximal lineages. The genealogy of the royal subclan at Ankpa, given on page 80, contains examples of both kinds of development.

Changes in clan structure can also occur through deviation from the agnatic line, leading to the incorporation and eventual assimilation into the clan of lineal segments that are originally related through uterine links. The Igala frequently say that uterine kin cannot succeed to titles, *ọmonobulẹ a jofẹn*, but many clan genealogies contain instances of this type of succession. For instance, in a recent title contest at Idah, one of the two maximal lineages in the Okweje clan presented two candidates. As figure 16 on page 160 shows, one was *ọmonobulẹ* and the other *ọmẹnẹkẹlẹ*. In considering their claims the Ata accepted the principle that a uterine kinsman became eligible to contest the succession if the elders of the clan were in full agreement. But it is clear from other title cases that full agnatic membership is usually the first qualification demanded, and that deviations from this rule are regarded as exceptional and permissible only in special circumstances. Moreover, once the uterine group has been incorporated into the main clan it tends in time to become completely assimilated. It is extremely rare in Igala to find a maximal lineage whose members admit to being incorporated into a title rotation through uterine links, and one can conclude from this that by the third or fourth generation uterine segments of the clan tend to become accepted as full members, genealogically as well as politically.

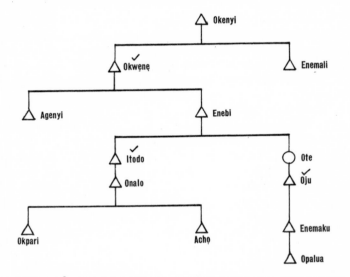

FIGURE 16. ASSIMILATION OF UTERINE KIN INTO THE
OKWEJE CLAN

$\sqrt{} = titleholder$

In untitled clans, and in periods of interregnum in titled clans, the office of *onu anẹ* tends to be separate from that of the *ogujo olọpu*, and to be transmitted through a different pattern of succession. Whereas the latter moves laterally rather than vertically through the descent group, from the most senior member to the next senior in age, the position of land chief tends to be hereditary in a direct line and to stay within the limits of a single maximal lineage.

In the Ọjọ clan, for instance, over the last generations the office of *ogujo olọpu* has been taken by members of five different lineages. But in the same period the functions of land chief have been monopolized by the maximal lineage descended from Achadu. And its members regard the office as their prerogative to such an extent that an heir apparent, Eicha, has already emerged within this line. It is common in this area for the land chief to employ either his eldest son or the eldest son of a previous office holder to represent him, *ekoji*, in a number of official capacities. And the person so employed forms the natural heir to the post when the incumbent dies.

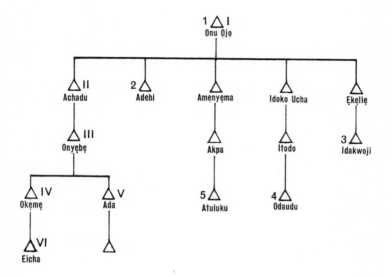

FIGURE 17. SUCCESSION TO OFFICE IN THE ỌJỌ CLAN

In this clan the division of corporate clan functions between two offices was a source of constant friction, and the relationship between successive holders of the different posts was strained and uneasy. As senior member of the clan the *ogujo olọpu* claimed a share of the tribute and other perquisites accruing to the land chief. But the allocation of these resources was continually disputed. Following a quarrel over tree crops brought to Ọkeme by the women of the village, Idakwoji resigned his position as ritual elder and left Igebije. His successor encountered the same problem, and quarrelled first with Onyẹbẹ and then with Ada over his share of the ẹnwu irẹ.

The monopoly of this important office, which controls the economic resources of the clan, ultimately affects the whole pattern of clan segmentation by preventing the emergence of a rotating system of succession within which the structure of the different lineages can be defined. In the Ọjọ clan the dominant lineage, founded by Achadu, had an unbroken residential connexion with the clan centre whilst the other lineages were widely dispersed in other districts. These dispersed groups were correspondingly attenuated genealogically, and their total known membership was not much greater than the past and present membership of the Achadu line on its own.

In the culminating stages of the disputes that attended the division of corporate responsibility in this clan, Odaudu made an attempt to revive the extinct title of Onu Ọjọ, so that the two clan offices would be reunited in a single office. If this had been successful the office would clearly have gone to a lineage other than the dominant one, and the nucleus of a new rotation would have been created. The dominant lineage was, however, so strongly entrenched in the district through its kinship connexions with the different hamlets, and particularly through its kin links with local branches of the royal clan, that it was able to resist this move to transfer rights over the land of the district from its own members. In the face of a threat by the other hamlet heads in the area to boycott the representative of any other lineage, the Ata concluded that the clan was unstable internally and that Odaudu's claim on the title had not been proved genealogically to the point where it could justify reviving this office. He therefore asked the clan members to decide amongst themselves who should succeed to the office before he could agree to award a title which would effect a major change in the structure of the whole group.

Palace officials.

In the royal court at Idah the hereditary officers of state did not attend the king personally outside the context of official government activities; neither did custody of the royal household form any part of their duties. The royal councillors, kingmakers, and heads of subsidiary clans all had their own compounds outside the walls of the palace, and their attendance on the king was limited, physically, to a comparatively restricted area of the royal compound. The king's titled siblings, who were more privileged in this regard than other titleholders, could move freely through most parts of the palace. But they were excluded from the morning *okwuteͅ* ceremony in which the king communed with his ancestors, and from any room in which the Ata was in the act of eating or sleeping.[1]

The organization and maintenance of the royal household at Idah was the responsibility of a group of non-hereditary officials, divided into the two grades of *eͅdibo*, or royal clients, and *amonoji*, palace eunuchs. The first of these grades also occurs in the Achadu's court at Idah, and in the courts of some of the provincial chiefs. But the second grade is exclusively royal, and the right to retain eunuchs in his service is a privilege belonging uniquely to the Ata.

The two grades of palace officials maintained the actual fabric of the palace, organizing repairs and rebuilding, and supplying most of the labour and materials required by calling upon their own followers. They also controlled the domestic economy of the palace outside the sphere that was under the authority of the king's wives. The king's personal safety and the security of his treasures, shrines, regalia, and other property were also their responsibility. And in this capacity the palace officials regulated access not only to the king himself but to all royal buildings and to the area of the palace in general. In a literal and physical sense they were the chief intermediaries between the king and his people, and occupied a correspondingly important place in the machinery of central government.

In local government also, the Ata used his palace officials as intermediaries, interposing their delegated royal authority between the hereditary officers of state and the clan heads in

---

[1] The conditions governing access to the inner royal apartments closely parallel the prohibitions associated with the *anuͅku* or inner courtyard in commoners' houses. See p. 140.

charge of local districts. *Ẹdibo* and *amonoji* were employed as messengers and agents in contacts between Idah, the provinces and the outlying districts of the metropolitan area. The second grade also co-ordinated the payment of tribute, through a system of permanent relationships between the different hereditary titles and various titled offices held by the senior eunuchs. Palace officials were thus directly responsible for the economic resources of government. From this they financed their own system of offices, by taking a share of tribute paid to the king, by collecting fees from petitioners at the court, and by customary payments received in connexion with the award of titles. In addition when travelling on the king's business palace officials were authorized to make direct levies, *edinya*, on goods displayed in the market or being carried to market.

Membership of the *ẹdibo* grade in the king's service was acquired by paying a fee and taking an oath of personal loyalty to the king. It was possible for any free-born male to become a member, and in this sense membership was unrestricted by factors of descent and birth. But the majority of *ẹdibo* claim some form of kinship connexion with the royal clan, and kinship links between the outlying settlements of the royal group and the non-royal descent groups were a decisive factor in the recruitment of clients. The importance of kinship factors in this grade of offices led Clifford to regard this form of service as originating in the Jukun custom of employing uterine kin as palace retainers in place of the king's sons, who are debarred from living in the compound. But although this class of kin is specially favoured within the grade, it is equally the function of the office to recognize distant ties of cognatic kinship, and in this connexion the Igala do not regard either of these two kinds of relationship as being logically or historically prior to the other.

The most closely related or specially favoured *ẹdibo* lived in the palace and attended the king constantly, whilst other members of the grade lived elsewhere in the capital, or in their own villages, and saw the king less frequently. They were obliged, however, to be present at festivals, and to supply labour and materials when required on other occasions. They were organized under a leader with the title of Ouchalla. But the grade did not develop a strong corporate organization.

It had no lodge or other permanent symbols of its own identity, and its members were essentially clients of the king and not participants in an independent society. This institutional weakness is possibly related to the strength of the kinship structure underlying the client tie, which provided a means of differentiating *ẹdibo* from one another without creating separate offices, and also tied the grade's organization to the rotation of offices within the ruling subclan. When the king died, his *ẹdibo* had to renew their oath of loyalty and make a further payment before they were recognized by the next king. And in practice the grade seems to divide informally into four sections which come into office with the particular lineage towards which each section is oriented.

All *ẹdibo* enjoyed personal immunities and other privileges in relation to the local district administration. Traditionally, cases in which they were involved were heard by the royal court rather than by the local district head. They could claim immunity from local taxation, by virtue of their direct contributions to the economy of the palace. And during the great royal festivals they enjoyed a specially privileged position. Seton said of the royal *ẹdibo* that during the Ogaingain festival they were licensed to seize children and sell them into slavery. And of the Achadu's *ẹdibo* he wrote that they could take any man's goods without his daring to complain, or take a woman to wife without paying the customary bridewealth.

Clifford wrote of the privileges of the royal *ẹdibo* that they 'held themselves to be independent of the authority and jurisdiction of the hereditary fief-holders in whose territory they dwelt'.[1] And in an unpublished report he added, 'The Onus are terrified to take disciplinary action against them and until recently it was a brave man who dared lay a complaint against any of them.' Clifford also estimated that the total numbers of *ẹdibo* had risen from about 200 in the Ata Amaga's reign to over 500 by the year 1930, when Ata Obaje was on the throne. The entrance fee had also risen from '20 brass rods, with 5 brass rods and a cock to the chief eunuch' to a cash payment of £2 10s. upwards, with gifts at festival times to the Ata of a goat or a cock and bundles of yams or guineacorn, in addition to money.

Of the two grades of palace officials the group of eunuchs

[1] Clifford, Miles, op. cit.

was relatively more important than the association of *ẹdibo*, possessing relatively greater independence of the crown, and achieving a much higher degree of corporate organization. The status of the *amonoji* was enhanced in relation to the hereditary titles by the same factors, and to the same extent, as the status of the royal clients. But they derived additional strength and influence from being independent of the system of rotating succession in the royal house. The royal eunuchs supplied more executive continuity between reigns than the royal clients, since their offices did not change when the king died, and were vested with important duties affecting the succession and investiture of the new king.

The importance of the eunuchs in the traditional system of government appears clearly in the development of an elaborate hierarchy of titles for this association, running parallel in functions and status to the titles held by the hereditary officers of state. Newly created eunuchs were placed in the charge of one or other of the titled eunuchs, and could in time hope to be appointed to one of the junior offices in the titled series. The five senior posts were usually filled only by promotion from a junior title. Some differences of opinion exist about the order of seniority below the first five titles, but the generally accepted ranking order amongst the titled eunuchs is as follows:

Title	Salutation
Ẹnẹfọla	Ọda
Ọrata	Uchiba
Ogbẹ	Iche
Ugbọla	Utoodo
Ochẹjẹ	Chaiaagwu
Ẹnẹkadugbo	Aloji
Ọkwu (Oyikwu)	Ọta
Ọkọtọnọwa	Ẹde
Elakwu	Oduma
Adenyi	Oliko
Eju	Ebije
Mamẹjẹ	
Agbaru	
Ọdachi Ata	

With the exception of the last office, the eunuchs lived in close proximity to the palace, and their traditional compounds,

166

okẹte, formed the first ring of buildings outside the palace wall. As the map on page 169 shows, their settlements follow the wall closely on three sides following in the direction of the Idah cliffs, and then open out towards the frontal approaches where they become interspersed with the compounds of some of the hereditary chiefs.

Before the practice of castration was abandoned at Idah, eunuchs were made from the class of those who offended against the king's prerogatives by levying war, embezzling royal monies, or committing adultery with the king's wives. It was regarded as a less severe form of punishment than sale into slavery or execution, and is said to have been chosen by some criminals in preference to these alternatives. The following list of individual cases shows that slaves could sometimes be made eunuchs after purchase, but the instances given are of slaves brought to the king as compensation for a rebellious act. I give the eunuch's own name first followed, in brackets, by that of the title or titles held, and then by a brief statement of the individual's offence and background.

Akwu (Ẹnẹfọlạ)	A Hausa slave. Possibly one of nine slaves given by the Abokko clan to the Ata as a peace offering.
Aruna Ẹre (Ogbẹ)	Of Nupe descent and related to the Ulimam clan at Ikagbo. Punished for committing adultery with the king's wives.
Aduku Imutsa (Ogbẹ)	Free-born member of the Atẹbọ clan. Punished for complicity in a local rebellion at Ọta village, Ibaji District.
Onuchẹ Ukpo (Ogbẹ)	Free-born member of the Abọkkọ clan. An accomplice of Aduku Imutsa.
Amẹ (Ochẹjẹ)	A former *ẹdibo* in charge of the king's treasury. Found guilty of embezzlement.
Atumeyi Odo (Ọrata)	Unable to discharge his debts to the Ata Ochẹjẹ Nọkpa, and reputed to have volunteered to become an *onoji* in order to restore his family's fortunes.
Ọmakoji (Ugbọla)	Free-born from Egume. Offence unknown.
Ocholi (Ẹnạkadugbo)	Igbirra from Koton Karifi. One of nine slaves brought by Abọkkọ clan as a peace offering.

167

The titled eunuchs were the chief executive officers of the Ata in his capacity of territorial sovereign and acted as the formal intermediaries between the king and his district heads. In this role they were known as *ohiegba*, 'the one who receives the answer', and controlled access to the king on all formal business involving district affairs. The tribute, *ęnwu ire*, paid annually by the district heads had to be presented to the king through the *ohiegba* of the title concerned, as did any gifts sent for the ritual or celebrations connected with the great festivals. In principle judicial business and formal complaints similarly required the *ohiegba*'s services, although there were, as I show later, ways of bypassing this formal avenue of communication with the king. In the same capacity, eunuchs played an important role in title disputes and in determining succession to clan offices. Every hereditary title in Igala, down to the present time, has its particular *ohiegba* among the eunuchs, who presents candidates for vacant titles to the Ata, guides them through the intricacies of title litigation at court, and finally administers the oath of loyalty and performs the actual investiture[1] ceremony for the candidate approved by the Ata. In the case of the great office holders at Idah, the *ohiegba* also officiates at their burial ceremonies, reversing some of the rites of installation so that the title can be regarded as being formally vacant.

As *ohiegba* or intermediaries, the eunuchs were kept informed by the king of all decisions affecting the areas within their respective spheres of jurisdiction. And if a serious dispute broke out, or the king wished to demonstrate his authority formally for some other reason, the *ohiegba* responsible would be sent to the area concerned with the king's instructions. One procedure for dealing with local rebellions, was for the Ata to send some of his eunuchs with their own followers to call out the local population against the rebels and organize this force into a punitive expedition. The dispatch of these agents was in itself a token that the rebel leaders were regarded as

---

[1] Newly appointed chiefs do not encounter or even see the king during the investiture ceremony, even the oath of loyalty being administered by the eunuchs. The first meeting with the Ata is on the day following the investiture when the new chief attends the morning audience (*ugwa odudu*) and announces his own new *odu ukpaihi* or cognomen.

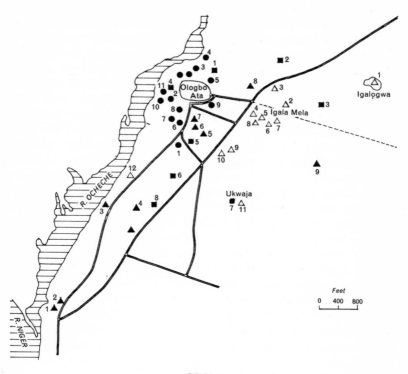

TITLES

■ Royal	△ Kingmakers	▲ Subsidiary	● Eunuchs
1 Ọmakoji Ata	1 Achadu	1 Ọmọgbajẹ	1 Enẹtọla
2 Ondomata	2 Ẹtẹmaihi	2 Ewọ	2 Ọrata
3 Achainyata	3 Aleji	3 Abọkkọ	3 Ogbẹ
4 Ohiemogbolo	4 Unana	4 Abọkkọ	4 Ochẹjẹ
5 Inalogu	5 Achanyuwọ	5 Ohiuga	5 Ugbọla
6 Odokina Ata	6 Agbẹnyọ	6 Atẹbọ	6 Ọkọtọnọwa
7 Amanata	7 Onubiogbo	7 Agaidoko	7 Agbaru
8 Ochai Ata	8 Ochẹjẹ	8 Ulimam	8 Mamẹjẹ
	9 Ochijenu	9 Onu Ohiji	9 Elakwu
	10 Obajadaka		10 Ọikwu
	11 Onẹde		11 Enẹkadugbo
	12 Ashadu Kịkịlị Ukwaja		

FIGURE 18. IDAH, SHOWING SITE OF PALACE AND CHIEFS' COMPOUNDS

169

outlaws by the king, and also carried the threat of a full-scale onslaught from Idah if the rebels were not contained and subdued locally. It was the death of two eunuchs on an expedition of this kind that led the Abokko clan leaders in Amaga's reign to go into exile and sue for terms which would permit their return.

Formerly access to the king at Idah was restricted and controlled mainly by the palace eunuchs, who admitted only titleholders and the Ata's own kinsmen to the morning and evening salutation ceremonies held in the palace. On every *ede*, completing an Igala week of 4 days, the king held a wider audience in the reception hall known as *ogwede*. Complaints could be made publicly on this occasion, as they could privately on other days, but discussion was usually limited to a number of serious cases, selected from those brought privately before the king. The eunuchs played a considerable part in introducing cases and litigants on these occasions, and one of the senior titled eunuchs, Ogbe, acted together with some of the other traditional councillors, as a presiding judge. Many accounts suggest that the Ata sometimes delegated his own role of president at these sessions to Ogbe, who thereby came to be regarded as chief judge in the Ata's court at Idah. But the final verdict was the Ata's and informants today insist that Ogbe did not preside over the court in his own right, but only as the king's deputy on occasions when the Ata chose not to direct the investigation in person.

The control that the palace eunuchs exercised over access to the Ata was a function of their responsibility for the king's welfare and safety. They were in constant attendance upon him during the day, and arranged the guard that watched over the palace at night. Igala notions of vulnerability to attack include the whole environment in which a person moves and lives, since sorcery can be put into effect by placing medicines in any room or across any path which the victim habituates. Again, the sacred duties of kingship occupy such an important place in concepts of royal welfare that any interference with the cult symbols, shrines, or medicines kept in the palace could have disastrous effects for the king himself. Igala tradition makes it clear that it may be necessary to spoil a person's protective medicines before his political downfall can be accomplished. Similarly it is notorious that adulterous wives expose their husbands to the risk of sorcery by their lovers and play an active role in plots to kill or harm the husband by mystical means.

Amonoji are responsible for the king's life to the extent that the Igala believe that no attempt to assassinate or replace an established king by assassination or personal injury could succeed without the eunuchs' consent. The traditions recording the murder of the Ata Ekalaga state that the plot was conceived by the next branch in line to the throne, approved by the Achadu and Igala Mela, and finally put into effect by the eunuchs, whose consent had also been obtained previously. One tradition says that in the period after the murder, before the Akogu lineage was expelled from the palace by the incoming heirs to the throne, the dead king's eldest son had two of the senior eunuchs, Ogbe and Ocheje, executed for their part in this conspiracy, whilst the other senior eunuchs defected to the new ruler.

The employment of eunuchs was one of the few governmental institutions in Igala that was exclusively monarchial and had no counterpart or imitation among the provincial governors or in the Achadu's palace. Eunuchs could only be made on the king's orders, and any man punished in this way automatically entered the king's service and took a personal oath of loyalty to the king. From one point of view this rule created a class of executive officials who were absolutely dependent upon the king, and who could not hope to transfer their loyalty and services within the existing framework of authority. This royal prerogative functioned in the same way as possession of the royal insignia and custody of the royal shrines and burial grounds, to uphold the institution of monarchy against the centrifugal tendencies created by delegation of authority to the provincial chiefs, and by the dispersal of the royal clan. Provincial administration in the kingdom duplicated the government of the metropolitan area in most respects. But it remained subordinate in status without the office of eunuchs to complete the administrative hierarchy.

The effect of allocating these ceremonial, domestic, and administrative duties to palace officials is to separate the king's office from the other great offices of state in the actual detailed workings of government. And the separation is made complete

171

by the fact that the *amonoji*, in addition to their other duties, are also responsible for practically all the ritual that is carried out within the palace precincts. There is thus no sphere of government activity in which palace officials are not to some extent interposed between the king and his councillors. Although the gap between the king and his hereditary officials, as representatives of a descent system, is not a great one in principle, in practice the royal councillors and titled clan heads participate in the work of government only in a comparatively restricted context.

The palace division of the royal ancestral cult, which is concerned mainly with the daily rites of ancestor worship, was maintained by the king in association with the five senior eunuchs. The latter were the custodians of the palace ancestral staffs and of the other utensils used in connexion with these symbols. Attendance at the morning *okwute* ceremony, at which the Ata offered to his royal predecessors, was limited to the titles Ọrata, Ọgbẹ, Ochẹjẹ, Ugbọla, and to any specially favoured *ẹdibo* in the king's personal following. These senior eunuchs were also responsible for the ritual of purification, *erọla*, that preceded the *okwute* ceremony.

The palace eunuchs are also responsible for the royal masquerades, Egwu Ata, which represent the king's ancestors at the great annual festivals, and form one of the most important aspects of the palace division of the ancestral cult. With two exceptions, the royal masquerades were in the custody of the eunuchs, who maintained the head-dresses and costumes, and produced the actual dramatic performances by supplying the chief maskers and attendant drummers, singers, and other followers. Responsibility for the masquerades was divided amongst the *amonoji* as follows:

Masquerade	Custodian
Ekwẹ	Ẹnẹfọla
Ọchọchọnọ	
Inyẹlikpi	Eju
Ẹpe	Ọgbẹ
Agbanabo	Ochẹjẹ
Isawulu	Ugbọla
Odumadọ	Ọrata

172

The two exceptions to this monopoly by the palace officials were the masquerades Ikeleku Ahuma and its 'child', Jamadeka, which were cared for by Agaidoko, one of the subsidiary clan heads.

Finally, there are a number of other shrines and fetishes, associated with tutelary spirits and protective agencies, that are also in the eunuchs' custody. The most important of these, the Ọbade shrine, is situated at the edge of the palace, and is maintained by the eunuch directly. The other shrines, located further away, are also maintained by them, but indirectly through resident priests who in some cases hold minor titles. The responsibilities of the different eunuchs, and the situations of the various shrines for which they are responsible, are as follows:

Shrine	Location	Custodian
Okuta Alechi	1½ miles inland from palace	Ẹnẹkadugbo
Owalika	Source of Inachalo stream	Ẹnẹkadugbo and Ogbẹ
Okwutadẹkọ	Near Owalika	Ẹnẹkadugbo and Ogbẹ
Ọbade	Palace outskirts	Ẹnẹkadugbo and Ogbẹ
Olifẹ	Across R. Niger	Ọrata
Maboro	Anambra river	Ọrata

TABLE 15. ROYAL SHRINES NEAR IDAH

When an Ata died, the palace eunuchs were responsible for most of the ritual performed within the palace, and also took charge of the royal regalia and other palace symbols of kingship. In the interregnum the locus of government was kept unchanged through the fiction that the Ata was indisposed. And the business of government was carried on by the senior titled amọmata in co-operation with the chief eunuchs and other palace officials. In the ceremonial transfer of authority from the dead king to his successor, the senior eunuchs were present at both the burial ceremonies and the accession rites. They make most of the arrangements for burial, sending for the ẹdibo to dig the grave, and other titleholders whose task it is to prepare the coffin and its supports. Then, after closing

173

the grave, they later attend the new king at Ofuloko, assisting him to robe, and handing over the regalia and insignia of office which they received from the dead king.

It is clear from this brief outline of their activities that the palace officials formerly exercised great responsibility in many fields of government activity, and that their offices had begun to evolve beyond the stage of complete dependence on the king's favour. In particular, the posts held by the senior eunuchs ranked high in the system of titles, and provided the king with his chief executive officers. The functions of the traditional councillors were, by comparison, advisory and limited in their authority. And in one sense the Ata's titled siblings were more dependent upon the king's favour than the senior eunuchs, whose offices did not change with the king's and who had a permanent right to mediate between hereditary titleholders and the crown. The councillors and the eunuchs were to some extent rivals for power and influence within the central government; one group representing the nexus of hereditary ties that united the king with his people, and the other group representing the system of formal territorial relationships between the capital and the other areas of the kingdom.

The senior eunuchs had their own local following of supporters and clients who assisted them in the performance of their official duties, and also participated in the rivalry for influence and prestige at court that characterized their relations with the other officers of state.

Each of the eunuchs' titles had a small fief or 'farm', *oko*, attached to it, comprising a village or group of hamlets whose heads accepted the eunuchs' authority in political matters, and assisted them economically. The eunuchs called on the villages for assistance in building their own compounds and in maintaining the palace, and were entitled to a large share of the tribute that was paid by these subordinate communities. They also recruited clients, *abimoto onoji*, through this system of local contacts. Adult men could enlist in the eunuchs' service and in return for patronage and protection worked for them personally, either in the capital or on the farms that they maintained in the subordinate villages. Men in this position seem to have either begun as members of the tributary

174

villages, or to have become assimilated as full members of these communities.

The fiefs held by the different eunuchs, in the last few decades of this system,[1] are as follows:

Title	Fief
Ẹnẹfọla	Okpe
	Idekenyi
Ọrata	Ẹgọbada
	Atẹnegoma
	Abujaga
Ogbe	Okogbẹ
	Achago
	Orunu
Ugbọla	Ibochi
Ochẹjẹ	Okochẹjẹ (Inẹnẹ)
	Igbudukaji (Inẹnẹ)
	Okpẹ Adige
	Okpẹ Ọjẹdẹgbe
	Okpẹ Apata
Enekadugbo	Okwutalechi
Oyikwu	Ọgaaji
Ọkọtọnọwa	Ejefe
Adenyi	Anike
Elakwu	Agbanaka, Oguma

A final indication of the eunuchs' high status in government is their right to bestow minor titles on their own followers. These titles duplicated the names of titles held by the royal councillors, so that Ogbẹ, for instance, appointed an Amana Ogbẹ, an Ọmachi Ogbẹ, an Ochai Ogbẹ, and an Odoma Ogbẹ. Some of these titles were hereditary and were held mainly in the eunuchs' fiefs, by the 'people outside', *abo ki dọdọda*, whilst others were held for life only by clients living in the capital, the 'followers in the inner courtyard', *abimọtọ ki def'anuku*.

---

[1] With the death of the last eunuchs, in the first two decades of this century, the *ohiegba* lost most of their executive power, but the offices have survived and are filled today by clients who deputize for their former masters, without being formally invested with the eunuchs' titles.

The influence of rank.

The division of functions between central and local government corresponds, as we have seen, to the difference in status between the royal and non-royal clans. This division is validated in Igala myths of origin and also upheld by the ritual arrangements that oppose the royal clan to the kingmakers, and to other clans with specialized functions. And it is also perpetuated by the factor of heredity, which vests each set of functions in a cluster of descent groups and makes their corporate existence depend upon the continuance of this division of power.

The Igala summarize the difference of political function between the royal and non-royal clans by saying that the former does not 'own land', *enanę*. Its members, in other words, possess no hereditary rights of local sovereignty, but are free, as the Igala say, to settle where they like and farm without paying tribute to the local district head. In practice, the influence of rank is such that princes and other royal settlers of the highest rank tend to become politically dominant wherever they live. And the balance of power between the royal and non-royal clans has to be worked out and adjusted continually between each localized segment of the royal group and its non-royal neighbours. In this section I shall illustrate this process of adjustment from districts in the metropolitan area. But the same pattern repeats itself throughout Igala, wherever segments of the royal clan, or of the other aristocratic clans, are established. Before going into these examples in detail it should be emphasized that the constant extension of royal influence, which is characteristic of this system, does not overthrow the descent system on which the transmission of political power is based. The descent principle is sufficiently flexible to accommodate a process of growth in the royal clan at the expense of the local descent groups. And it is this structural process that ultimately consolidates the royal clan's local political gains, and leads to the establishment of permanent centres of royal influence.

In the metropolitan area a considerable proportion of members of the ruling house, who have no direct connexions with its political leaders, are dispersed through non-royal villages and hamlets. As in-laws and kinsmen of the local population they are completely integrated into the political, social, and economic life of these non-royal communities, and are only loosely connected with the royal clan through the elders of the major or maximal lineages to which they belong.

A smaller proportion of members of the ruling house live in separate communities that are strongly patrilineal and exclusively royal in relation to the transfer of offices and corporate responsibility. In the Ọjọ district, for example, there are about thirty royal homesteads dispersed through the various non-royal villages and hamlets in the area. But there is also one hamlet, Icalaba, sited close to the district centre, whose inhabitants are classed as *amọmata*, in the political sense of the term. They are descended, as the genealogy in figure 19 on pages 178–9 shows, from two princes who were sons of the Ata Aku Odiba, and form a small extended family with a total membership of about thirty adult males. One of the two founders, with whom the other lived, was a member of the royal council during his father's reign, and held the title of Amanata. But when Aku Odiba died and the Ocholi lineage went out of office, Ọgaaji and his junior brother moved from the capital to live near Ọgaaji's wife's kin, and founded a new hamlet at Icalaba.

Hamlets of this type tend to be unstable by comparison with the district centres and other major villages in these local areas. In the district, for example, Icalaba is the third in a series of royal hamlets, the other two having broken up within a generation or two of their foundation. Oral tradition records a close link between Igebije, the district centre, and a hamlet of the same name that was founded shortly before the reign of Aku Odiba. This community was established by Egwu Ọnọja, who belonged to the same major lineage in the Ocholi descent group as the founders of the hamlet of Icalaba. His own father was the son of a king and had held the title of Ọmakoji Ata. When Aku Odiba came to the throne Egwu left Igebije and became a member of the royal council with the same title that his father had held three reigns previously. But after his death the hamlet that Egwu had created at Igebije was abandoned, since his sons chose not to remain there and dispersed to other areas.

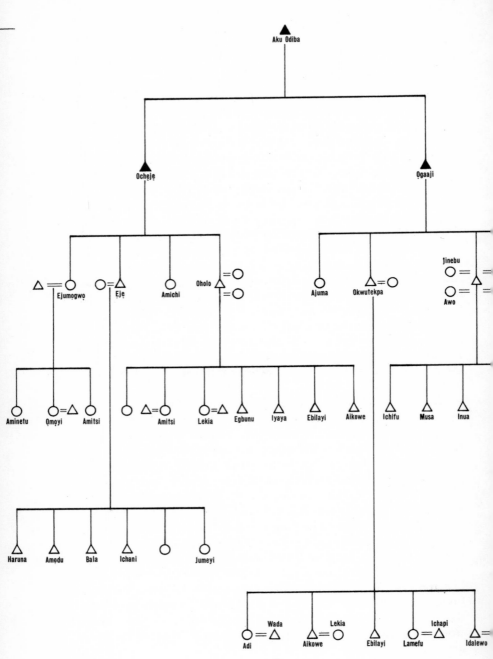

FIGURE 19. COMPOSITION OF THE ROYAL HAMLET
OF ICALABA

○ △ *Living members of the hamlet*

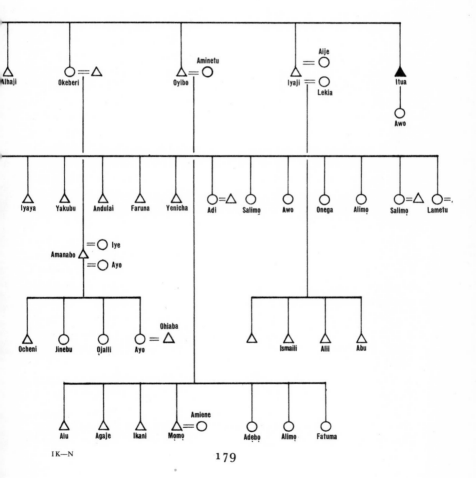

The other royal hamlet that grew up in the Ọjọ district was founded by a prince belonging to a different maximal lineage in the ruling house. Ayagba, son of the Ata Okoliko, held the title of Ọmakoji Ata in his father's reign, before moving to Igebije and settling with his children at Ofagba, a short distance from the district centre. But this settlement lasted for less than one decade, since the founder moved, with most of his followers to an adjoining district shortly before his death. Oral tradition rationalizes his withdrawal by attributing it to sickness and other misfortune. But it is possible also that the success of a related royal group in a neighbouring district attracted the population of Ofagba. Again, the Ọjọ district is traditionally allied with the Ocholi lineage rather than the Amachọ group to which this settlement belonged, and the strength of this alliance may also have contributed to the decision to withdraw.

It is significant that all three of the royal hamlets in the Ọjọ district were sited near the district centre, and maintained close social relations with the head of the landowning clan. The land on which their members built and farmed was allocated to them by the District Head himself, and the royal hamlets were free of any territorial tie with the subordinate villages and hamlets in the district. This pattern recurs in all parts of the metropolitan area. At Ajo, for instance, the royal hamlet of Agbenẹma is situated within easy walking distance of the central village, and has closer contacts with the district centre than with any other community in the area. Similarly at Okenya, Okpachala, Ofenya, Gwolawo, and many other district centres there are satellite royal hamlets so closely connected with the nuclear village that they are sometimes regarded as an extension of the central community.

The proximity of the royal hamlets to the centres of local government is at once an instrument and an expression of their involvement in the political aspects of district affairs. Through the high rank of their founders as princes of the blood, the royal hamlets have a profound influence on the conduct of local politics and counterbalance the authority of the local district head. Informally, and in varying degrees, their leaders represent the authority of central government, and frequently exercise functions that are nominally divided

180

exclusively between the officials at Idah and the clan heads who are in charge of districts. They play, for instance, an important part in settling disputes, and continually threaten to usurp the land chief's own judicial functions by the frequency with which they are asked to intervene on litigants' behalf, or to settle cases informally.

Much of the influence that royal hamlets wield in district affairs derives from their lineage connexions with the capital, which provide the centres of local government with an alternative channel of communication to the formal system of links through palace officials. In the Ọjọ district the clan head was subordinate to the eunuch holding the Ogbẹ title, who was the official intermediary between the Ọjọ clan and the Ata. But this relationship was limited to the formal contacts occasioned by the payment of tribute and by the procedure of title taking. And outside this relationship the clan had a wide range of contacts with the court through the agnatic relatives of the royal extended family of Icalaba. The most important of these, through which much traditional business was transacted, were with other descendants of Ọgaaji Aku.

Through intermarriage between the royal lineages and members of the non-royal clans in outlying districts this alternative system of communication with the capital is developed and to some extent institutionalized, as a network of kinship and marriage ties. The nexus of local ties between the royal hamlets and district centres becomes the pivot of a wider system of lineage oppositions, involving major lineages in the royal clan and maximal or major lineages in the non-royal descent groups. In the Ọjọ clan at present the alliance between the village head of Igebije and the agnates of the Icalaba settlers is focused on a link of uterine kinship. Atidọga, a grandson of Ọgaaji Aku, who now lives in the capital, is *ọmonobulẹ* to the Achadu lineage of the Ọjọ clan, and the clan head is reciprocally his *omenyi* or mother's brother. This relationship is invoked to justify the mutual assistance that these two kin groups constantly give one another. For instance, in the title dispute initiated by Odaudu's lineage against Ada's descent group, Atidọga took the side of his *omenyi* and was instrumental in keeping the court informed of the strength of local opposition to the office of land chief being transferred. On another occasion, when the clan head forwarded gifts of game to the Ata, he notified the king through the same relative before formally handing over the gift to his *ohiegba*. Similarly when trouble threatened the clan head over a minor shooting accident that occurred in the annual hunt, *ọde ọdọ*, he immediately notified the head of the Icalaba community, and their mutual kinsmen at Idah.

In this district relations between the royal hamlet of Icalaba and the district centre are not competitive, and the leaders of the royal group accept and uphold the rights of local sovereignty vested in the head of the Ọjọ clan. The former attend the land sacrifices and hunts organized by the latter and recognize his authority over the land by making occasional gifts of beer and kola nuts on ceremonial occasions. At one stage of a local inquiry appointed by the king to investigate Odaudu's claim on the Ọjọ clan title, the Icalaba community sent one of its senior members to testify in Ada's favour, and claimed publicly that the hamlet had paid tribute regularly to the land chiefs from Ada's lineage. Similarly in matrimonial disputes and other legal quarrels they made no attempt to bypass the *onu anẹ*, but consulted him fully and referred cases from their own hamlet to him for settlement.

This relationship of political equality obtains in many other districts between the royal hamlets and local district centres. In the Ajo district, for instance, the head of the royal group at Agbẹnẹma is in a similar position in relation to the head of the Ohiuga clan, who controls the whole district. The royal group has on a number of occasions acted on behalf of the latter in a dispute over fishing rights with the head of a subordinate hamlet. But the head of the royal group emphasizes the separation of his own interests and those of his lineage from the interests of the Ohiuga clan by claiming that he acts only as *ọmonobulẹ*, to protect the rights of his father's mother's agnatic group. At Ofenya and Okenya, similarly, the royal elders freely admitted their subordination to the local land chief and disclaimed any interest in local jurisdiction or in control of the land.

In other districts, however, royal hamlets have come to dominate the partnership with local clans to such an extent that they have supplanted the land chief administratively, juridically, and even ritually. The influence of these royal settlements in district affairs is in proportion to their influence at court, and where this is exceptionally great the balance of power in the districts tends to be tipped in favour of the royal settlers.

In the Oba district (Anoba) adjoining the Ojo area the royal hamlet of Iga has gained so much influence at the expense of the traditional district centre, the village of Oba, that the latter has been virtually abandoned, and Iga has become the new centre of political and administrative control. This change is fully apparent in the fact that the modern office of *gago*, which is to some extent a modern continuation of the land chief's office, has become hereditary in the royal section of the district community, so that administrative control has been transferred entirely from the landowning group to the royal group. The founder of this royal hamlet, Amonojio, was exceptional in being related to the ruling house on both sides, paternally to the Itodo Aduga branch of the Ajaku lineage, and maternally to the Ocholi lineage. Amonojio retained the post of royal councillor for three reigns, and was given titles by the Atas Aku Odiba, Okoliko, and Amocheje successively.

In the face of powerful competition from the hamlet led by Amonojio the landowning clan in this district seems to have fragmented and become widely dispersed through the migration of its members. The remaining members of the clan placed themselves under patronage of the royal group, and came increasingly under their dominance until they finally abandoned their traditional clan centre and moved to Iga, where they now occupy a subordinate hamlet. Their duties at present are purely ritual in character, and administrative duties connected with the land, including the collection of tribute, have been taken over by the leaders of the royal group.

To take a different example, in the district of Oju-Ocha, as I indicated briefly earlier, there is rivalry for political control of the district between an untitled clan whose members are regarded as the traditional *amomonuane* and another clan that traces its ancestry agnatically to the famous hunter Otigba, and by a link of matrifiliation to the Ocholi lineage of the ruling house. The latter group acquired power through the marriage of its founder's son with Omigbi Aku, the eldest daughter of the Ata Aku Odiba. And it was subsequently able to consolidate and extend this position through the support of the Niger Company and other trading groups, who accepted Omigbi's children as the Ata's representatives in the area. When colonial administration was established, from 1900 onwards, Otigba's clan was given the office of *gago* or administrative head, and the traditional landowning clan was overlooked. This division of authority has been challenged in the last few years by the present head of the *amọmonuanẹ*. But the court ruled that in this case the administrative functions of collecting tax and representing the area in the modern court system had become separated from the traditional office of *onu anẹ*. There is thus a recognized land chief, who carries out the traditional duties of office except in so far as these have been modified by the appointment of a separate administrative head, from a different clan.

In another district in this area, formerly centred on the village of Igoti, there is a long history of rivalry for local control between the royal hamlet of Ofoke and the landowning clan which was centred first on Igoti and later moved to the site of the district market, at Adum. Ofoke, like Oju-Ocha, benefited greatly in the nineteenth century from the expansion of European trade along the main route leading into the interior from Itobe, and its royal connexions gave it an advantage over other groups in the area in exploiting this traffic. For almost two generations Ofoke dominated this district to such an extent that the traditional clan at Igoti was virtually supplanted administratively and juridically. But in recent years the balance has shifted again, and the administrative office of *gago,* which was for a time held by the Ofoke group, has been reunited with the traditional land chief's title of Ochabe.

The development of Ofoke provides an interesting case study of growth and accretion within the royal clan, and its structure repays detailed analysis as an illustration of the processes by which the royal clan recruits and assimilates a proportion of its members. The hamlet was founded by Apẹ, a male slave of the Ata Idoko Adẹgbẹ, who was commissioned to farm for the Ata in this area and provided with capital for trading on his master's behalf. Historically, the hamlet achieved its greatest expansion in the next generation under the dynamic leadership of its founder's daughter, Ochonia Apę, who was given the royal title of Akuma Ata and greatly favoured in other ways by the Ata Oboni. Ochonia accumulated great wealth first as wife of an alien District Head at Dekina and then through trading. She was later made the administrative head of the entire Itobe District, with the modern title of Onu Itobe. In Amę's reign, when the Ocholi lineage came back into power, her fortunes declined, and she lost this adminis-

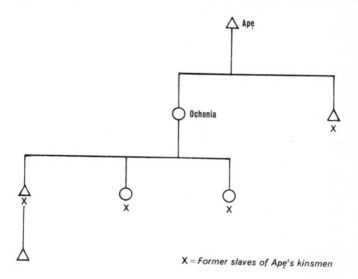

X = *Former slaves of Apę's kinsmen*

FIGURE 20. ASSIMILATION OF SLAVE-BORN FOLLOWERS

trative post, and, in the next reign, the office of *gago* when this was returned to the landowning clan at Igoti.

In the last few years of Ochonia's life, the hamlet of Ofoke comprised about fifty households. Most of the heads of families in these units claimed full membership of the Ocholi lineage through Apę, the founder, who was regarded by this time as a free-born son of Idoko Adegbe. Amongst these households at least four were founded by slaves belonging to various descendants of Apę, but the individuals concerned claimed free-born status as shown by the genealogy above.

Actual relationship   Modified version

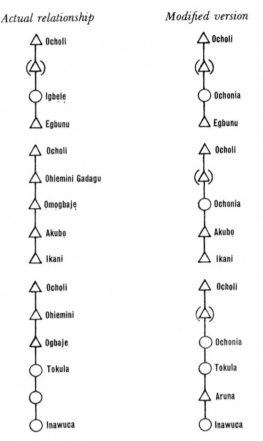

FIGURE 21. MODIFICATION OF GENEALOGIES IN THE
OCHOLI LINEAGE

A further four households were founded by kin from other branches of the Ocholi lineage or by blood kin distantly related to Apẹ's putative branch of the Ocholi lineage. In these cases the genealogies given modified the actual kin ties as shown in figures 21 and 22, to give subsequent descendants the status of full members of the kin group founded by Apẹ himself.

The extension of royal influence in outlying districts is correlated, as we saw earlier, with the development of kinship ties that perpetuate the system of links created by marriage between the royal and non-royal groups. In cases where royal hamlets become locally dominant this network of kinship ties tends to spread beyond the district in which the hamlet is situated, and gives rise to loose cognatic kinship groupings that ramify over a wide area. These groupings are described

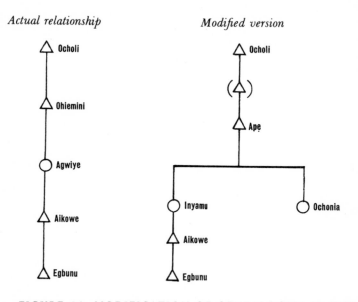

FIGURE 22. MODIFICATION OF GENEALOGIES IN THE
OCHOLI LINEAGE

by the term *aju*, which basically means grandchildren or descendants in the sense of a nuclear agnatic group, together with its *ǫmonobulę*, or uterine kin.

In the Ọjọ district the kin network of the royal hamlet of Icalaba overlaps with another network of royal kinship ties which centres on the village of Iga, in the neighbouring district of Ọba. The *onu anę* in Igebije is *ǫmonobulę* to the Amonojio group at Iga, and this extraneous kinship tie provides an important alternative to his alliance with the Ogaaji Aku branch of the Ocholi lineage. Furthermore, through this tie the District Head participates in the loose cognatic grouping

187

formed by the descendants of Amonojio, who are known collectively as aju Amonojio. This group affiliation is not important outside the borders of his own district, but within the Ojo area the group of hamlet heads who share kinship ties with Iga form a closely united body.

CHAPTER FIVE

IGALA CONCEPTS OF KINGSHIP

IGALA kingship has frequently been cited by students of comparative ethnography in proof of the supposedly widespread belief in Africa in the divinity of kings. Frazer included the Ata of Idah with examples of kingship that were listed together under the heading, 'human gods in Africa'. And he quoted a statement taken down by the early explorers from the Ata which seemed to show that the Igala king believed in his own divinity.[1] Seligman was able to elaborate this reference by using the detailed ethnographic material made available by Clifford after Frazer's time. An account by Seligman of the installation procedure at Idah forms one of the most detailed pieces of evidence in his analysis of divine kingship in the Western Sudan. He modified Frazer's interpretation of the somewhat scanty earlier references by concluding that the Igala kingship had fallen away from its complete and earlier form in which the king was ceremonially slain. But he accepted the basic hypothesis that the king was regarded as quasi-divine. Seligman wrote: 'the remainder of the formulae of the Divine Kingship (his freedom from human needs—his control of the elements and so of the harvest, etc.) were kept up'.[2]

In a recent study of kingship in Africa,[3] Dr Irstam has carefully synthesized the criteria of divine kingship employed by earlier English and German writers, and created an index of typical features which is extremely useful in comparing the Igala system with other sacral or divine monarchies in Africa. Dr Irstam includes the Igala in his examples, and suggests that it conforms to the ideal type of this institution in respect of the following major categories:

The coronation ceremony.
The king has a special sceptre, throne, and crown.

[1] Frazer, Sir J. Y., *The Golden Bough,* 3rd edition, 1912, Vol. 1, p. 396.
[2] Seligman, C. Y., *Egypt and Negro Africa,* 1934, p. 48.
[3] Irstam, Tor, *The King of Ganda,* 1944.

The king was killed.
The king's death was kept secret.
The king's office was sacral or quasi-divine.[1]

Using sources that were not available to Dr Irstam we can extend this list by including further criteria of his that seem to be relevant to the Igala case. Using his typology, the kingship shows the following special characteristics in addition to those already noted by Dr Irstam:

Succession is paternal.
The king wore a lion or leopard skin (a symbolic one).
The king wore moon ornaments.
The king's death was not to be mentioned.
The king was believed to be transformed after death into a lion or a leopard.

Typologies and comparative studies of this nature serve a useful purpose in drawing attention to the ritual aspects of kingship in Africa and to the fact that the king, in a typical kingdom, is directly or indirectly responsible for festivals and religious acts on which the welfare of the whole community is thought to depend. But they tell us little about the religious conceptions actually involved. And it is surely unjustifiable and extravagant to assume that these notions, if better known, would amount to what Dr Irstam calls belief that 'the king was the living expression of a permanently divine principle, which was considered to have begun with the primeval father and to continue in all eternity'.

The theory of divine kingship has many methodological weaknesses, but is particularly vulnerable with regard to the methods adopted to account for discrepancies between the hypothetical ideal and the living reality of kingship ceremony and ritual in different parts of the world. Frazer used an evolutionary model to overcome this difficulty, explaining discrepancies and missing links in the ethnographic data by the hypothesis of development from a public magician through the priest-king to the divine king. But, as Seligman shows by reversing part of the order of evolution, this sequence is an assumption that cannot ultimately be proved or disproved,

[1] Irstam, Tor, *The King of Ganda*, 1944.

and if this is the case it follows that the whole process of explaining discrepancies is largely one of a priori rationalization.

Other writers, of whom Dr Irstam is the most systematic in his methods, have tried to avoid this same difficulty by regarding the divine kingship as an ideal type that has become modified in the process of historical diffusion from a particular source. But apart from the impossibility of locating this source and of proving the course of the supposed diffusion, it is extremely doubtful whether the connexion between the examples cited and the ideal type of the institution is sufficiently close to justify regarding the model as a true empirical abstraction from the facts available. In most cases the comparisons are so loosely controlled that resemblance is proved only in a number of general features, and not in a sufficient number of particular details to be definitive. This is especially true of writers like Frazer and Hocart who equate one principle with another in such a way that detailed analysis of the examples cited becomes superfluous. In the more carefully controlled comparison made by Dr Irstam, the degree of conformity between the examples and the ideal type is still so slight that the reality of the model must be suspect. For instance this author compares the coronation ceremonies of sixty-two different African tribes against a list of twenty-seven items that are supposed to represent the stages of development of the coronation in the ideal pattern of sacral kingship. But it is clear from Dr Irstam's own table that the degree of correlation with this ideal type is extremely low. Fifty-five of the sixty-two tribes each display less than a third of the traits listed. The remaining seven score less than two-thirds of the maximum of twenty-seven traits, and there is no tribe with more than seventeen of these stages in its coronation ceremony.[1] This failure of a critical and disciplined attempt at comparison inevitably arouses suspicion of the much looser comparisons made by the earlier writers.

This methodological weakness points directly to the fact that divine kingship theory is often contradicted by the empirical evidence. And this is true in particular of its basic premiss that the king is universally believed to incarnate a deity or divine

[1] ibid., p. 56.

principle in his own person. On the one hand this view has had to be modified by the admission that many kings are not divine in this sense, but that they are rather, in Seligman's phrase, priest-kings. On the other it has been maintained in this restricted application by a kind of special pleading that relies on esoteric facts such as the supposed ritual killing of kings and conservation of personal divinity by other means. The interpretation of this kind of evidence is, to say the least, open to question since in general the studies cited are not sufficiently detailed to place it beyond doubt that the peoples concerned actually hold the kind of beliefs attributed to them. Professor Evans-Pritchard has suggested an alternative interpretation of the symbolism of king-killing notions held by the Shilluk, and Dr Lienhardt has similarly thrown doubt on the Frazerian interpretation of these customs among the Shilluk.[1] Among the Igala, similarly, the possibility of assassinating a king is related to the effects of a long or oppressive reign on the balance of power between lineages within the ruling house and the abstract notions that Igala hold on this subject are diametrically opposed to Frazer's hypothesis that the king's subjects fear a diminution of royal power.[2]

The root of this matter seems to be that the terms divine and divinity have no meaning in relation to kingship except as a loose but convenient way of referring to the complex spiritual qualities and principles that uphold systems of monarchy in Africa. If we accept the view that belief in the sacredness of the king's office is commoner than belief in incarnation of an actual deity, and that there is no historical or evolutionary connexion between these different forms of the institution, then it is clearly necessary to establish the ritual difference between the king and his subjects empirically before any valid generalizations can be made about the religious symbolism of

[1] Evans-Pritchard, E. E., *The Divine Kingship of the Shilluk of the Nilotic Sudan*, 1948, and Lienhardt, G., 'The Shilluk of the Upper Nile' in *African Worlds*, ed. Forde, D., 1954.

[2] In this rotating system of succession any king who lives too long blocks the way to office for the elders of an entire maximal lineage. Of the Ata Ekalaga, who was murdered for this reason, the Igala say that the king's medicines were in this case more powerful than those of his rivals and they imply that the king gained rather than diminished in ritual power as his life was prolonged.

kingship in the various parts of Africa. The early explorers,[1] and many subsequent writers, have been so impressed by the difference between the ethos of acephalous political systems in Africa and the apparently deeper spiritual qualities of centralized monarchies that they have assumed the existence of a spiritual gulf between the king and his subjects in the latter type of system. But in Igala at least, the king's religious duties are congruent in every respect with those of clan and lineage heads in the society as a whole. And it is only as a symbol of the interdependence of parts in the whole system of ritual and political offices that the king is responsible for the welfare of the nation.

The symbolism of kingship in Igala falls naturally into two major divisions centring on the king's role as clan head and on his position as head of a centralized system of territorial administration. On the one hand the king's ritual status is defined by his relation towards the royal ancestors, whose cult is one of the central themes of the national religion. On the other hand he is the ultimate custodian of the national land shrine, erane, which symbolizes the moral and spiritual welfare of the Igala as members of the same political community. The polarity of this ritual dichotomy appears in the existence of two major royal festivals, one oriented towards the king's ancestors and the other towards the land shrine and activities associated with the communal use of the land. On the day of the king's installation, similarly, there are two major stages, one in which the king halts at the boundary of the royal burial ground, where the king is invested, and another at the site of the land shrine, where the king delays again to receive the homage of the kingmakers and the other traditional officers of state. The ritual objects used by the king in the palace likewise fall into two distinct classes, expressing the dichotomy of the king's ritual functions. Nevertheless although there is an intellectual separation in Igala culture between these aspects

[1] The speculation that occurs in the early records of Niger exploration about the Ata's divinity may well have been inspired by the contrast that met the expeditions, between the freedom of the Eze's subjects at Aboh (downstream from Idah) and the devoted submissiveness apparent in court procedure at Idah. The explorers regarded the system at Aboh as a monarchy in name only, whilst the Igala type fulfilled their highest expectations of an African ruler's authority and position.

of kingship which justifies dividing them for description and analysis, it must be emphasized that the two are complementary and that the reality of kingship is represented more accurately by talking of their fusion and interpenetration than by thinking of them as distinct. It is the fusion and inter-action of these two sets of ideas which largely accounts for the ceremonial aspects of the kingship; the regalia and insignia of office represent the undivided aspect of kingship and symbolize the merging of different ritual and political capacities in the image of a single institution.

It will be useful to preface a detailed analysis of the king's ritual duties with two general remarks. The first is that the Ata is not regarded by the Igala as being divine in the sense of incarnating a god or deity in his own person. A remark made by the Ata to the officers of the 1841 Niger expedition has been quoted by several writers to prove that the Ata regarded himself as divine. He said, 'God made me after his own image; I am all the same as God; and he appointed me a king.'[1]

The contemporary writers who recorded this statement seem to have regarded it as an arrogant metaphor rather than as a claim to godhead, and the metaphorical character of the remark appears clearly in the use of the pidgin English phrase 'I am all the same as' which implies comparison and not identification. However one interprets this statement, and as Frazer himself saw, it is equivocal as it stands, and can be read to mean that the Ata accepts no higher authority than that of the creator. It is also possible that the king was using an alien conception of the nature of God to demonstrate the nature of the Igala social order. In many proverbs and ritual sayings the Igala introduce concepts from other languages to portray their own ideas metaphorically. For instance one of the Ata's praise names says—

> Ata, olisa okẹ, i a kpẹ i a du.
> Ata, God the great, he shares out and takes away.

The term for God, *olisa*, is a Bini or Western Ibo category.[2] Its introduction, in place of the normal Igala term, Ọjọ, can

---

[1] Allen, W. and Thomson, T. R. H., *Narrative of the Expedition to the R. Niger in 1841*, 1848, Vol. 1, p. 288.

[2] *Okẹ* is probably the Ibo term *okẹ*, 'male or masculine', used here in the sense of masculine and powerful.

be regarded as a poetic device to compare the role of the Ata with that of the supreme God without actually identifying him with the deity. The second phrase expands the metaphor by saying that the king is his own arbiter in deciding what people deserve; there is no appeal from his decisions.

The second preliminary remark is that the Ata himself does not make any ritual offerings or perform sacrifices in public.[1] Each shrine or cult object with which the king is concerned has its own custodian who is responsible for the oblations and other forms of direct contact. The procedure followed when the Ata goes to the shrine in person is for the priest to kneel or squat in front of the central point of the shrine whilst the Ata sits slightly to one side, and passes his offerings to the priest for presentation or sacrifice. After handing over the ritual offering the Ata makes an invocation, *i agule*, which is recapitulated by the priest before the offering is brought in contact with the shrine.

This procedure is not unique, but follows the pattern standard to all ritual activities in Igala in which the hereditary element is pronounced. In ancestral rites, for instance, the ideal procedure is for an *ǫmonobulę* to perform the oblation whilst the family head sits outside or at the entrance to the ancestral shrine, *unyi ibegwu*. The acolyte repeats the latter's invocations and ritually presents whatever has been offered to the cult symbols. Similarly at district land shrines, the District Head makes his offerings and invocations through the intermediacy of a uterine kinsman.

One function of this division of labour is to stress the interdependence of the two principals and to symbolize their different contributions. In the case of royal ritual the division has political associations symbolizing and giving effect to the king's dependence upon his officers of state. But this custom also emphasizes the impersonal character of ritual and places the act in a dimension which transcends the limitations of the actors' own personalities. The king's ritual acts, like those of the individual family head, recreate what Malinowski termed a greater and more relevant reality, a mythical situation in which the king's role and that of his office holders are identified with

[1] The only ritual performed by the Ata himself is the daily offering of kola to the royal ancestors.

the parts played by the founders of the Igala state and with their successors who have upheld the continuity of these arrangements. It is in this sense that the Igala praise Ayagba by saying:

> Ayagba ọm Idoko, i ajẹ eyi egwu, i ajẹ eyiile.
> 'Ayagba, son of Idoko, (who) rules over both the dead and the living.'

Kingship and the clan system.

Igala myths describing the origin of the kingship and the subsequent emergence of the state imply harmony and co-operation in the fusion of indigenous and immigrant elements; the transfer of sovereignty to the royal clan was made voluntarily and the indigenous clans were incorporated with their basic structure unchanged. Idah, the capital, has an almost sacred significance to the Igala because of its great antiquity as a centre of government, predating the emergence of the ruling dynasty, and because its features symbolize the participation of the different hereditary groups of clans in the work of government. At the hub of the traditional layout the Ata's palace symbolizes the co-ordinating role of the royal clan and the Ata's own position as head of the clan system. Ritually it forms one of the principal centres of the royal ancestral cult, in which the king is so closely involved that it determines the broad pattern of his daily activities. The prohibition on the king's sleeping in another man's house, for instance, is related to his religious duties; it bears out the ideal that when a person is appointed head of his own clan, egba konẹ gbogujo olọpu, he returns to look after the home of his forefathers, i wa de unyi amukwọnw, and takes over the ritual duties of clan head, i wa chuchẹbọnwma.

The royal ancestors are represented in the king's palace by a set of okwutẹ, brass-bound wooden staffs that are wrapped individually in red cloth, ododo, and stored in the ancestral shelter, unyi ibegwu.[1] Offerings are made to these cult objects only during the Egwu festival, when they are displayed publicly. But symbolically they participate in the daily ritual of the same

---

[1] For an illustration of the royal okwutẹ see 'The Rise and Fall of the Igala State', Nigeria Magazine, no. 80, 1964.

name, *okwute*, which the Ata performs in the morning before holding his first audience, the *ugwa odudu*, or morning salutation.

Before performing the *okwute* ceremony, the Ata has to be ritually cleansed of any contamination incurred during the preceding day and night through sexual intercourse or through contact with any unclean agency. After being woken by Ogbe, the king dresses and goes into the next room where Orata takes chalk, *afu*, and the seeds of *ainwili*, for the purification ritual, *erola*. He first touches the king's forehead with chalk, then taking the *ainwili*, he touches the king's forehead again, followed by his shoulders, chest, sides, and knees. In performing this second act Orata repeats the formula:

ola we ki bie, u na gwo rinyoyi, era, era, era.
'Body yours that is spoiled I am cleansing thoroughly now, you be clean, be clean, be clean.'

This ritual of purification is not exclusively royal, but is used throughout Igala to remove contamination from individuals, cult objects, and also from herbal medicines. For instance, in preparing medicines, the last and most important stage before the herbs are cooked or infused is the *erogwu*[1] ceremony, in which the owner of the remedy ritually invokes the medicine, explaining the nature of the disease and saying what action is required of the medicine itself. *Ainwili*, or, more commonly, *ata* (alligator pepper) seeds are used as the medium of the incantation. They at once convey the force of the spell uttered by the owner, and ritually cleanse the medicine of any impurity that would affect its qualities and spoil its action. The vessel in which the medicine is to be cooked is usually included in this ceremony, consecrating it to its ritual task by removing the contamination incurred through mundane uses and through contact with women in an unclean condition. Both *ainwili* and *ata* have the quality of heat in common, their seeds contain volatile, peppery oils which burn the mouth and symbolize the ritual force of the invocation. Cleansing in this sense is virtually synonomous with activating; the ritual liberates qualities which are inherent in the individual or thing concerned and enables it to fulfil the function for which

[1] From the verb *era,* to purify, with the noun *ogwu,* medicine.

it was created. One could translate the imperative, *ẹra*, by the words 'be active' without distorting its sense in Igala.

One account of this royal purification ceremony claims that Ọrata masticates some of the *ainwili* seeds before invoking the substance with which he touches the Ata's body. This version says that the ritual ends with Ọrata holding the Ata's outstretched hands and ritually blowing, *efafu*, over them. This procedure is part of the purification ritual in connexion with medicine; the magician chews alligator pepper or *ainwili* and sprays juice over the bundle of herbs by blowing, *efia ru*. But it is unusual for this to be done in connexion with purification of persons, and there may be some confusion here with the act of blessing a person which is also performed by ritually blowing into their hands, *echadu wa*.

Following the *erọla* ceremony, the other senior eunuchs arrive, bringing a short brass staff, *ajibo*, and an iron cannon ball, *oyọ*, with kola nuts, *obi*, a small brass bowl, *anẹ*, and a cast brass cylinder, *akpa Ayagba*, for use as a stool. Sitting on this stool and facing the eunuchs, with the iron ball in front of him, the Ata begins to invoke his ancestors. One of the eunuchs breaks kola nuts and places them on the iron ball, whilst the Ata recites the praise name, *odu ukpaihi*, of a particular ancestor, striking the *ajibo* heavily on the ball at the conclusion of the verse. The eunuchs interject their own ceremonial greetings from time to time, with one person leading and the others replying in chorus, as in the following:

SOLO: *Ogbẹ gwata.* 'Ogbẹ salutes the Ata.'
CHORUS: *Gabaidu.*
SOLO: *Ọrata gwata.* 'Ọrata salutes the Ata.'
CHORUS: *Gabaidu.*

The reply uttered in chorus uses the normal royal salutation, *agabaidu*. This formula is repeated by the different eunuchs in turn, using their own titles, but there are also two variants which can be introduced at any stage. In contrast to the other greetings their symbolism is religious rather than political.

SOLO: *Okẹgga gwata,* or, *Okẹgga gwagu.* 'Okẹgga salutes the Ata.'
CHORUS: *Fiiid.*
SOLO: *Ojọ gwata.* 'God greets the Ata.'
CHORUS: *Gabaidu.*

The meaning of the first phrase is obscure to most Igala, and few informants could offer any interpretation. One possibility is that it preserves the salutation of an obsolete title, *okęggakini*, that used to be held by the head of the Ata's slaves. But this suggestion is usually rejected by the Igala, who associate *okęgga* with the cult object of the same name sometimes found on Igala shrines. *Okęgga* is an Igala version of the Ibo *ikęnga* and has similar associations with masculine achievement and individual good fortune. The Ibo derivation also appears in the word *agu*, leopard, which is used in the alternative as a synonym for Ata. We can perhaps translate this first phrase loosely as 'Let good fortune attend the Ata.'

Both this greeting and the second variant, *Qjǫ gwata*, are not restricted to the *okwutę* ceremony alone, but occur in any ritual performed by members of the royal clan. The second phrase is even more widely distributed, being repeated during ancestral rituals by clans that are not related to the royal group as a mark of respect to the Ata and as a token of their submission to his authority. *Qjǫ gwata* uses the verb *gwa*, to salute, in the sense of bestowing blessings upon, or showing goodwill towards. It can be translated, loosely, as meaning 'May God attend the Ata and bring him good fortune.'

In invoking the royal ancestors the Ata uses the cognomen adopted by each king on appointment as Ata and recites the particular verse or proverb associated with this nickname. These *odu ukpaihi*, 'names of power', tend to be abstruse and in many cases are untranslatable because they use phrases from other languages, Igbirra, Idoma, Ibo, and possibly Nupe. Alien phrases of this kind are usually followed by an Igala sentence which roughly defines what the Igala believe to be the sense of the borrowed words. But through this process of reinterpretation, the borrowings have become conventional ritual phrases which are not easily recognized by a speaker of the language concerned, and in many cases the original meaning is still unknown.

The invocations begin with four verses addressed to the land, which is represented at the *okwutę* ceremony by a small brass bowl, *anę*. These are followed by verses containing the praise names of Ayagba ǫm Idoko and his descendants in order of succession. These are uttered in the order given, so that the most recent Ata is always the last to be invoked in the ritual.

1. *Anẹ ki jonu anyudẹ, ki jonu anyi itẹkẹlẹmi.* 'Land that eats up the chief who wears copper (anklets) that eats up the chief who wears (fine) slippers.'

2. *Uwo nana togọ lị ma Ohiẹmini nana tọkọkọlọ lị.* 'A hill is greater than a valley, and the Niger is greater than any single-stick bridge.'

3. *An'ajibo chukpodu.* 'The land of *ajibo*[1] is the land's name-sake.'

Meaning that the land ruled by the Ata is fundamentally the same as the land of other kingdoms.

4. *An'Ayagba ọm Idoko.* 'Land of Ayagba, son of Idoko.'

5. *Otutubatu, ọmagili gbajẹ gbajẹ. Ma mata ki binw ma miye ki binw.* 'Otutubatu, that pounces suddenly and devours abruptly. Of unknown father and unknown mother.'

Otutubatu is the name of the ritual staff kept by Atẹbọ that I described earlier as representing the protodynastic ancestors collectively. This praise name, in association with the next verse, which is related to it, emphasizes the spiritual, almost psychic quality of the staff's attributes.

6. *Imọtọ rule omi kafu kẹrẹbọ.* 'The child runs from the rain, but the wind (that goes with the rain) catches up with him.'

This is a second praise name for the protodynastic ancestors, represented by Otutubatu. In one sense it refers to the king's own position in relation to his ancestors, and in another sense to the mystical sanctions underlying the king's authority over his subjects.

7. *Akp'Onu Apa ki a kp'Onu Ichi.* 'Whoever kills the Jukun chief (chief of the East) will also kill the Ichi chief (chief of the West).'

For Ayagba ọm Idoko, who conquered the Jukun and so established Igala autonomy. *Apa* and *Ichi* frequently stand for East and West in everyday speech, although there is no people with the second name in the West corresponding to the position of the Jukun or Apa in the East.

8. *Ajeyi egwu ki ajeyi ile.* 'Ruler of the living and the dead.'

9. *Ayagba Ọbaka ela ina abotifi gọnọ gọnọ.* 'Ayagba Ọbaka, sacred animal with long, thick, tail.'

---

[1] *Ajibo* is a short brass ritual staff, used by the Ata.

Ayagba Ọbaka is sometimes said to be the name of the legendary figure who saved Ayagba ọm Idoko from assassination. In this context he is identified with the leopard, mythical founder of the royal clan.

10. *Onu, akpaku maku bi.* 'Onu, the one who makes the fence knows how to open it.'

This verse praises Ayagba's eldest son, Onu, by referring to the popular tradition that he fortified Idah and built the ditches and walls that surround the city.

11. *Onu, hiuku hiuku.* 'Onu, the mighty one.'

12. *Ọkanigbogbo na ka hiẹtẹ hiẹtẹ.* 'The casqued hornbill says *hiẹtẹ hiẹtẹ* (a harsh sound).' See next verse.

13. *Irereku tagẹgẹnẹ ki agbanodo.* 'Spreading *irereku* that takes over the land of (one's) dwelling.'

These two verses are for Akogu, Ayagba's second son, who is traditionally supposed to have conquered the outlying areas of the kingdom.

14. *Akwa hioji ochimọgwa owẹhe tabo tabo.*
Meaning obscure.

15. *Ohiemi ocholi ẹbije, ki ma jebu.* 'Ocholi, iron of the finest grade, that never rusts.'

This and the verse above, are spoken in praise of Ocholi, Ayagba's third son.

16. *Idoko Adẹgbẹ ki chele agadagbolu.*[1] 'Idoko Adẹgbẹ whose gift-giving was astounding.'

17. *Ugbiti ọnye ka kade ugbogbo aji.* 'Mighty crocodile that stops us at the water's edge.'

My informants commented. 'If a person is seized by a crocodile the people who run to his help are powerless to do more than stand at the water's edge.'

18. *Uchiya miyanw ko.* 'The player has gone and taken his entertainment with him.'

The king is the source of his peoples' pleasure as well as of

---

[1] Some Igalas read this as *ki chele agadabulu*, 'who made gifts like the pigeon-pea plant', and relate it to the proverb—

> *agadabulu ki a gwodunw eju*
> pigeon-pea that strikes its master across the face.

This reference to the pigeon-pea's springy branches and bushy habit would imply ingratitude on Idoko Adẹgbẹ's part to an unmentioned patron or protector.

occasional sorrow. This and the preceding two verses are all spoken in praise of Idoko Adẹgbẹ.

19. *Agada Ẹlamẹ ọkpọku ki dalunọjẹ.*

Obscure to most Igala, and to Igbirra speakers, although one informant translated it as an Igbirra verse meaning 'clapper that is inside the bell'. Agada Ẹlamẹ is one of three kings who died without issue.

20. *Aji ina ki dan'Idoma.* 'The sacred (or, great) stream that is in Idoma land.'

This is spoken in praise of Agada Ẹlamẹ, and possibly refers to the tradition that he died in the Agatu area and is buried at Amagẹddẹ, near the river Benue. Idoma in this context is the ancient kingdom of Idoma, north of the Benue, which has now given its name to a wider tribal area.

21. *Onuche ohiegba okẹkẹnẹ ẹpu.*

Meaning obscure. Refers to the Ata Onuche.

22. *Obojoguu ki achoga ijẹlẹ.* 'Ball of medicine that cures the *ijele* sickness.'[1]

A praise name for the Ata Onuche.

23. *Mageni aganoku negba echi igabọ ki ma denyi gwẹgwọla.*

Meaning obscure. A praise name for the Ata Ẹkalaga.

24. *Amochẹjẹ adeji makwu kailo a bẹkẹta.* 'Amochẹjẹ took two and tied them up to make the third one afraid.'

25. *Aku otẹmẹjẹ ọm'Idoko. Odiba kwu kafu kpẹnẹ alimeji.* 'Aku the mighty, son of Idoko. When the one at the side died the one at the centre began to feel cold.'

Aku Odiba's second name, *odiba*, is taken from the proverb which is quoted in the second sentence.

26. *Okikilinyẹ ki ma diba nwafu.* 'Small tree stump that does not fear the wind.'

This is a second praise name for the Ata Aku Odiba.

27. *Okoliko uwa jeji k'ejiji jaga, ojika kpechi om'ohiegba* (or) *ojika kpechi om'Ayagba.* 'Okoliko, the world changes as fashions change; small bag (that is) child to the *ohiẹgba*, (or) that is child to Ayagba.'[2]

28. *Ame adenyi tọla ne daba loji. (Ame olofia deji tọla ki ma dabolache.)*

---

[1] *Ijẹle* is the term for a bobbin or spindle and may imply giddiness in this context.

[2] The first section is in the Ibo language, the second is in Igala.

A praise name for the Ata Amaga. Meaning obscure.

29. *Ọgbọwu ki a leku dẹbẹ, ẹbẹ ki ma leku dọgbọwu.* 'Aardvark that goes on its knees for the mound of earth, although the mound does not go on its knees for the aardvark's sake.'

Implying that the Ata is made great by the respect and efforts of his people in the same way that the mound left by the aardvark (which tunnels into the ground) is the most obvious sign of its activity.

30. *Ochẹjẹ, idu okakpuru ọnya,*[1] *una ki ma li ẹgben ki manẹ du jo.* 'Ochẹjẹ, lion that roars an unanswerable challenge, fire that saw no grass to burn and burnt the ground instead.'

31. *Ajidudu ki a bugbodu ailo.* 'Deep stream that frightens the clumsy person.'

32. *Oboni agwoshishi nẹ findẹgeli, udachi ane akpa ki cholugbo akpa.*[2] 'Oboni like a snake that lies across the path, wherever the solid trunk of a hardwood tree falls, there it will lie and enjoy old age.'

33. *Oguchẹ akiko ki akoji baba.* 'Oguchẹ, young child that will represent his father.'

34. *Atakpa awule ma ji agbiti.* 'The strong man is buried in the lazy man's parlour.'

Another praise name for the Ata Oguchẹ.

35. *Atabọ okọchiku ne tagba ojiji mu, mojiji kimọtọ mọọna da.* 'Atabọ, old and bent down catches a fearful thing, a fearful thing that would have made a youngster give way to it.'

36. *Obaje ọbagu tegwegwọ ki akponu oko ẹdọ biẹ.* 'Obaje, Patas monkey that moves stealthily and breaks the farmer's heart.'

37. *Ọgọ ina ki akp'aakpa biẹ.* 'Mighty flame that destroys the maize.'

This compares the Ata Obaje to the flame of a great bush fire that destroys maize in the farm.

38. *Amẹakpoli ugbakolo ki ma bun, ki aro ulaka ulaka.* 'Amẹ (nicknamed the) waves. Like the *ugbakolo* tree that does not flower but fruits by hatred.'

39. *Ogwu ku ma neju ọgwa ki dufu ejubi.* 'The war that they expected in front broke out behind them.'

A second name given to the Ata Amẹ.

---

[1] *Idu okakpuru ọnya* is an Igbirra phrase.

[2] *Agwoshishi nẹfindẹgeli* is an obscure phrase, not in Igala. Several informants suggested the translation given here.

In choosing an *odu ukpaihi* on acceding to the throne each king adopts a traditional saying which seems appropriate to his own conception of royal power. The complete series therefore comments, in poetic metaphors, on the nature of the Ata's power in general and of his relations with his subjects. But the verses also reflect the lineage and sibling rivalries created by the Igala pattern of rotating succession to the kingship. Sometimes in commenting on the significance of these praise names, the Igala refer to the events that led up to the accession. For instance Amocheje's praise name (24) is associated with the war that he had to fight against two of the ruling lineages before he was secure on the throne. Again, many of the verses refer obliquely to the element of chance in the succession, created by the situation in which the strongest and most likely candidate dies before his turn comes, leaving the opportunity to a younger brother. Atabo, for instance, was junior to a famous prince, Aku Agaru, but outlived him and so came to the throne. This explains the reference to the 'fearful thing', *ojiji*, which he shunned in his youth but grasped firmly later in life. Similarly, the Ata Ame was not expected to become king because he was a second son and his elder brother, Acho, was a comparatively young man when the preceding Ata, Obaje, began his reign. This explains his second cognomen which refers to war breaking out in an unexpected quarter.

When the *okwute* ceremony has been completed the Ata goes to an outer room and receives his traditional councillors, the *amomata*, and other visitors who may include titleholders from outlying areas. After this formal audience the king then breakfasts by himself, and receives visitors in private or rests until early evening when another audience, the *ugwa ane*, or evening salutation, takes place. There are no further ritual observances after the *okwute* ceremony, apart from the fact that any food or drink taken by the Ata is symbolically shared with the ancestors by placing a portion in the *ane*, a small brass bowl that forms a palace representation of the land shrine.

In the theory of divine kingship, one of the most important tokens of the king's divinity is his freedom from human needs, including the need for food. Customs of eating in seclusion, and of referring to the king's meals by euphemisms are interpreted in this approach as attempts to conceal the king's humanity behind a façade of separateness. In Igala, customs of this nature are well established conventions which do not serve the purpose of concealment since everyone knows and respects them. In general the Igala do not refer to the king as eating food, but say that he drinks air, *Ata a mafu*. Within the palace similarly the king's need of food is always referred to euphemistically. If he withdraws from company to eat it is said that the king is 'nursing a sick eunuch, Oyikwu', *i achudu Oyikwu*, or that he is busy, *i liọwọn*, 'he sees no chance', or, *i dejefu*, 'he is inside (the palace)'. If his wife wishes to announce that food is ready she sends a message to say *udu biẹ*, 'the thing used in nursing is ready'. Another conventional way of referring to the Ata when he is in the act of eating is to say *afu aju*, 'the wind is blowing'.

This avoidance of discussing food and the question of eating in public is widespread in Igala and is not confined to the royal clan. A family head will eat in the presence of his own sons or close kinsmen, but not in the presence of clansmen or of strangers, and to avoid causing embarrassment if meals are either ready or in course of preparation, the subject is usually not discussed outside the intimate and narrow circle of those who will eat together. If visitors arrive at a compound and the person that they wish to see is indoors, eating a meal, euphemisms similar to those used in the palace are employed. The person's family reply to the visitors, *i dejefu*, 'he is inside (the house)', or *i a chudu*, 'he is taking care (of himself)'. If the second phrase is used it is immediately obvious that a meal is in progress; the first phrase could simply mean that the householder is busy, performing a rite or some other intimate task and cannot be disturbed. In either case the remark is also an indication that the visitor should sit and wait for a little while and that the person he wants to see has been notified of his arrival.

This conventional avoidance of the topic of eating has certain ritual associations that could be regarded as the ultimate cause of the formal behaviour in which these notions are expressed. Fear of sorcery is a primary motive in the custom of eating privately and in seclusion. There is a class of sorcery causing 'food sickness', *ọga ujenw*, which operates through charming a person's food, and it is believed to be sufficient for the sorcerer to see the person eating at a distance to cast the spell which introduces sorcery into the food and makes the victim ill. Suspicion of sorcery and witchcraft is especially strong between clansmen, and Igalas have often commented to me that they would rather eat in the presence of a complete stranger or a distant blood relative than in the presence of their own collateral agnatic kin. Clan heads, and others in positions of responsibility are particularly exposed to the dangers of sorcery. The sibling and lineage jealousies engendered within the clan focus on the clan head and the succession. But in addition, there are other kinds of evil magic, meant to influence judicial decisions and an official's public actions that need to be taken into account.

The ritual aspect of eating has a positive as well as a negative aspect in Igala. The meals taken by a person responsible for ancestral cults form a kind of communion with the ancestors, to whom a portion of the food is dedicated by placing it on the ground.[1] This custom is not widely observed in practice, but it nevertheless forms part of the ideal of the dedicated life that is led by an elder who takes over the family ancestral cults. The Igala say that when a man becomes old he no longer goes about but remains at home, and if in charge of the clan's *okwute* staffs, he frequently takes his meals in the room where they are stored. In a general sense, also, the restrictions on eating help to differentiate ritually the inner part of a man's house, the *anuku*, from the public part, *atakpa*, where he receives strangers. This is an important distinction in Igala compounds, it being a grave breach of etiquette for anyone other than *omonobule* or a close associate to enter the *anuku* without invitation. This inner courtyard is the centre of a man's ritual activities, the home of his protective medicines and personal shrines and of the ancestral cults on which the collective welfare of the family depends. The fact of withdrawal into this area at mealtimes symbolizes the essentially religious character of an adult man's life. Far from creating a gulf between the king and his subjects, as Frazer's theory would imply, the avoidances connected with the king's meals epitomize the basic religious functions of every clan head. The euphemisms

[1] In the Ata's case this token offering is placed in the ritual vessel, *ane*.

that are employed in this connexion reconcile these duties, and the restrictions imposed on a public figure by Igala notions of witchcraft and sorcery, with the conventions of hospitality and politeness to strangers and with the norms of co-operation and mutual trust between clansmen.

In addition to the palace symbols of the royal ancestor cult, the king's forbears are also represented ritually at Ojaina, by a set of nine graves and nine associated staffs, okwute. And the ritual staff, Otutubatu, that is kept by Atebo in a compound outside the palace forms a third distinct branch of the cult. During the king's lifetime these different cult symbols receive daily offerings and are cared for separately by different office holders, the Ojaina shrines by Eguola, the palace symbols by the Ata and his senior eunuchs and Otutubatu by Atebo. But once a year, and again when a new king is installed, these different manifestations of the royal ancestors are symbolic- ally reunited and combined through the participation of their custodians in a common festival. The annual ceremony, Egwu, and the accession rites are so similar in respect of offerings made to the okwute, staffs, and other permanent symbols that we need describe only the former in detail here.

Until they were abolished by law in 1956,[1] the Egwu and Ocho ceremonies at Idah were the two principal festivals of the Igala year, forming the year's seasons into a cycle alter- nating between the ritual of clan ancestors and the ritual of the land. The first of these festivals, Egwu, took place annually towards the end of the sixth lunar month, around August, when the rains were at their height and new yams had become plentiful. On the first day of this month the king sent a palace official to announce in Ajaka market, 9 miles from the capital, that *Egwu bojo ogwu nyeyoka inyini*, 'the Egwu festival will begin

[1] The abolition of these festivals was recommended by the Igala Native Authority Council after complaints had been received about cruelty in the method of sacrificing a goat at the Ocho festival. An unfounded accusation that the king made human sacrifices at these festivals also contributed to the abolition movement. These complaints and rumours were symptoms of a much deeper lack of confidence in the reigning king, Ame, who had quarrelled with most of his own traditional councillors and with the progressive elements in Igala. Opposition to Ame's rule caused the govern- ment to withdraw its recognition of the Ata in the same year and this was followed by Ame's suicide in June 1956.

in twenty-five days' time'. This proclamation set in motion the following train of events:

Day of month	Ceremony
1st	Proclamation made at Ajaka market.
21st	Offering made at Ojaina, the royal burial ground, to Otutubatu and the last nine kings.
25th (ede)[1]	Egwu Ata. Offerings are made at a special enclosure in the palace to Otutubatu and the last nine kings, followed by offerings to the remaining royal ancestors.
27th (ukwo)	Egwu Ayagba. A ritual performed at Ekwe's compound, commemorating Ayagba Obaka. Egwu Igala. The Achadu, Igala Mela, and Igala chiefs offer to their own ancestors, in a separate ritual.
28th (ede)	Ojo Ata. The Ata offers to his own ojo, representing his personal destiny.
3rd (ede)	Omakoji Ata returns from defence post outside the town.
4th (afo)	Ogbadu. Ritual by the Ata and all the Igala for ancestors who died violent deaths. Consecration of iron implements to Ogu.
5th (ukwo)	Ojo amomata. Royal clansmen offer to their own ojo, and to the ancestors of their own families.

TABLE 16. TIMETABLE OF THE EGWU FESTIVAL

The calendar dates of this festival are adjusted to fit the days of the week, shown in brackets, so that the ceremonies in which the Ata is involved fall on ede day, traditionally the most propitious day of the week. Afo is avoided on the other hand, because it is ritually unpropitious for the royal clan. But its unlucky associations make afo an appropriate day for the ogbadu festival, which has associations with war and sudden death.

I give below fuller notes on the individual stages of the Egwu festival, showing the part played by different officials, and also discussing the underlying ritual symbolism.

[1] The names in brackets are those of the appropriate day of the Igala week.

Ọjaina.

Four days before this offering is made, the palace eunuchs and *ẹdibo* go to the royal burial ground to clear the path leading into the grove, and to repair the small shelters housing the graves of the last nine kings. Soon after this, Atẹbọ brings the ritual staff, Otutubatu, to Ọjaina in readiness for the offering. On the day of the ritual he and Eguọla go with an assistant, Adọkpulu, to the grave of the Ata's father. The staff, Otutubatu, is stood on a stone, leaning against the wall, and offerings are made near its foot. Gifts are then brought forward from the Ata, comprising a goat, kola nuts, and an *okpẹ* cloth. The goat is killed at this grave, and kola nuts are offered before the group moves on to place kola on the graves of the other eight kings. Later, when the goat's flesh has been cooked, a portion is placed on each of the graves, together with cooked yam.

Egwu Ata.

Before the day of this ritual, two temporary ancestral shelters, *unyi ibegwu,* are erected in the Ata's compound by the palace eunuchs. These are made of palm fronds, thatched with grass, and house the *okwutẹ* or ritual staffs which are transferred here from the palace for the week of the festival. The two houses are screened by a fence hung with cloth, the enclosure thus formed being called *udọja.* In transferring the *okwutẹ* they are divided so that those representing the ancestors of the Akumabi moiety are in one house whilst those of Akogu and Ocholi lineages are placed in the other. One informant claimed that there are three houses in *udọja,* one for each of these three groups. But the principal participants denied this, and their own statement, that there were two houses, is in closer accord with the physical division of the palace area into two.

On the day of the ritual, the king, senior eunuchs, Eguọla, and Uchalla, representing the *ẹdibo,* wait for Atẹbọ, who is summoned from his house by Ogbẹ with a gift of kola nuts. Atẹbọ twice refuses to come, but at the third request goes to the *udọja,* carrying Otutubatu. The king and these officials then process three times around the enclosure before entering it, and finally go in and enter the *unyi ibegwu* of the king's own

209

ancestors. Ten kola nuts are given to Atẹbọ, who divides the first one at the foot of Otutubatu. Four or five nuts are then divided by Atẹbọ and Eguọla alternatively, placing fragments on the *okwutẹ* of the king's immediate ancestors. Before the kola are divided, the king invokes his ancestors, and his prayer is repeated by Atẹbọ. After this, four or five nuts are broken in the same way in the next hut for the immediate ancestors of the other reigning branch.

After the kola nuts have been offered, nine goats are sacrificed by Elakwu, with the assistance of Atẹbọ and Eguọla. This is done in two stages, following the same procedure as the division of kola for the last nine kings. After this a further fifteen goats are sacrificed for the remaining royal ancestors, half in the first shelter and the rest in the other house.

The Ata then leaves the *udọja* and goes to a separate shelter where he is acclaimed by the titleholders and their followers. They come up to the king in order of precedence, with the royal masquerades arriving first, followed by the *amọmata*, then by the Achadu, Igala Mela, and Igala chiefs. The leader of each group is given a calabash of kola nuts by the Ata, together with three or four pots of beer or wine, and after greeting the king and prostrating before him the group withdraws to one side, leaving the centre free for new arrivals to approach the king; and for the royal masquerades to dance in his honour.

Egwu Ayagba and Egwu Igala.

The separation of the ritual activities on this day into royal and non-royal elements provides a key to the symbolism of this stage of the festival. The Achadu, Igala Mela, and Igala chiefs offer to their own clan ancestors individually, staying at home in the morning to perform the ritual in their respective *unyi ibegwu*. In the afternoon the *amọmata* gather at Agaidoko's compound and wait there whilst the Ata goes in procession from the palace to *okẹt'Ẹkwe*, Ẹkwe's compound.[1] The latter group, accompanying the Ata, comprises Atẹbọ, and five senior eunuchs, followed by the other eunuchs leading a rider-

---

[1] Before the procession moves off Ẹkwe ritually purifies the Ata by touching him with a whip, *itali*.

less horse. This represents a legendary incident in which Ayagba Ọbaka, a contemporary and friend of the Ata, Ayagba ọm Idoko, gave his life by impersonating the king on an occasion when it was known that there was a plot to kill him. This legend relates that the king's son, Ọgadọ, had conspired to kill his father when the latter rode out in procession. But the second Ayagba took the king's place and was speared to death whilst riding on horseback, dressed in the royal robes.

This Ayagba, the 'king's friend', *onukwu Ata*, is commemorated by an *okwute*, staff, kept by Atẹbọ, and by the association of his grave with Ẹkwe's[1] shrine, which is under the jurisdiction of Ẹnẹfọla. On the day of Egwu Ayagba, the Ata offers a goat and kola nuts at this shrine, addressing the invocation to Ayagba Ọbaka (Ayagba *onukwu Ata*) and returns afterwards in procession to the palace.

This ritual and ceremony symbolize the danger to the unity and well-being of the royal clan of rivalry over the succession, and associate the royal ancestors with ritual sanctions against conspiracy by any member of the clan. The legend of Ayagba *onukwu Ata* forms one among many stories of attempts by heirs in line to eliminate their rivals and seize the throne. But from one aspect it is unique in referring to the founder of the dynasty, it is thereby associated with the clan as a whole, and not with a particular lineage, as the other stories of succession rivalries are.

The burial of Ayagba in Ẹkwe's compound identifies his rescuing of the king with the protective influence of the royal ancestors, and also incorporates protection of the king's life in the ritual functions of this masquerade. Ẹkwe, like Otutubatu, is a visible manifestation of the ritual authority that is vested in the royal ancestors, and the masquerade portrays dramatically the ancestors' watchful interest in the affairs and conduct of their descendants. On the one hand Ẹkwe disciplines the king himself, in the sense that he maintains the ritual purity of the palace and of the king's own person. But on the other hand, Ẹkwe also symbolizes the ritual sanction behind the king's authority over his own clansmen. The association of Ẹkwe and Ayagba *onukwu Ata* testify to the benevolent

[1] Ẹkwe is the senior royal masquerade, and in the case of Ẹnẹfọla, the shrine of Ẹkwe forms part of Ẹnẹfọla's compound.

intervention of the king's ancestors on behalf of the greatest of the Igala kings. And the legend, recreated annually by the Egwu ritual, contains a quasi-mythological precedent for the inevitable failure through their intervention of attempts on the king's life by his own clansmen.[1]

Significantly, this ritual occurs on a day when each clan is concerned with its internal hierarchy of spiritual authority, and not with the opposition of clans to one another. The Igala Mela and Igala chiefs do not visit the Ata collectively on this day, but celebrate their own ancestral rites privately. The only way in which they participate in the royal ceremony at *Okẹtẹkwe* is as follows. In the evening after dark, when the Ata has returned home, Aleji goes from Igala Mela and makes a circumference of the palace, playing a large iron gong, *enu*. The present clan head commented that this was done to 'close the road to evil' and to any trouble that might afflict the Ata, *i akpoọna ẹbili kpai ẹnwu bibi ki fa kẹrẹbọ Ata*. Aleji then goes to *Okẹtẹkwe* and searches the shrine until he finds a thigh of the goat sacrificed there earlier in the day. This portion had been concealed by Elakwu, Atẹbọ, and Ẹnẹfọla when the goat was divided between them. The meat is taken home by Aleji but is not eaten by him; the Ata redeems it from him the next day by sending a messenger with a gift of kola and some other meat.

The clandestine aspects of this minor ritual can be associated with the fact that there is no formal public co-operation between the royal clan and the Igala Mela on this day. As a body, the kingmakers have no connexion with the ancestral sanctions that function to maintain the solidarity of the royal clan. But they are indirectly involved in the Ayagba incident through the expulsion and punishment of the son who conspired against the Ata. Tradition records that Ọgadọ was executed by the Ochai Ata, and that his corpse was buried outside the boundary of the palace area, formed by the wall running between Idah and the Igala Mela quarter. The head was interred at Ukwaja,

---

[1] Writing of this ceremony Seton said that a goat was sacrificed over the grave (which is traditionally located in Ẹkwe's compound) and that the Ata made the following invocation—'If my successor desires my death that he may have my title, may Ajẹgba Akwabobo slay him'. Seton, R. S., 'Notes on the Igala Tribe', *Journal of the African Society*, Vol. XXIX, 1929–30, p. 155.

which is an extension of the Igala Mela area, guarded by the Amanata, a senior royal councillor. But the body after the head had been removed, was buried separately in Ayija, the traditional seat of the Aleji titleholder, and at a site near the centre of the Igala Mela area. In view of these associations, we can regard Aleji's role in the ceremony as expressing his association with the punishment of the Ata's son. The goat's leg that is hidden is a symbolic payment for his ritual services, acknowledging the king's debt to him without admitting a public involvement on this occasion between the royal clan and the corporation of kingmakers. The playing of the *enu* symbolizes the protective role discharged by Aleji as custodian of a somewhat sinister royal grave,[1] and renews this ritual bond between his own title and the king's.

Ọjọ Ata.

In Igala religion the term *ọjọ* has two distinct connotations. One use describes the supreme god, *Ọjọ*, who is the creator of mankind, and, in a looser sense, of the world as a whole. The second use, which is usually qualified by a possessive pronoun, noun, or person's name, refers to the relation between an individual and a particular ancestor who is believed to control or predispose the person's destiny, and who is in some respects reincarnated in the individual concerned. *Ọjọ Ata* uses the term in its second sense of the king's personal destiny, symbolized by a special relationship with one particular ancestor.

This concept, like the concept of royal ancestors in general, is in most ways parallel to the beliefs held about *ọjọ* in Igala society as a whole. Every Igala has an *ọjọ* and makes offerings to this ancestor at regular intervals, as part of the ritual of ancestral festivals, and also at other times on the advice of the Ifa oracle. One respect in which the Ata's cult is different is that it has a permanent symbol of the ancestor, in the form of a miniature box-stool, covered with red cloth. But this is used in association with the standard forms of approach to *ọjọ*, which consist of using an *okwute*, or a grave-mound, *ojinoji*, or simply of scraping a small hole in the earth in a spot intimately

[1] This gong belongs to the class of ceremonial *enu* gongs that are played at chiefs' installation and funeral ceremonies.

associated with the ancestors or with the domestic life of the person concerned.

On the day of Ọjọ Ata, the king goes in the evening to the *udọja*, together with the senior eunuchs and Uchalla. The cult symbol representing the king's *ọjọ* is taken into the shelter of the ancestor concerned and placed on the ground in front of the *okwutẹ* representing him. After kola nuts have been broken and offered to convey the king's invocation to his *ọjọ* a goat is sacrificed by Elakwu, and some of its blood is allowed to run into a small hole dug in front of the cult symbols. The Ata then retires to the public shelter outside the *udọja*, and is greeted there by his titleholders, following the same order of precedence as on the first day. On this occasion the *amọmata*, kingmakers, and other chiefs bring gifts individually, usually a bowl of kola nuts each, with a small sum of money added, and a pot of beer or calabash of wine. In return the Ata provides food, which is shared amongst the different sections of titled men. Of the royal masquerades only Ẹkwe comes out on this occasion.

Ogbadu.

On the evening before the Ogbadu festival, one of the traditional councillors, the Ọmakoji Ata, ceremonially returns to the capital from a defence post which he is supposed to have been occupying throughout the Egwu ceremonies. It is his task to watch over, *ede*, the town in case of surprise attacks by the king's enemies. But this duty lasts only whilst the king is personally engaged in ritual, and with the completion of the *ọjọ* ceremony, which nominally goes on until the eve of Ogbadu, he is free to return home. This re-entry to the capital is greeted with triumph by the members of his own lineage, and the Ọmakoji Ata is also welcomed by the Isawula masquerade, belonging to his *ohiegba*, Ugbọla.

The next day, at about eight in the morning, the two eunuchs Oyikwu and Elakwu fetch an iron staff, *okpa Akpakumabi*, from the palace, and plant it in the ground in Oyikwu's compound. They set it up on the site of a former shrine of an *ẹbọ* called Ọta, whose main shrine is at Ogurugu. This *ẹbọ* is believed to furnish portents of the Ata's death or of any other serious misfortune, in the form of shooting stars or meteorites that fall from the sky into the river Niger. On this day it is identified with the palace by the iron staff, which is decorated by Oyikwu with stripes and dots in red and white. After decorating the staff, the eunuchs sacrifice three cocks provided by the Ata, one for each of the major branches of the royal family, and also offer *igballa* (a paste of ground corn and palm oil), *okwuchu* (boiled yam sliced into pieces and served with palm oil), and kola nuts. When the Ogbadu ceremony was revived in 1961 the following invocation was made for this offering:

> *Alii donę wa ęcheyi kanę kinyọ, kanę ki ọchọlaafia, kọga ki tenyubi, kọla bibi ki akpanę bię ki tęnyubi. Eju ki liwa ọdoyi ki liwa ọdọmunę kano lia kawa chabęlę gę.*
>
> Alii (the reigning king) called us here to do this so that the land may be good, so that sickness may go back again, so that any evil matter which might spoil the land may go away. May the eyes that see us this year see us another year, so that we will come back again, and again make this (offering).

Following this ritual, the two eunuchs return home and wait until the evening before continuing with the second stage of the ceremony. Meanwhile, Igalas everywhere carry out the domestic ritual of Ogbadu, by consecrating iron implements at their own household ancestral shrines. Each householder places a token number of the iron tools, weapons, and other iron articles that he uses in ordinary life before the *okwutę* or *ojinoji* in the *unyi ibegwu* for which he is responsible. They are consecrated to Ogu, the god of iron and of sudden death, by painting them with red and white stripes in the same manner as the decoration of the iron staff at the king's Ota shrine. This is preferably done by an *ọmonobulę*, since the rite comes within the class of ancestral ceremonies. With the *ọmonobulę* officiating at the shrine, the householder then makes the usual preliminary invocation with kola nuts, followed by the sacrifice of a goat or a cock, according to the individual's means. Yams are also offered in different forms, first as plain roast yam, *iyalu Igala*, then as *okwuchu*, and finally, when the meat of the offering has been cooked, as pounded yam with a meat sauce, *ọję*.

In the evening, when all the household ceremonies can be

presumed to have ended, the royal part of Ogbadu continues, with the two eunuchs taking the iron staff from the palace to a spot near the Inachalo stream known as Alaku Agwe. A ford across the stream at this point used to be one of the main entrances to the capital, and is traditionally supposed to have been the centre of the Jukun attacks on Idah during their long siege of the capital. On reaching this spot Oyikwu plants the staff in the ground and sacrifices a tortoise to the land, repeating the invocation that was made earlier in the palace. From the stream the eunuchs retrace their steps along the main footpath to the palace until they reach ẹranẹ. Here the procedure is repeated, a second tortoise being offered, together with kola nuts.

In the palace, whilst the eunuchs are away, the king comes out to the shelter erected for his public appearances and sits there with his councillors, and a large gathering of chiefs and their followers. The royal masquerades come out, and go towards ẹranẹ to welcome Oyikwu at the completion of the sacrifice to the land. They lead him, holding the spear, in procession through Igala Mela, and receive kola nuts from the kingmakers as they pass their respective compounds. After all the masquerades have entered the palace area, Oyikwu also enters, dances around the ụdọga, and stands the staff in the ground before the Ata, where it remains until the gathering disperses.

In explaining the symbolism of the Ogbadu festival the Igala say that it is for the ancestors who died a sudden or violent death, *ma che todu abo kukwu achigili kpa·ma lẹ*. They include in this category people killed in war, or in accidents, and the victims of murder together with those executed for murder. For instance, the two graves of Ọgadọ are repaired for this day, if dilapidated, and Aleji includes Ọgadọ's name in the invocation made at his ancestral shrine. At Ukwaja the Amanata and Ọmakoji Ata go together to offer a cock at the site of Ọgadọ's burial, and on the way back make a pretence of quarrelling about their relative seniority and order of precedence. The Igala say that the ghosts of all ancestors in this category come out on Ogbadu day, and that anyone who goes into the bush before the offerings have been completed runs a grave risk of being made ill by them. The festival emphasizes

216

notions of spiritual anger and ferocity that are otherwise of little significance in Igala doctrines about the ancestors.

Ọjọ Amọmata.

On this day, following Ogbadu, the Ata's clansmen offer to their own *ọjọ* individually, presenting kola, a cock or goat, and then cooked yam, *ọjẹ.* Some informants regard this ceremony as an opportunity to invoke their own ancestors, and therefore perform the ritual in the *unyi ibegwu.* Others regard it as being confined to their individual *ọjọ*, and effect this exclusion of the other ancestors by making the offerings inside or near their houses instead of going to the ancestor shrine.

In the afternoon of this day Ẹkwe comes out for the last time and ends the festival by going to the various titled *amọmata*, to receive a share of the meat, kola, and beer or wine offered to the ancestors in each compound. We can relate this visitation to the appearance of ancestral masks at funeral rites to 'accept the rites', *egbicholo*, although it does not fall into exactly the same category. The Igala say that 'Ẹkwe blesses the *amọmata*', *Ẹkwe a dẹnyọnwuma (nwu amọmata).* The ritual nature of this visit also appears in the custom of pouring palm oil at the threshold of the compound, for the mask to make a footprint, which is later dusted with millet flour and left unswept until the rain washes it away.

The Egwu festival occurs at a time of the year when new yams are beginning to be plentiful, and we can regard it as a festival of thanksgiving because of its association with renewed prosperity and the restocking of household food stores. But it is not a first-fruits festival in the strict sense of the term. The Igala term for the ritual presentation of first-fruits, which are previously prohibited as food, is *ekahiana*, and this is rarely, if ever, used in speaking of Egwu. One informant said that until Egwu had been performed he would not store any quantity of new yams at home. But there is no prohibition on eating new yams before the festival. The Igala say, when asked this question, *awa chane juchu kpọkpẹ mẹ*, 'we have already begun eating new yams (before the festival)'. And this view is borne out by the popular names of the months that succeed the famine period. The fourth month, in which food supplies

217

are at their lowest, is sometimes called, *ukpọta ina*, 'the great famine'. The fifth month can be called, *urojẹ*, 'I begin to eat again', and the sixth month, in which Egwu falls, *urojẹ gbolo*, 'I eat plentifully'.

Egwu is a national festival for the Igala in the sense that it forms an occasion for ancestral ritual to be performed throughout the kingdom, and marks a principal stage in the sequence of the year. But it is of less importance to the landowning and other non-royal clans than to the royal clan itself and its immediate allies. The ancestral cult takes a slightly different form among the non-royal groups in charge of districts, and one of the major points of difference is that the non-royal groups have their own ancestral festivals, held at a different time from the festival of royal ancestors. Clans whose political functions are similar to those of the royal clan, and who govern at the provincial level rather than the district level, tend to conform to the royal model. Amongst the kingmakers, for instance, the Achadu keeps Egwu as the main ancestral ceremony for his own clan, whose titled members gather at Idah on this occasion in the same way as the Ata's own clansmen. But the Igala Mela keep a different festival, Okula, as their main ancestral celebration, and although they participate in the Egwu rejoicings, and make ancestral offerings on this occasion, the Okula rituals are their primary clan feasts, and they regard Egwu as a royal festival.

Ultimately, therefore, the ritual of this great ancestor festival stresses the separateness and individuality of clans in Igala, and also emphasizes the superordinate position of the aristocratic clans in charge of central government. In the metropolitan area and in the provinces the subordinate, non-royal clan heads send gifts of produce and game to the Ata and the provincial chiefs for Egwu, to recreate the relationship that existed between their own founding ancestors and the mythical leaders of the royal dynasty. The Achadu and other non-royal provincial chiefs participate in this ritual recognition of central authority. But the central importance of the royal ancestors in this festival shows that the notion of central authority is expressed mainly by the uniqueness of the royal clan and by the concept of unbroken royal descent.

Kingship, sovereignty, and the title system.

In connexion with the palace symbols of the royal ancestor cult the king maintains a small shrine of the land, *ane*, in the form of a small bowl into which portions of the king's food and drink are dropped. Writing of this cult symbol, in 1929, Seton says:

> There is a small brass pot, covered with cowries, called the Ane (not the same Ane as previously mentioned) believed to have been brought to Idah by the first Attah. A minute portion of whatever the Attah eats or drinks is placed in this. It is in charge of the Okoto (pronounced Awkawtaw). Nawa (one of the eunuchs, the Orata-chief of the eunuchs) takes charge of it on the death of the Attah. It is part of his duty to see that there is always water in it.[1]

Clifford writes similarly:

> a small portion of everything he eats or drinks is placed in a covered brass receptacle known by the name of 'Ane' which is held to be extremely sacred; it is never washed out but is kept filled with water. It is said that he spits the food and drink into the bowl and in so doing is ritually feeding the spirits of the ancestors—hence the extreme sanctity of the vessel.[2]

Both writers also comment on the fact that water from the vessel can be administered as an oath, Clifford describing this water as an 'oath-binder of great potency'.

This ritual sharing of the king's food with his ancestors is equivalent, as I indicated earlier, to the widespread conviction that meals taken by the senior member of a clan or lineage are a form of communion with the ancestors; an ideal which is expressed by his eating in the *anuku* and breaking-off morsels of food and placing them on the ground. Similarly there is the less formal custom of invoking the ancestors whenever hospitality to strangers is offered in the form of drink or kola nuts. The senior person present invokes the ancestors, *i a gule ibegwu*, before the gifts are shared out. If wine or beer is involved, a libation is poured on the ground, *ma cherane*. If kola is presented, the senior person present first splits the

[1] Seton, R. S., 'Notes on the Igala Tribe', *Journal of the African Society*, Vol. XXIX, 1929–30, pp. 162–3.
[2] Clifford, Miles, 'A Nigerian Chiefdom', *Journal of the Royal Anthropological Institute*, Vol. LXVI, 1936, p. 410.

kola into its component pieces, then holds them together to form a complete nut whilst he invokes the ancestors, and finally allows the nut to fall apart, *ekpa*, in a bowl placed on the ground. This ceremony of dividing kola, *ekpobi*, is an important rite of hospitality, and the fall of the kola segments constitutes a minor oracle for the business in hand and for the health of the one who presented the nuts, usually the head of the household.

The use of water from the *anę* in oath-taking is a special case of the form of oath known as *emunę*, 'drinking from the land'. Families or individuals wishing to settle a long-standing dispute arrange for the principals on either side to swear that they have settled their mutual quarrel, and they invoke the land itself to kill the guilty party in future if one transgresses against the other. To seal this compact, two small holes are dug in the ground, inter-connected at the bottom by a horizontal tunnel. When this has been filled with water, the principals drink simultaneously from opposite sides, so that they share the liquid with each other and with the earth at one and the same time. On account of his unique social position the Ata cannot take an oath in this form with his subjects. But the same purpose is achieved by using water which is symbolically in contact with the land, and ritually identical with water that the Ata has drunk.[1]

We can sum up the symbolic associations of the *anę* vessel in which the king places food and drink at every meal by saying that it symbolically unites the Ata with the land in which his ancestors are buried, following the normal Igala convention of regarding the floor of houses in the inner courtyard, *anuku*, as dedicated to the ancestors through the association of their residence and eventual burial in this area. This aspect of the land, *anę*, is different from that represented elsewhere in Idah by the national land shrine, *ęranę*, which is the royal counterpart of the district land shrines maintained by the heads of local political communities. The palace representation of the

---

[1] Seton writes that in administering oaths of loyalty to a member of a different branch of the royal family, water to which water from the *anę* had been added was poured over the *okwutę* or ancestral staffs of the person's ancestors. Seton, R. S., 'Notes on the Igala', *Journal of the African Society*, Vol. XXIX, 1929–30, p. 163.

land is not a direct manifestation of the latter shrine, but bears the same relation to it as domestic land shrines in general to the land shrines in each locality. This ritual vessel forms one of the exclusive insignia of royalty which by emphasizing the notion of descent help to assert the royal clan's supremacy and its inherent right to rule. The land shrine, on the other hand, symbolizes the royal clan's membership of a wider political community, and, by its association with the kingmakers, under-lines the essentially contractual nature of royal power in the Igala state. This difference is expressed neatly in the tradition that Ayagba stole the royal vessel, *ane̩*, from the Jukun palace, whilst he based his relationship with the kingmakers, and so with *e̩rane̩*, on his forefathers' own compromise with the indigenous, landowning population.

Offerings are made at the national land shrine whenever a new king is installed, at the Ogbadu stage of the annual Egwu ceremony, and also on any occasion when the Ifa oracle attributes misfortune to the ritual pollution of the land. The principal festival of *e̩rane̩*, however, is the Ocho ceremony, which represents the king in his capacity of territorial ruler, and draws a parallel between his position and that of the *onu ane̩* in non-royal ritual. It brings together the two principal ritual functions of the land chief, centring on hunting and on the local land shrine, and ritually inaugurates the new farming year in the same way that the *onu ane̩* concludes the communal activities of the dry season by initiating the *o̩de̩ o̩do̩*.

The Ocho festival complements the Egwu ceremony in the ritual cycle of the year in the same way that the land rituals performed by local communities are complementary to the festivals of clan ancestors performed separately by the in-dividual clans and clan segments in each neighbourhood. The ritual of the land is directed ultimately towards the collectivity of ancestors and symbolizes the participation of descent groups in a common political community. This symbolism comple-ments the expression of the different kind of loyalty created by the descent tie, to the group of one's birth, and to past and present members of this patriclan.

Like the Egwu festival the Ocho cycle overlaps two lunar months in such a way that its main stage coincides with the end of one lunar month and its concluding stages with the beginning of a new month. As the timetable shows, the date is announced on the first day of the twelfth lunar month, *ochu ęgwejï*, and the main events are arranged to occur on the twenty-fifth day. The later stages are more sharply divided, ritually and terminologically, from the central rite than the corresponding stages are separated in the Egwu sequences. But they nevertheless form part of a single cycle, whose events follow one another at fixed stages of nine days, *ojǫ mela*.

12th lunar month. (*ochu ęgwejï*)

    1st day.   Announcement of the date of Ocho.
    16th day. Obajadaka masquerade comes out.
    24th day. Offering made to the Obade *ebǫ*, behind the palace.
    25th day. Ocho ritual, performed at *anocho* and *ęranę*.

13th lunar month (*ochu ęgweta*)

    5th day.   Ogaingain festival.
    14th day. Offering to Inikpi, at *ogwega* (waterside).

TABLE 17. TIMETABLE OF THE OCHO FESTIVAL

Obajadaka.

On this day the Achadu Kịkịlị Ukwaja brings out a masquerade, Obajadaka, for which his clan is responsible, and takes it through the town. Popular accounts of this masquerade describe it as a single masked figure in the form of a narrow fabric cylinder capable of elongating its body to a height of 15 feet. In addition to this magical property of changing shape, the Igala say that the mask can alter its weight so that from being a crushing load which is beyond the strength of its supporters it can become so light that one man picks it up on the palm of his hand. The attendants and followers of the masker carry long peeled wands with which they flog one another viciously so that blood flows and the whips break into pieces.[1] This flagellation is a necessary part of the ritual.

    Obajadaka is a unique masquerade, in the sense that there

---

[1] The broken wands are sometimes incorporated, after the festival, in fetishes used to protect farm crops against theft. Another magical feature of the flagellation is that the wounds are always said to heal within a few days, no matter how grievous they are when first inflicted.

is no other masked performance of this character in Igala. But it has affinities of a general nature with ancestral masquerades and with nature spirits, *ẹbọ*, and seems to represent a compromise in this specialized genre between the two sets of ideas. In name the masquerade is identical with the ancestral masks of the Achadu's clan that appear singly when any member of the clan dies, to accept the funeral ritual on behalf of the clan ancestors.[1] But in spite of this parallel, the Igala regard the masquerade as an *ẹbọ*, or nature spirit, rather than an ancestral masquerade, *egwu*. The distinction turns on the fact that Obajadaka seeks out witchcraft in the manner of an *ẹbọ*, and is not concerned only with the welfare of members of a particular clan, but with preventing the action of witchcraft in society at large. *Ẹbọ* perform this function, Igala say, 'by seizing the witch and making the person confess', *ẹbọ a mu ajochu ki dalunw ka*. Similarly Obajadaka is believed to seek out witchcraft, and to make whoever is responsible ill until they confess their actions.

> When Obajadaka comes out, he passes through the town, and goes to the houses of witches. Later, the witch falls ill and begins to see Obajadaka at night in her dreams. The sickness continues until the witch takes a cock, kola, and other gifts to Obajadaka and offers them at the shrine.

The implication of this statement, in the context of Igala witchcraft beliefs, is not that the masquerade hunts down individual witches in the manner of a witch-finder, but that it creates a ritual condition which witches in general cannot tolerate. In Igala belief, for an *ẹbọ* to bring retribution upon a particular witch it is necessary for a person wronged by this witch to invoke the *ẹbọ*, *egẹbọ*, describing the harm done, and inviting the spirit to discover the person responsible and make her confess. But the *ẹbọ* also acts against witchcraft in general, at the request of its own priest, *atama*, who makes regular offerings to the spirit and maintains its shrine. Obajadaka's appearance at Ocho exemplifies the second rather than the first type of protective function, in which the *ẹbọ* comes out on behalf of the king to purge the land of witchcraft, *ochu*, and all

---

[1] The name of these masquerades means literally *obaje* (a man's name), *adaka*, (that goes) around.

evil magic, *inacha*. Four days after this appearance the king sends to the shrine of Obajadaka in Igala Mela a goat, a cock, an *okpe* (cloth), wine, and kola, to form the basis of one of the two main annual offerings that are made to the *ẹbọ*.

In the spiritual dimension that is represented by the masked plays in Idah, Ẹkwe and Obajadaka are complementary to each other, and the Igala recognize this by calling them husband and wife, *ọkọ nwọya*. Ẹkwe is the male and senior partner because of its identification with the royal clan, Obajadaka is female and junior because it belongs to the politically inferior group, and also because the associations of *ẹbọ* are mainly with femininity. One symbolizes the ritual authority latent within the royal clan, the other portrays the notions of moral and ritual community that underlie the cult of the land and the opposition of the kingmakers to the royal clan.

In the wider context of masquerading throughout Igala, Obajadaka's closest affinities are with the Abule, or land masquerades that were described in an earlier section. These two classes of masked play are different in form. Obajadaka is played by daylight and uses visual devices, whilst the Abule come out at night and are heard rather than seen. But they are similar in ritual function, and above all in their preoccupation with the problem of witchcraft in the community. They make a positive contribution to the moral and spiritual welfare of the community by lessening the incidence of *inacha*, the combination of ill-wishing, envy, and malice that predisposes people to commit acts of witchcraft and sorcery. And in their ownership they also reflect the responsibility of the *amọmonuanẹ* for the welfare of the whole community. Ultimately the division of functions between Ẹkwe and Obajadaka, the two principal Igala masquerades, reflects the distinction between particular groups of ancestors and the collectivity of ancestors. And this distinction, as we saw earlier, forms a paradigm of the two principal aspects of political structure in Igala.

Obade.

This ceremony is a comparatively minor one in the Ocho cycle, being restricted to the Ata and his wives, together with the palace officials and his senior royal councillors. For a description of its events I quote an eye-witness account pre-

pared by a detective during police investigations into allega-
tions of human sacrifice[1] that were made against the Ata Ame
Oboni.

At about 1700 hours the same day, the Ata went to a mud-
walled enclosure, some little distance from his compound, to
worship an idol (two small clay pots buried up to the neck)
called Obade. Four women (Ata's wives) had previously made a
fire just clear of the enclosure, they were chanting and incense
was being burned. On the arrival of the Ata the four women held
up their cloths in a ring around the fire. He passed them by,
entered the enclosure through a cloth covered gate, sat down and
exchanged greetings with about fourteen relatives grouped around
inside the enclosure. A white cock was killed by Ogbe (keeper of
the Obade juju) and some blood and feathers put on every one
of nine stones buried around the enclosure. The Obade was then
given some dried fish, meat, and kola nuts. There were about 200
people present.

This *ẹbọ*, like Obajadaka, is associated with the prevention of
witchcraft, and has the special function of guarding the king
against the practice of evil magic or witchcraft by his own
wives. In the past when the sasswood oracle, *oraci*, was employed to detect witchcraft, the Obade shrine was one of the
two sites at which the oracle was consulted where royal wives
were concerned. If the Ifa oracle indicated that witchcraft had
caused the death of an Ata or of an *ọmata,* sasswood was prepared at one of these two sites by Ogbẹ and Eju, and given
to the wives to drink. Those who were guilty of witchcraft
died on the spot, or became so ill that their lives had to be
saved by giving emetics; those who were innocent vomited
the poison of their own accord.

This ritual at Obade, which the Ata performs before leaving
his palace for the main Ocho ceremony, is in the nature of an
annual thanksgiving for protection against witchcraft in the
preceding year. But it also invokes the *ẹbọ* in particular to
avert witchcraft from the Ocho ceremony and to disclose
whether there is any evil influence present that will cause the
ritual of Ocho to miscarry. When the cock offered at the
shrine is inspected in the usual way to see whether the sacrifice
has been accepted or rejected by the spirit, if the testicles

[1] These accusations were eventually proved to be without foundation.

225

within the scrotum are clean, *fe*, it is a good omen for the ritual of the next day, and auspicious for the Ata to leave the palace. But if the testicles are 'spoiled', *kpabie*, by blood spots or other marks, the refusal on this occasion is an omen of witchcraft. In this event the Ata sends for Ohiuga to consult the Ifa oracle before proceeding with the Ocho ceremony, and does not leave the Obade shrine until a further sacrifice is propitious.

Ocho.

In principle after making a successful offering at Obade the Ata does not go indoors again, but leaves at once for the temporary camp in the bush, *anocho*, where the first stage of the next day's ritual is celebrated. But this condition can be met by leaving before dawn, so that the party in the camp is complete before sunrise. I give below in full a continuation of the report quoted earlier describing the events that occur on this day.

On 16 April 1955, at about 0400 hours Ata led a procession of about 250 people to a spot between his compound and the G.R.A. (government residential area) known as Ane Ocho, where a red blanket tent had been set up for him. (Corporal Shado inspected the tent beforehand, and it contained a bed and the same red bag, brass horn with bells and the iron ball used in the morning ritual.)

On the arrival of the procession, a trumpet sounded to inform the people of the Ata's safe arrival and to indicate where the Ocho ceremony was taking place this year. People rapidly began to assemble and just after the sun came up food and drink were brought and everyone ate and drank. Between 0800 and 0900 hours a canvas tent was erected about 100 yards away from the first tent, and the Ata entered this tent at about 1200 hours. Various juju drummers and dancers played and performed before the Ata during the day.

At about 1300 hours, the Ata, dressed in his ceremonial titular robes, left the tent and sat on a chair placed in a circle of burning grass and incense. An outer circle of men with cloths spread behind them made an enclosure. The ashes of the grass were blessed by the Ata and then taken by the watchers, rubbed on their faces and bodies. The Ata then prayed and a black goat, which was tied on to a bench of sticks and twine was killed by the Ohuga

226

who first cut its throat and then cut it open down the centre of its body. It was then covered with a white cloth. After an interval the Ata returned to his tent and took off his ceremonial robes. Juju drummers performed again and at about 1600 hours the procession left for the palace, stopping at Ere-Ane, where a tortoise was sacrificed by the Ataibo, and at Alu-Aku near to the entrance of the palace where a white cock was sacrificed by the Ogbola. Final prayers were said, and the ceremony ended at about 1700 hours. The Ata entered the palace and the people dispersed. The remainder of that day was taken up with general festivities locally.

This description agrees in most important respects with Clifford's account of the ceremony and with my own notes. But on this occasion the ritual seems to have omitted one traditional stage, before the sacrifice, in which the king is blindfolded and shoots an arrow at the black goat whilst it is still tied to a tree.

The symbolic aspects of the Ocho ceremony can best be explained by relating it to the hunting festivals for which each *onu anẹ* is responsible in his own district. In the traditional cycle of the year, throughout the kingdom, when the savannah grass became dry enough to burn thoroughly each District Head fixed a day for the land sacrifice in his own area. On this day the senior men from each extended family in his village, together with representatives from the subordinate hamlets and villages in the district, attended the land shrine in the morning with offerings of a cock, beer, kola, and symbolic payments of tribute, *enwu ire*, in the form of yams, guineacorn, or millet. After a cock had been sacrificed to the land, and found to be clean, *fẹ*, the men dispersed to hunt in the area of the shrine by burning a wide tract of savannah grass and driving the escaping animals towards a line of concealed marksmen. Any animals killed were then taken to *ẹranẹ*, the liver of some of the larger animals was placed on the shrine, and some of the meat cooked and eaten before the men finally dispersed.

The second annual hunting ceremony for which the *onu anẹ* was responsible was done in connexion with the opening of the reserved, and best, hunting lands towards the end of the dry season. For this, the greatest hunt of the year, the men who took part withdrew from normal life by camping in the area of the reserve, so that this hunt was associated with creation of an entirely masculine community, drawn from the population of the surrounding area as well as from the district owning the land in question. In principle the camp lasted 9 days, but in practice it went on for as many days as was necessary to beat and hunt over the area of the reserve and its environs. Hunting usually went on for at least 3 days, but the duration was ultimately determined by the abundance of game, and the way in which they dispersed after the first day, coupled with the numerical strength of the hunting bands, and their efficiency.

The royal camp at *anocho* is symbolically equivalent to the establishment of these district hunting camps, and the withdrawal from ordinary life and from contact with women is symbolized by the rule that the Ata must pass the night there, and reach the camp secretly. The site of *anocho* is changed annually, the exact spot being determined by Ohiuga's Ifa oracle in the same way that the choice of sites for the district camps and for the first day's hunting is submitted to the Ifa oracle before a final decision is taken.

The ritual preparations that are made for these hunts are many-sided and place great emphasis on medicines, *ogwu*, and fetishes, *ode*, owned individually, and also upon individual consultation of the Ifa oracle. But there are also public rituals, of two kinds, for which the *onu aṇẹ* is responsible. In the first place a temporary land shrine is established at the hunting camp, and tended by the district head himself. Secondly, there is usually a particular medicine or fetish, privately owned, which is employed on behalf of the whole community on this occasion, and is regarded in general as the senior hunting medicine in the area.

A land shrine, *ẹraṇẹ*, is set up in the hunting camp by clearing a small space at the foot of one of the tree species associated with this cult. On the first day of the hunt, the *onu aṇẹ* buries here a small leaf bundle containing shot and arrow poison collected from all the hunting groups present. A black hen is sacrificed over the spot, and the land is invoked to make the hunting successful by averting witchcraft and any evil magic that might cause accidents. Subsequently, kola nuts are broken

228

and offered at this shrine every day, and in addition any tortoises caught in the hunting field on the previous day are also offered to the land. In addition the *onu ane* consults the Ifa oracle daily, and any other offering that it may prescribe is made before the hunters leave camp.

The royal hunting ritual at *anocho* combines the symbolism of this class of land ritual with that of the earlier festival, in which offerings are made at the permanent land shrine of each district. The rites of burning the grass in a circle, and of killing a black goat condense the morning and evening stages of the latter ceremony, the goat being both the main offering to the land and a symbol of the animals killed and brought back by the hunters in the evening. Of the blindfolding of the king and the symbolic shooting of the goat, my informants said,

egba k'Achanyuwọ kiwọnw ru, Ata chanẹ dọdẹ, i a tọfa ifela kpe mẹ.
'When Achanyuwọ has burnt the grass, the Ata begins to hunt, he shoots an arrow and kills an animal straight away.'

But these events take place within a camp, and the offerings are made at a temporary land shrine, not at the regular Ẹranẹ, which transposes the symbolism into a different context. Similarly, after the animal has been killed it is placed on a stick framework, *akpata*, of the type that is erected in the hunting camp for smoking the game to preserve it. We can conclude from this that the ritual at *anocho* has associations with both the inaugural rite of hunting and with the land rites that are performed when the preserves are opened.

The protective fetishes, *ode*, used for hunting vary in name from one district to the next, but are usually in the form of an animal horn filled and bound round with dried vegetable substances that are believed to have magical effects. An Igala king may own fetishes of this type privately, but there is nothing comparable among the hereditary royal cult emblems and insignia. Instead, the ritual functions of *ode* are performed during Ocho for the king by the protective *ẹbọ*, Obade, and by a medicine, *atẹkpa,* which is prepared by Achanyuwọ, one of the Igala Mela chiefs. When the king goes to *anocho*, this medicine is carried in nine small pots and is sprinkled over each of the paths that the Ata takes on his way to and from the hunting camp. *Atękpa* is a specific and widely used antidote for *iwǫ*, a type of sorcery in which magical substances are buried across paths to kill or harm an enemy. In this context it is effective against all bad medicine, *ogwu bibi*, and fulfils the same role of ritual protection as the *ode* employed by individuals and by the land chief in hunting as a district activity.

The final stage of Ocho, in which a tortoise is sacrificed at Ęranę, combines the symbolism of hunting rites with that of the accession ceremony performed at the same site. On arriving at Ęranę from Anocho, the Ata is greeted by the Achadu, and goes with him and Atębǫ into the walled enclosure. The Achadu takes a tortoise provided by the Ata and ritually touches it against the king's forehead, saying:

Oji ǫyami ki dǫmǫ nwumi, ki kpoji olugbo efofę.
'May my wife stay alive for me, and grow old in the title.'

The Ata himself invokes the land:

Oji mi ki dǫmǫ, eju ki limi ǫdoyi ki nǫlimi ǫdǫmunę. Oji ane mi chaka, ki chębębǫ.
'May I live long, let the eyes that see me today see me another year. Let it be cool throughout my land.'

Atębǫ recapitulates this invocation, and then sacrifices the tortoise over the land shrine. He also breaks kola nuts, reciting the praise names of the land, and lets the segments scatter on the ground so that the kola oracle can be interpreted.

On leaving Ęranę, the king is greeted by all the royal masquerades and by his royal councillors. He then makes a triumphal re-entry into the capital, as on the occasion of his accession, passing through the Igala Mela quarter to receive the homage of the kingmakers, and then riding up to the main entrance of the palace where the titled heads of the Igala clans, together with Inalogu, wait for his return. Socially and politically, the last stage of the ceremony, at Ęranę, is more significant than the stages completed at Anocho. The royal councillors, for instance, do not attend the latter as a body, although a few intimates of the king may go there individually. Similarly, Atębǫ does not attend Anocho, nor does any other Igala Mela chief than Achanyuwǫ. There is a quality of secrecy and concealment about the ceremonies at this symbolic hunting camp which can be related to the notion that ritual sovereignty over the land is shared with the kingmakers. They emphasize the king's dominance in the political system, and symbolize his right to co-ordinate the activities of his subjects that are based on spatial arrangements. But this right is subordinate to the constitutional rights of the kingmakers, in the same way that the temporary land shrine at Anocho is junior to Ẹranẹ as the permanent centre of the land cult.

Ọgaingain.

This ceremony is a comparatively minor stage of the Ocho festival, attended by smaller numbers than the preceding and subsequent stages. There is no special ritual for Ọgaingain, but the king's masquerades appear, and thus create the direct bond between the Ata and his ancestors which is implicit in all their public performances. The central ceremonies of this day consist of an exchange of greetings between the Ata and his titled chiefs. For this exchange the king sits in the Ocho tent, *unyi abo,* which is re-erected in his compound. He first receives the homage of the masquerades and their attendants, then of the titled men in their usual order of appearance. But attendance on this day is not obligatory, as it is on the day of Ẹranẹ, and the major groupings of titleholders may be represented by a few of their number. On this occasion the king reciprocates gifts made to him during the earlier stages of the festival. But the symbolism of the ceremony emphasizes his position as territorial overlord. The re-erection of the Ocho tent within the palace identifies the Ata's hereditary prerogatives with the political privileges of the *onu anẹ,* or land chief. Ọgaingain is also the occasion on which the king reminds his subjects publicly of their duty to pay tribute, and of any shortcomings in their past behaviour in this respect. Finally, the palace officials, who are the king's executive agents in the tribute system are privileged on this day and have licence to behave much as they like without giving offence to the inhabitants of Idah. The *ẹdibo* and the eunuchs' followers, *abimọtọ amonoji,* can appropriate wine, kola, and any other minor property that they desire by touching it with the peeled wands that they carry for the festival. If we regard the earlier stages of Ocho centring on Anocho and Ẹranẹ as stressing the king's dependence on the Igala Mela, the Ọgaingain festival redresses the balance by symbolizing the king's assumption of political sovereignty.

Inikpi.

For the concluding rite of the Ocho festival the Ata goes in procession with his councillors, the palace officials, the Atẹbọ, and the royal masquerades to the waterside to the shrine marking the grave of Ayagba's daughter, Inikpi. In the king's presence Atẹbọ and the priestess of the shrine[1] make offerings of a goat, a hen, kola nuts, and palm oil. They invoke Inikpi to avert witchcraft and all misfortune from Idah and from the kingdom in the year to follow, so that the land might be fertile, the numbers of children increase normally, and the king rule in peace. Emerging from the shrine the king is formally acclaimed by his councillors and by the riverain chiefs, Abọkkọ, Ọmọgbajẹ, Agaidoko, and the lesser titleholders. After the king has returned to the palace the priestess prepares the flesh of the creatures sacrificed by Atẹbọ, with yam and palm oil, and makes a further offering, with little ceremony.

Inikpi is associated ritually with the land cult rather than with the cult of royal ancestors. Although the best known of the royal princesses, in oral tradition, her name is not included in the list of ancestors recited in the daily *okwutẹ* ritual. Nor is she named or offered to at any stage of the Egwu ceremony. Inikpi's grave complements the symbolic function of the main land shrine, which stands for the normal and settled aspect of communal existence, by representing the possibility of 'restoring the land' once the normal relationship has been disturbed by strife and bloodshed. Her apotropaic functions also reflect the symbolism of the earth cult, which is specially directed towards prevention of witchcraft and the evil effects of *inacha*.

In terms of the ritual structure of the Ocho festival, Inikpi's position as an ancestor is analogous to that of the dead who are commemorated in the Egwu cycle by the Ogbadu festival. It is significant that both festivals close with offerings to spirits who are excluded by the manner of their death from normal ancestral

---

[1] The priestess is appointed from among the clients or followers of the palace officials, and is usually an elderly woman. The office is not hereditary and has no special title. The last holder, Iyechọja, was a Nupe.

status. They represent the dimension of social and political relationships in which conflict occurs, and to which both the state and the local community are perpetually vulnerable.

We can conclude and summarize this outline of Igala kingship ritual by saying that the king is involved in two sets of ritual duties, centring on the one hand on his relationship to the royal ancestors and on the other on his relationship to the land. This division corresponds to the polarity expressed in Igala origin myths between the position of the immigrant royal clan and that of the indigenous landowners. These notions in turn conceptualize the basic division of power in Igala between a few large-scale, aristocratic clans and a great number of small, low-ranking clans vested with rights of local sovereignty.

In describing these royal rituals I have partly sketched in the background of purely ceremonial actions and observances against which these ritual acts are performed. And it will be useful next to consider the ceremonial aspect of kingship in greater detail since the ceremonial procedure that surrounds the king's actions elaborates the ideas that are set out in their simplest form in ritual. And, more importantly, this ceremonial has the important function of uniting the two themes pursued separately in ritual, and of presenting the underlying philosophy of kingship as a unified whole. This appears clearly, for instance, if we analyse the praise names that titleholders and others traditionally use in greeting the king. In the set of typical greetings given below, the verses combine references to both aspects of the king's power, to his relations with his own clansmen, and to his territorial sovereignty over the whole kingdom. His position as Ata, as unique ruler and the source of all patronage, is due, they imply, to a combination of the different elements that are portrayed metaphorically in the praise names.

The commonest of the salutations or 'names of power', *odu ukpaihi*, used in addressing the king are as follows:

1. *Ata, Agabaidu.* 'Ata, lion of lions.'

This is the standard form of salutation, used by all the Igala, whatever their rank or sex, in addressing the king.

2. *Ata, Agabaidu, amideju, ayele achele.* 'Ata, lion of lions, let me live, O maker of gifts, O giver of gifts.'

This is used by women in general, and emphasizes the fact that women are dependent on men for the performance of rituals and hence for their relationship with the spiritual forces that are believed to maintain life.

3. *Ata, olisa oke, i a kpẹ i a du.* 'Ata, (like) God, he gives out shares and takes away (as much as he likes).'

This, and all the following praise names, are the prerogative of other titleholders, clan heads in general, and other distinguished elders. It would be considered presumptuous for any commoner, unless in the king's favour to address him by any of these other aphorisms.

4. *Ata ọkpaka, a moli ẹgbe d'olubọ.* 'Ata (like) climbing bean, that makes a withered tree give shade again.'

This describes the Ata as the source of all patronage and also implies that families or individuals whose fortunes decline in one reign may fare better when a new branch of the ruling house comes to the throne.

5. *Ata, ododo ki ma maja ajan.* 'Ata, red blanket that does not hide in the market.'

Ododo is the name of a red felted cloth traditionally reserved to the king and his leading councillors. A piece of it worn or displayed for sale in the market would stand out from all other cloths because of its colour and associations with rank.

6. *Ata, imogili i kpagili.* 'Ata, who pounces (lit. seizes) suddenly and kills suddenly.'

7. *Ata, fai fai, i chogwu ifai.* 'Ata, soon soon, he is the medicine of immediacy.'

8. *Ata, ẹnyaro gidiba.* 'Ata (like) breasts full to overflowing.'

9. *Ata, edaku ebije ki ma lọ, ugbodu a tun.* 'Ata, knot of iron that is not pliable, an unskilled person cannot untie (it).'

10. *Ata, ọkẹẹlẹ ki a laboji aboji; ukokolo ki a ma ẹfodudunan.* 'Ata, curving flight that comes from the wrong side; kite that does not end up in the smoke of the fire.'

This is one of a group of aphorisms stressing the Ata's tactical skill and resourcefulness in Igala politics. The first verse combines two metaphors, of a missile reaching its target by a curving flight, and of water being drawn with the mouth of the pot facing downstream instead of upstream, which is the usual way. The second verse refers to the kite's skill in swooping through the smoke of bush fires to catch the insects and small rodents driven out by the conflagration.

11. *Ata, ẹgbo ki adagbiti uja.* 'Ata, weak one, that overcomes a strong man in the fight.'

12. *Ata, ojiji akafili.* 'Ata, a terror of the unbelievers.'

13. *Ata, ojiji Idoma.* 'Ata, a terror to the Idoma.'

This may be the older and original form of the previous salutation which reflects Moslem influence and is probably more recent.

14. *Ata, adagba a bọ laawu laawu.* 'Ata, elephant that trumpets *laawu laawu.*'

15. *Ata chimi chimi jowali, i fọkpa ka je ma fu ta.* 'Ata (who) takes counters frugally, he takes only one piece and they play on.'

This metaphor uses terms from the mancalla game, *ichẹ*, to suggest that the most skilful player is the one who wins although his play gives the impression of losing.

16. *Ata komi ka i abata d'Idan.* 'Ata, of whom I was about to say that there is no king at Idah again.'

17. *Ata, akpuluka tọmẹ.* 'Ata, (like) the crab that is greater than boundaries.'

Whatever boundaries men may fix, the crab is not affected by them and goes on its way regardless.

18. *Agbo ogbaala ki ajẹnw oona jiji.* '*Agbo* (a kind of lizard?) that eats up things at a distance.'

19. *Ata jaichi jaichi dagbudu.*

Meaning obscure. *Jaichi* is corrupted from the Hausa word, *zaiki*, meaning lion. *Dagbudu* may similarly be a corruption of the Hausa *dabubu*, many or numerous.

20. *Ata, ọmichẹkpa.* 'Ata, child of *ichẹkpa.*'

Ichẹkpa is a mythical creature that lives in the bush and surpasses all other creatures in knowledge of the bush, including knowledge of medicines.

21. *Ata, Agaba kpa ki du mufa.* 'Ata, lion that kills and drags away (its prey).'

22. *Ata chi alu kojẹ kpọ.* 'Ata (you) open mouth and food becomes cheap.'

Referring to the Ata's right to commandeer provisions for his messengers and agents, and also to the lavish hospitality which is provided for the king and his followers on tour or during a campaign.

It is perhaps significant that although these royal praise names lay stress on the uniqueness of the king's office, they do not associate it solely with overwhelming power in the physical or military sense. Instead they maximize the qualities of sagacity and political expertise, and balance the king's control of patronage and justice against the limitations imposed by the segmentary nature of the political system. A further limitation on royal power is also apparent in the wider ceremonial context of the king's public appearances and relations with his subjects. The opposition of the king to his titleholders, which is a constant feature of his public appearances, in one sense underlines the differences of functions between clans and reproduces the hierarchy of descent on which the distribution of power is actually based. But in another sense it stresses the basic congruence between the office of the king and those of his titled clan heads whose duties, like the king's, combine the functions of the ritual clan head on the one hand and of the land chief on the other. The king's office, though unique in many respects, shares the attributes of titles in general, and is described by the same term, *ofẹ*. The Ata's regalia includes the items of dress common to all titleholders, *amajofẹ*, the wrist and neck beads, *ọka,* flywhisk, *otihi*, and ornamental hat that is worn with a fringing circle of red feathers, *okẹbetsi*. The royal ceremonies not only distinguish the king from the rest of his subjects, they also oppose the whole class of titleholders to the rest of the population. And within the framework of a unified title system the Ata is *primus inter pares* rather than an autocrat. The same limitation is apparent in the king's title itself, which in its traditional form is Ata Idah and not Ata Igala. This habit of defining royal sovereignty by reference to the powers of indigenous landowning groups sums up the king's position at the apex of interlocking systems of territorial and genealogical control.

TEXTS ON SUCCESSION TO THE KINGSHIP

TEXT ONE. *Succession among Idoko Adẹgbẹ's children, in Ocholi lineage.*[1]

Ọgaaji chọma Idoko Adẹgbẹ. Amọgbe chọma Idoko Adẹgbẹ. Abu katama j'Ata, atama wa lekwu, eyi ogujo ma f'odunw kọ Ọnọja i mamefunw ko manyọla. Iii onw a tini, i chẹnw omi gbo mẹnomi j'Ọmakoji Ata nwatami. Ọnọja ọm Idoko akayi o. I f'Ọgaaji ki charononw dọ, i f'Amọgbẹ ki rọnọ Ọgaaji dọ, i mu ma ko nyi ef'Ifa. Abu ki a b'Ifa ma f'Ọnọja ọm Idoko dọ mayi uwẹ lekwu, i yown ma. Ma f'Ogaaji dọ, mayi uwẹ lekwu, i yown ma. Amọgbẹ, mayi uwẹ lekwun, Amọgbe a kwun gbogbo gbogbo tak ile olọpu Ocholi wan. Amọgbe nayọ. Mayi, ama, ọfẹ Ata doji wẹn, ukpaihi wẹ i jẹ kọfẹ Ata doji wẹn. Ẹnẹ nọma kẹkẹ ki dubi mẹ ki. Mayi, 'Aku Odiba', Mayi, O, ọmata wẹ dẹyi, i yẹlẹ ii, Idoko Adẹgbẹ bi ọma kẹkẹyi. Ẹnẹ ki ajọfẹ Ata dẹ. Own Amọgbẹ yi, Ii, own a jọfẹ Ata, nyọ, i ka nyefunw.

Ma li ny ogwega Mabolo ny agwọla, i fọwọ t'Aku Odiba i mudu rọ tomi. I lekwu fa mi fajọfẹ Ata kin. Ma na kpọgu, Amọgbe mokịkịlịnw du rọ tomi. Okịkịli nw omi mu du cha na gbaju ejiji takamonẹ nyọmọ ma rule efomi ma na mudu. Ọnọja ọm Idoko kaki Ii, Amọgbẹ a cheyi i a folọpu mi kpa tẹgbe, idabẹlẹ me f'Amọgbẹ kpa. Ma f'Amọgbẹ li ku ma kpa, ailo jẹ ku ma kpan, own ma fu ji, ma fu ji wa. Okịkịlịnw ku ma dọ Ọgaaji, 'Uwẹ m'Aku Odiba dalo ny ngbo ku wẹ kwo wa, uwẹ jẹ k'Amọgbẹ ki wọmọ gẹ no. Amọgbẹ li ọmọ i f'okịkịli wẹ akpa ọfẹ wa la fa linyo'—Ọnọja i ka nw okịkịlịnw ku ma dọ Aku Odiba, 'Ichẹnw kọfẹ lia ọfẹ Ọmakoji komi jeyi uwẹ mọfẹ Ata du, ẹ mọma mi ọma wẹ i che kio, ẹ mu du jẹ Ọmakoji Ata koji mi'. Aku Odiba yi 'O'.

Ab'Amochẹjẹ wa lekwu, ẹgba eyile amefunw chaka ma lekwu, ibonw, ibo Amọgbe, own ma f'Aku Odiba dọ wa, ki wa jọfẹ Ata. Amọgbẹ kaki 'Ii, omi ki chogujo daneyi k'Ifa ka lẹ, omi a jẹn'. I muja ko wane tamonoji t'am Igala Mela ma jigidi manyu Amọgbẹ, ma fu ne toko tak' Aku Odiba fọfẹ jẹ, tak i m'Egwu Ọnọja, ọm achọgwanw, i mudu jẹ Ọmakoji Ata.

[1] By Amana Edime, my chief informant.

Ọgaaji and Amọgbẹ were both the sons of Idoko Adẹgbẹ. When their father, the king, died, Ọnọja brought his relatives together. He said that he wanted to know if he grew old whether he would take his father's title of Ọmakoji Ata. Ọnọja summoned Ọgaaji who was next to him in seniority, and also sent for Amọgbẹ, who was the next in line again, he sent for them to consult the Ifa oracle. The diviners put Ọnọja's name to the oracle and gave the answer that he would not live; he accepted this. They put Ọgaaji's name with the same result. They addressed Amọgbe and told him that he would not die, but when he began to rejoice at this they also told him that he would not become king because it was not in his destiny to hold this office. The diviners then asked about the parentage of a small child who was also present, and when they had confirmed that this was another son of Idoko Adẹgbẹ's they announced that this would be the eventual heir to the throne. The child was Aku Odiba, Idoko Adẹgbẹ's son. Amọgbẹ heard the verdict and thought, 'We will see'.

One day when they went to the waterside to wash in the river Anambra, Amọgbẹ seized Aku Odiba and threw him into the water, thinking that this was his best chance of dictating the succession. The people shouted that Amọgbe had thrown his younger brother into the water, and on running to help him found that Aku Odiba had been carried by the current against the branches of a tree. So they were able to rescue him. Ọnọja was summoned and commented that as Amọgbẹ was trying to destroy the family he himself should be killed. They found Amọgbẹ and could have killed him, but became afraid, and so brought him back bound. The younger brother, Ọgaaji, ordered that Aku Odiba should be sent away and kept safe from Amọgbẹ, so that the kingship should not be lost to them. Then Ọnọja petitioned Aku Odiba to regard Ọnọja's children as his own and select one, whenever he came to the throne, to succeed Ọnọja in the title of Ọmakoji Ata. Aku Odiba agreed to this.

By the time that Amochẹjẹ died and the throne became vacant, most of Aku Odiba's brothers were also dead, and Amọgbẹ's people sent for Aku Odiba to be king. Amọgbẹ himself refused, because he was the elder, and he went to war over this. But the eunuchs and Igala Mela fought against Amọgbẹ and overwhelmed him. Aku Odiba came to the throne and appointed his brother's son, Egwu Ọnọja, to be Ọmakoji Ata.

TEXTS ON SUCCESSION TO THE KINGSHIP

TEXT TWO. *Succession among Ẹkalaga's children, in Akogu lineage.*[1]

2a. Ab'Okoliko lekwu, Amaga wa ki wa jọfẹ, okịkịlị Amaga ka dọmọ, ma dọ Aku Ọchu, i li ki wa b' Amaga gbọfẹ jẹ. Abo Idah, abe Igala Mela, ma jeju, ma chuji; mayi, 'Akwu Ọchu, i muwa ọla gbẹ, i chenyọ ki j'Ata'. Own Amaga gbọ, kaki, 'Eeh, ma che ku ma chuji nyi mi, najẹn, abẹ k'Idahyi ogwu i che nwomi kpai ama. Tak i mu du dufu ma fọla ji du dufu kpai ebijẹ ịyanga nyanga nyanga. Tọ, ma dẹ, ma nẹkẹ kọla gẹn, own Amaga f'Ata jeyi ki o. Okịkịlịnw lẹ ki bọ gbọfẹ, tak'Amaga la wa wẹwe wẹwe kpai amonẹ, ẹnw ki che kailo b'abe Idah tak Amaga fọfẹ atanw jẹ dẹ o.

When Okoliko died Amaga came to take the title and was on his way when his younger brother, Akwu Ọchu, tried to wrest the succession from him. The people of Idah, the Igala Mela, met and conspired, deciding to favour Akwu Ọchu. When Amaga heard of their treachery he threatened them with war, and armed his people outside. When they saw these preparations, the Idah people kept quiet and accepted Amaga; when Amaga came with a great following they were afraid and let him take his father's title.

2b. Atami Amaga ki j'Ata, ọjọ ku ma nyadọ ki awa, Akwu Ọchu ch'ọm Ẹkalaga, Amaga chọm Ẹkalaga. Akwu Ochu ma mudu gugu oji ọpata ma mudu maja, abe Igala Mela mayi ẹlẹlẹ aj'Ata amala kponẹ, nyadọ Amaga kw'Ife todu ki lawa j'Ata. Ubilẹ ma nwọ fu gwọgwọ, ma m'Akwu Ọchu du ubinw, todu ki j'Ata, ẹgbọ. Own Amaga gbọ own i wa eju ọkpẹ ọọna Ojekpodu Iyọku. Own yẹlẹ Iii, amarọlọ ma wa rọ kaki uwẹ ma kwanẹn olikitsi abẹ ku wẹ j'Atan, ọbata amẹlẹ chuẹwẹ wale. E gbọ, chai Akwu Ọchu ẹlẹ chẹnẹ kamalẹ du maja todu kẹlẹ kij'Ata. Own Amaga yi, taa, own a li eyin, abẹ kẹlẹ lafa che ẹnw du kẹlẹ ma chen ẹ lafa che, own ama ọna. Amaga fọlogwu ji, i m'ikapa du tunyọwọ, i m'adakanw du, adaka ki a du dọdẹ kwubi, i mu du nika, abokolobia mejọ ma fọla ji cha chaka. Own ma wa bọ Achadu, ẹgbọ, Igalọgwa, own i Achadu ma nya dẹlẹ fai fai todu k'Achadu i e kị dufu ki wa gwonw eti du ki. Achadu kaki, Ahah, eyi ki tọnọ. I yẹlẹ ma dufu wa kị wa gweti du inyinin abẹ own a jẹn abẹ kown meyilẹ du kpa, ownlẹ la mọleyinw du kpa inyini own ẹlẹ ama ọma k'Akpọtọ lẹ nẹ, Akpọtọ lẹ own kwo wayi. Ichukpẹ kẹlẹ mown du wa gugu ọọna own a chọbata, kẹgbo, ẹlẹla kponẹ a dọnw, abiche tak ẹlẹ ia nwọ dabi kwuji ẹla cheo kuwe chuji no, pio pio, fai fai, own a tini ku ma gweti du, chẹkponi ma kanw konw kpologboyi fọ.

---

[1] Text 2a is from Amana Edime, who belongs to a different lineage. The second and fuller version is from one of Amaga's own sons, Ubọchi Amaga.

Own ma b'Achadu, Achadu kaki, Ehhe, eh, iche ki a kuja wa, i abamin, tak i a momi du kpan, Akpọtọ dẹ, ẹnẹ bibi i che, kẹgbọ, e tọnọ, anẹ ma gweti du. I yẹl, Nnn, fai fai, ma gwudu ẹlẹ chọfẹ atanw lẹ dẹ. Own amẹ dọwn, ownlẹ la wa jeyi ẹgba kẹnw du lẹ la chen etinw lẹ a biẹ pio pio, ẹ gbọ, i neyi ẹnwọ nyi anẹ taku ma gwudu gen. I yẹl Tọ, ma gwudu kin, ẹlẹ mud ọga ọwọnwlẹ dọ gẹn. I yẹl eba, uwẹ kwulan, uẅẹ kpọla wẹ eyilẹn, efukpaihi own ili tak i dọfẹ atanw nwunw, own i gweti du tak i d'Igalọgwa lẹ fali fali, tak i lo t'Ojaina, tak i ny achubi.

Before my father Amaga became king he and one other son of Ẹkalaga's, called Akwu Ọchu, were involved in the succession. When the Igala Mela met to discuss the succession Akwu Ọchu was hidden in the roof of the house and heard them say that if he came to the throne he would kill people, so that Amaga should be sent for. After this message had been sent to Amaga, who was at Ifẹ, the Igala Mela deceived Amaga by choosing Akwu Ọchu in his place. Amaga heard this when he was on the road and had reached Ojekpodu Iyòku. He heard it rumoured that he would need to stir up trouble himself in order to meet the trouble that was brewing at Idah to keep him off the throne. Amaga swore that if this were to occur then nothing would be left untouched. So he prepared for war, putting on his fighting knife, and shouldering the gun that he normally used for hunting; eight young men also went with him, fully prepared as well.

They came to Igalọgwa to meet the Achadu and summoned him to come and pierce Amaga's ears. The Achadu sent a reply that Amaga should let the matter rest, but Amaga sent back again to say that if the Achadu did not come to pierce his ears he would have him killed so that he would learn what kind of children were brought up in Akpọtọ land, where he came from.[1] He would not sit on the road and suffer, since they had sent for him in the first place; if the Achadu was trying to change the earlier decision and deceive him he should give up the idea.

They met the Achadu again and the Achadu gave way, saying that Amaga was a typical Akpọtọ man and too dangerous to meddle with. He appointed the evening for the ear piercing ceremony. But Amaga refused and insisted that his ears should be bored at once. So the Achadu disclaimed responsibility for any sickness that might result and bored Amaga's ears. Amaga went on from there to stay in Igalọgwa, from there to Ojaina, and then performed the last funeral rites (of his predecessor).

[1] The phrase '*Akpọtọ land*' is equivalent to saying 'in the north'.

TEXT THREE. *Succession among Amochẹjẹ's children, in Ajaku lineage.*[1]

Todu ọla eyimi, Odokina Odoma, ọm Odoma Okolobade dẹ. Ateyimi kpai Ochẹjẹ Nọkpa nata, atemi kp' Ochẹjẹ ki natalẹ Odoma kp'Ochẹjẹ nata. Okwina chomehi ma own i chachọgwa ma chachaka, own ka kown a kpọfẹ nwamale, onw kpone datemi kakuwẹlia kuwẹlẹ nọfẹ Ata kown a duwe. Tak atami nyi ki wa Okwina mọfẹ lẹ du nw'Ochẹjẹ jẹ. Own atami ka kuwẹjẹjẹnw own ofofo chi, own a jẹ no. Abe kọlamayi la chajọ ka ma ka na ene ki tamalẹ ọla le ma kabẹlẹ gbogbo ny ngbo amẹnẹfu tak ẹnẹfu ka nwatami kiche nwọ dabi agbali ọwọ ofo alon uwe gọfẹ kerueju ki je kuwe je. Own atami wa jẹ Ọmakoji Ata nw Ochẹjẹ Onọkpa takọlama takpa. Efeyilẹlẹ ayi chaka takpa ku ma chaka feli ọlama ki kwogbadu ki chaka dujabọ todu eyile i jẹ wẹdọno todu alu keyiwa ka chamọmanw tod ẹgba ka nwọ dakubi wa gugu ojinw ojọna omunẹ. Ubi eyilẹlẹ abu kownma la nwọ dọmọni tak Obaje nwọ wẹki j'Atayi, ukpẹ katanw jẹyi omi la nwọ dakubi nyẹkẹ tini Ọmakoji Ata, eyi katami jẹ. Ọmakoji Ata lẹ, abu ki ma la mi du ni, onw i du Ọmọlọbu nwu mi, onw ch'Ọmọlọbu ku jẹ guguyi.

This story is told by me, Odokina Odoma, the son of Odoma Okolobade. My father and Ochẹjẹ Nọkpa had one father; Odoma and Ochẹjẹ were the sons of one man. Okwina was their father's sister, and the eldest of their father's siblings. She said that she would give out (lit. divide) the title to them; then she sent and called my father to come and take the title. But before he came she chose Ochẹjẹ, his brother, and made him king. Then my father refused to be left empty-handed and would not accept this decision. The matter was disputed on and on until they took the case to the Europeans who ruled that my father should stand down, promising him the choice of any other title that he liked to take. Then my father became Ọmakoji Ata, and the quarrel ended. He accepted this decision for the sake of his children in the future, when their turn should come again. After his death, Obaje came to take his own father's title and became a King. So I went to him and asked for the title of Ọmakoji Ata, that my father had held. This was not given me, but the title of Ọmọlọbu came to me instead, which I still hold.[2]

[1] Collected from Odokina Odoma, son of one of the contestants.
[2] The speaker had left Idah after Obaje's death and gone to live in the hamlet of Okpachala, a few miles away.

The above text can be compared with a contemporary account of the same succession dispute, written by Charles Partridge, an early administrative officer who was stationed at Idah at the time of the dispute.[1] This account confirms my informant's statement that Amochẹjẹ's sister, who was still alive when it came to be the Ajaku lineage's turn to provide the Ata again, played an important role in the succession procedure. And the two accounts show that a candidate for the throne needed the full support of his own royal lineage in addition to the consent of the kingmakers in order to overcome his rivals.

On 10 August 1901, I found myself in charge of the sub-district of Idah, embracing, on the left bank of the Niger, as much of Igaraland as lies within Southern Nigeria, and, on the right bank, a similar portion of Kukurukuland. It was a new station, having been a political residency only since the preceding November. My two predecessors had been in charge nearly three and nearly seven months respectively. I was destined to spend 9 months there. When I 'took over', the political situation was as follows: Atta Am Aga had been dead many months (eighteen, it was said); his embalmed body was lying concealed in the royal compound at Idah, and his only son, Aku Agaru, had retreated inland to Keffi with most of his people. There had been several candidates for the throne, and fighting would have ensued had no British Commissioner been there. The election was in the hands of the Princess-Royal, a clever old woman named Akwina, the eldest child of Atta Am Osejji, who would herself have been Atta but for their Salic law. The principal candidates were Osejji Onapa, Ondoma Korobad, and Aku Neddi. All bribed Akwina heavily, and at last, having got all she could out of them, she fixed upon Osejji Onapa. He was a fine, good-looking man, and the wealthiest of them all. Her choice had been ratified by the Government, and the disappointed candidates had been induced to come in from the bush and settle under the Commissioner's eye at Idah. Osejji Onapa could not, however, enjoy the title or power of Atta until after the burial of his predecessor; for the Igaras say, 'We cannot have two kings above ground at the same time.' During this interregnum, Osejji Onapa was called Adukina (Prince). He, too, had of course come in, and was living about a mile from the royal compound, being forbidden to enter until the

[1] Partridge, Charles, 'The Burial of the Atta of Igaraland, and the "coronation" of his successor', *Blackwood's Magazine*, CLXXVI, 1904, pp. 329-37.

dead body had received burial. The royal compound[1] (a collection of huts surrounded by a wall) stands within a large open space protected by earthen rampart and mud wall, and approached by two principal entrances—one from the water-side and the other from the Igara hinterland. Having been vacant for so many months, it presented a most dilapidated appearance: houses and walls and their thatched roofs were broken in many places, and the little courtyards and big open enclosure were overgrown with rank weeds and rushes.

My instructions were to keep the political situation as quiet as possible on account of the then pending Aro expedition, but to endeavour to bring about the burial of the late, and the peaceful accession of the new, Atta. It was added that the Igaras would probably try to offer human sacrifices at the funeral.

The first point was to make friends with the principal chiefs. This was done gradually: they called on me, and I returned their calls, squatting on a small stool in their compounds, chewing the (bitter!) kola-nut of friendship, and exchanging compliments and little presents. Of course they often lied and prevaricated, and probably they would have liked to relapse into slave-dealing when my back was turned; but I learned really to like some of them, and look upon them as friends. It was important to be on good terms with Akwina, the old Princess-Royal. I presented her with a large coloured portrait of Queen Victoria, sent out framed from home, and she was delighted with the blaze of orders and jewels, and her people gratified her by saying she was like 'the great white Queen'.

The next point was to make peace between Akwina and Ondoma Korobad, the most powerful of the disappointed candidates, and then to induce him and Aku Neddi to acknowledge the Atta-elect. On 14 October I spent an hour and a half squatting in Akwina's little audience-room, together with Ondoma Korobad and a few other natives, my orderly acting as interpreter, and eventually they agreed to 'Swear ju-ju' together. Akwina's Yoruba husband produced a beautifully illuminated copy of the Koran, which was laid in our midst on a goat-skin, and a kola-nut broken up into small pieces was placed on the top. First the old Princess, and then the chief, knelt down and took a solemn oath of mutual peace, and then ate the kola-nut. Then we all placed our right hands on the Koran as witnesses.

Aku Neddi soon afterwards made private submission to Osejji

[1] Illustration given in *Up the Niger*, by Captain A. F. Mockler-Ferryman, 1892, p. 223.

Onapa, but Ondoma Korobad's affair was publicly done. On the morning of the 17 October the procession started from my house, I riding my little black horse and accompanied by orderly and horse-boy, and Ondoma Korobad riding his white horse gaily caparisoned, and attended by at least 100 followers, many armed with long trade-guns, and others beating drums and shouting. The chief wore a robe of alternate broad stripes of scarlet and yellow, and on his head a huge white turban latticed with black cloth and stuffed with numerous ju-ju charms. We rode about 3 miles in straggling procession along the narrow 'road' winding through the bush. Crowds of people were squatting inside and all around the compound occupied by the Atta-elect. He and his chiefs received me in an innermost oblong hut, which was most unpleasantly crowded, and we all sat down, Ondoma Korobad, however, remaining in the courtyard just outside. At first the King was arrogant, and Ondoma passionate and noisy; but a little 'parable' made them laugh, and at last the ceremony was begun. A ju-ju man traced a sort of triangle on the ground outside, and various ju-ju things beribboned with bits of cloth were held up and shaken about. A man beat a gong, and Ondoma and Atta's son (representing his father) stripped themselves to the waist, and knelt on the ground. Then the Atta swore a long oath, enumerating various evil things which if he should do to Ondoma Korobad the ju-ju (spirit) would kill him. Ondoma and the boy repeated all this, and then drank something out of a wooden bowl, and then the liquid was sprinkled on their faces, chests, and backs. Ondoma fell on the ground, and made several obeisances to the king, which ended the ceremony.

Peace having at last been completed between the Atta-elect and Akwina on one side and the disappointed candidates on the other, there seemed nothing to prevent the long-delayed funeral taking place. But the West African native moves slowly. The whole conduct and expense had to be borne by the family of the late Atta. His only son, Aku Agaru, was living in retreat at Keffi, and was—as my messengers ascertained—really too 'sick' to superintend the arrangements in person. This duty therefore, fell upon his eldest sister Agwiei, who during the late reign was said to have ruled her father and the whole court. She came in from the bush, and, taking up her abode at Idah, began to prepare for the funeral.

BIBLIOGRAPHY

Allen, W., *Picturesque views on the river Niger*, 1840.

Allison, P. A., 'The Collection of Export Produce in an Agricultural Community, the Palm Produce and Rubber Trades in Igala', *Farm and Forest*, VII, June 1946.

Armstrong, R. G., 'Peoples of the Niger-Benue Confluence', in the series, *Ethnographic Survey of Africa*, ed. Forde D., London, 1955.

Baikie, W. B., *Narrative of an exploring voyage up the rivers Kwora and Benue in 1854*, London, 1856.

Beattie, J., 'Nyoro Kinship and Marriage', *Africa*, XXVII, 1957.

'Nyoro Marriage and Affinity', *Africa*, XXVIII, 1958.

Boston, J. S., 'Notes on Contact between the Igala and the Ibo'. *Journal of the Historical Society of Nigeria*, 2, December 1960.

'The Igala Oil-Palm Industry', *N.I.S.E.R. Conference Proceedings*, 1962.

'Notes on the Origin of Igala Kingship', *Journal of the Historical Society of Nigeria*, 2, December 1962.

'The Hunter in Igala Legends of Origin', *Africa*, XXXIV, 1964.

'Ceremonial Iron Gongs among the Ibo and the Igala', *Man*, 52, LXIV, 1964.

'Igala Inheritance and Succession', in *Studies in the Laws of Succession in Nigeria*, ed. Derrett, J. D. M., 1965.

Burdo, Adolf, *A Voyage up the Niger and Benue*, London, 1880.

Byng-Hall, F. F. W., 'Notes on the Okpoto and Igara Tribes', *J. African Society*, 7, 1907.

Clifford, Miles, 'A Nigerian Chiefdom', *J. Royal Anthropological Institute*, LXVI, 1936.

Unpublished reports and letters in administrative records at Idah.

Crowther, Samuel, Reports, letters and personal papers. Unpublished mss. in C.M.S. House, London.

'Report of the Annual Visit to the Niger Mission in 1873', *Church Missionary Intelligencer*, 1868, pp. 9–13 and 19–20.

'Bishop Crowther's Narrative of his Detention by the Chief Abokko', *Church Missionary Intelligencer*, IV, 1868, pp. 9–13, 19–20.

Crowther, Samuel, and Schön, J. F., *Journals of an Expedition up the Niger*, London, 1942.

Journals of an Expedition up the Niger and Tshadda Rivers . . . in 1854, London, 1855.

District Notebooks. Unpublished administrative records covering most of the major administrative divisions in the Igala area.

Dumont, L., 'The Dravidian Kinship Terminology as an Expression of Marriage', *Man*, 54, LIII, 1953.

Evans-Pritchard, E. E., *The Divine Kingship of the Shilluk of the Nilotic Sudan*, Cambridge, 1948.

Frazer, Sir J. G., *The Golden Bough*, 3rd edition, 1912.

Irstam, Tor, *The King of Ganda*, Stockholm, 1944.

Koelle, Rev. S. W., *Polyglotta Africana*, London, 1854.

Laird, Macgregor, and Oldfield, R. A. K., *Narrative of an Expedition into the Interior of Africa by the River Niger, 1832–33*, 2 vols., London, 1837.

Lander, Richard and John, *Journal of an Expedition to Explore the Course and Termination of the Niger*, 3 vols., London, 1832.

Levi-Strauss, C., 'The Structural Study of Myth', *J. American Folklore*, 68, 1955.

Lienhardt, G., 'The Shilluk of the Upper Nile', in *African Worlds*, ed. Forde, D., 1954.

Lugard, Frederick D., 'Northern Nigeria', *Geographical Journal*, XXIII, 1904.

Mockler-Ferryman, *Up the Niger. Narrative of Major Claude Macdonald's Mission to the Niger and Benue Rivers* (in 1889), London, 1892.

Monckton, J. C., 'Burial Ceremonies of the Attah of Idah', *J. African Society*, XXVI, October 1927 and January 1928.

Monsell, C. N., *Historical Notes on the Attahate of Idah*, ms., no date.

Murray, K. C., 'Idah Masks', *Nigerian Field*, 14 July 1949.

Nadel, S. F., *A Black Byzantium*, London, 1942.

Nevil, Sir William, *Nigeria under British Rule*, 1927.

Nigeria Magazine, 'The Rise and Fall of the Igala State', no. 80, 1964.

Partridge, C., 'The Burial of the Ata of Igalaland and the Coronation of his Successor', *Blackwood's Magazine*, 1904.

'A Note on the Igala Tribe', *J. African Society*, VIII, 1908.

Paul, Charles, ms., *Journal*, 1866.

Philpot, W. S. A., 'Notes on the Igala Language', *Bulletin of the School of Oriental and African Studies*, VII, 1935.

Seligman, C. G., *Egypt and Negro Africa*, 1934.

Seton, R. S., 'Installation of an Attah of Idah', *J. Royal Anthropological Institute*, LVIII, 1928.

'Notes on the Igala Tribe', *J. African Society*, XXIX, 1929–30.

Talbot, P. A., *The Peoples of Southern Nigeria*, 4 vols., London, 1926.

Temple, O., and C. L., *Notes on the Tribes, Provinces, Emirates and States of the Northern Provinces of Nigeria*, Cape Town, 1919.

Trotter, H. D., Allen, W., and Thomson, T. H. R., *A Narrative of the Expedition to the River Niger in 1841*, London, 1848.

INDEX

247

5/8   **DATE DUE**
